Fénelon

Fénelon

Moral and Political Writings

Translated and Edited by

RYAN PATRICK HANLEY

OXFORD
UNIVERSITY PRESS

OXFORD

UNIVERSITY PRESS

Oxford University Press is a department of the University of Oxford. It furthers
the University's objective of excellence in research, scholarship, and education
by publishing worldwide. Oxford is a registered trade mark of Oxford University
Press in the UK and certain other countries.

Published in the United States of America by Oxford University Press
198 Madison Avenue, New York, NY 10016, United States of America.

Library of Congress Cataloging-in-Publication Data
Names: Fénelon, François de Salignac de La Mothe-, 1651–1715. |
Hanley, Ryan Patrick, 1974– translator, editor.
Title: Moral and political writings / Fénelon ; translated and edited by Ryan Patrick Hanley.
Description: New York, NY : Oxford University Press, 2020. |
Includes bibliographical references and index.
Identifiers: LCCN 2019035355 (print) | LCCN 2019035356 (ebook) |
ISBN 9780190079581 (hardback) | ISBN 9780190079598 (paperback) |
ISBN 9780190079611 (epub) | ISBN 9780190079604 (updf) | ISBN 9780190079628 (online)
Subjects: LCSH: Philosophy, French—17th century. | Philosophy, French—18th century. |
Ethics. | Political science—Philosophy.
Classification: LCC B1878.5.F462 E5 2020 (print) |
LCC B1878.5.F462 (ebook) | DDC 194—dc23
LC record available at https://lccn.loc.gov/2019035355
LC ebook record available at https://lccn.loc.gov/2019035356

1 3 5 7 9 8 6 4 2

Paperback printed by Marquis, Canada
Hardback printed by Bridgeport National Bindery, Inc., United States of America

Contents

Acknowledgments

I am deeply grateful to a number of institutions and individuals for their support of my work on both this translation and its companion monograph. Fellowships from the National Endowment from the Humanities and the Earhart Foundation made possible invaluable periods of uninterrupted work. The Way-Klingler Fellowship in the Humanities and Social Sciences and the Mellon Distinguished Professorship of Political Science at Marquette University also instrumentally supported my work on several fronts, including my work in the archives. For their helpful assistance with this work I am grateful to the staff of the Manuscripts Department of the Bibliothèque nationale de France, and to Agnès Jauréguibéhère and the staff of the archives of the Compagnie des Prêtres de Saint-Sulpice. The Liberty Fund generously hosted a colloquium on Fénelon's moral and political thought, which enabled me to receive a great deal of useful feedback on the materials in this volume; I am extremely grateful to Christine Henderson for her efforts at bringing this colloquium to fruition, and to Mark Alznauer, David Carrithers, Aurelian Craiutu, Aymeric D'Alton, Eve Grace, Jennifer Herdt, Ourida Mostefai, Adam Potkay, and Kent Wright for many very helpful comments. Several other friends and colleagues read the manuscript in close detail, going well above and beyond ordinary duties of collegiality; for their efforts and their invaluable criticism and suggestions I am deeply indebted to Hank Clark, Charles Griswold, Christine Henderson, Chris Kelly, Catherine Labio, and John Scott. I must also record my debts to the late Patrick Riley for his pioneering work on Fénelon and the authors of his period, and also for suggesting to me, in the course of casual conversation at a 2008 conference in his honor, that an English translation of "On Pure Love" was especially to be desired. Finally, I am grateful for having been able to benefit from the assistance of several excellent research assistants, including Taylor Ahmed, Will Fitzsimmons, Michael Murillo, Anthony Lanz, Darren Nah and Kaishuo Chen.

Chronology

1651	Birth of Fénelon (traditional date: August 6)
1654	Crowning and consecration of Louis XIV
1663	Fénelon enrolls at the University of Cahors
1669	Fénelon receives his degree from Cahors
1672	Start of the Dutch War; not concluded until 1678
1674	Fénelon enters seminary of Saint-Sulpice
1677	Fénelon ordained
1679	Fénelon installed as head of *Nouvelles Catholiques*
1681	French annexation of Strasbourg
1682	Birth of the Duke of Burgundy
October 1685	Revocation of the Edict of Nantes
December 1685	Fénelon sent to Saintonge as head of mission to Huguenots
1688	Start of the War of Grand Alliance; not concluded until 1697
1688	Fénelon first meets Madame Guyon
1689	Fénelon appointed tutor to the Duke of Burgundy
1693	French famine
March 1693	Fénelon elected to the *Académie française*
Late 1693–Early 1694	Fénelon writes his *Letter to Louis XIV*
1694	Inquiry into Madame Guyon's writings begins
1695	Fénelon named Archbishop of Cambrai
January 1697	Publication of Fénelon's *Maxims of the Saints*
January 1699	Fénelon removed from position as royal tutor
March 1699	Pope Innocent XII censures twenty-three propositions of the *Maxims*
April 1699	Publication of *Telemachus*
1700	Duke of Anjou crowned Philip V, King of Spain
1701	Start of the War of Spanish Succession; not concluded until 1714
1707	Fénelon delivers his *Discourse* for the Elector of Cologne
1708	French famine
1710	Fénelon writes his "Memorandum on the Deplorable Situation of France"
Early 1711	Probable period of composition of the *Examination of Conscience*

Translator's Note

The process of translating Fénelon brought home to me, at nearly every turn, both the vast extent of Fénelon's genius and the severe limits of my own. Fénelon is not only a masterful prose stylist but also a sophisticated philosophical writer, one well aware that different methods of presentation are needed to speak to different sorts of audiences. Even as his moral and political writings advance a set of consistent, even systematic, substantive teachings (as I emphasize in my introduction to this volume and my monograph on his political philosophy) Fénelon uses several different voices to convey his teachings in the course of addressing different audiences with different needs. The tutor of the child for whom the *Fables* and *Dialogues* were written clearly spoke with a voice very different from that of the spiritual and political counselor of the young man for whom the *Examination* was written; so too the voice of strident admonishment and urgency that resonates across the *Letter to Louis XIV* and the Political Memoranda is far removed from the gentler but no less urgent voice of the moral and spiritual advisor on display in the essay on pure love included in this volume.

As translator I have sought at once to do justice to the unity of Fénelon's moral and political thought and also allow these different voices to come through and be heard. This goal compelled me to make several choices. In order to preserve and thereby convey the substantive consistency of Fénelon's moral and political thought within and across texts, I have tried, so far as possible, consistently to use the same English words for specific French words. But in an effort to preserve and convey Fénelon's different voices I have not aspired to a similarly slavish consistency in matters of syntax and punctuation, and have been freer in such matters in texts (like the *Dialogues*) that artfully employ conversational informality, and less free in texts (like the *Discourse*) that are more formal and technical.

My translations of Fénelon's quotations from classical philosophical texts as well as writings of the Church Fathers represent my renderings of these passages as they appear in Fénelon's own French. The accompanying notes are intended to provide interested readers with the information necessary to consult the originals directly; the chapter and paragraph numbering provided generally accords with the editions of these texts published in such established series as the Loeb Classical Library and the Early Church Fathers (the latter as publicly available online at https://www.ccel.org/fathers.html). The versions of Fénelon's biblical citations provided here, however, are drawn from the Douay-Rheims English translation of the Bible published in France between 1582 and 1610.

As editor of this volume I had to make difficult decisions about material to include and not include, knowing it would be impossible to do justice to all the riches available in Fénelon's collected works. The writings included here are those that I have thought most necessary for appreciation of the core claims of his moral and political thought and that do not currently exist in a modern English translation. The main exceptions to this rule are the selections from *Telemachus*, which, in the sketches they provide of various social orders and regimes, complement the other writings included here. The source texts for all of the translations are the published versions of these texts to be found in the collections listed in the guide to further reading; also consulted have been several alternate versions in various manuscript and published editions.

The editorial apparatus aims to be informative rather than interpretive, and seeks to provide basic information that may be helpful to nonspecialist readers. Some annotations provide further information on contemporary word usage. These are generally drawn from three dictionaries that have been invaluable to my work on Fénelon: Jean Nicot's *Trésor de la langue françoise* (1606), Antoine Furetière's *Dictionnaire universel* (1690), and the first edition of *Le dictionnaire de l'Académie française* (1694)—all of which are publicly available online through the University of Chicago's remarkable ARTFL resource (https://artfl-project.uchicago.edu). Other annotations aim to provide basic biographical information on individuals or background information on institutions. Several specialized reference works have been especially helpful in preparing these notes: Marcel Marion, ed., *Dictionnaire des institutions de la France aux XVIIe–XVIIIe siècles* (Picard, 1923); Lucien Bély, ed., *Dictionnaire de l'Ancien Régime* (PUF, 1996); and Simon Hornblower et al., eds., *Oxford Classical Dictionary* (Oxford, 2012). Other general reference works—including especially the *Encyclopedia Britannica*, the *Dictionary of National Biography*, and the *Encyclopédie* of Diderot and d'Alembert (similarly available via ARTFL)—have also been consulted. Finally, in some cases annotations provide references to authors and/or texts cited by Fénelon; in almost all such instances my notes follow the outstanding notes in Le Brun's edition.

The following abbreviations have been used in the notes:

A. S.-S. = Archives de la Compagnie des Prêtres de Saint-Sulpice
BnF = Bibliothèque nationale de France
CF = *Correspondance de Fénelon*, ed. Orcibal
OF = *Œuvres complètes de Fénelon*, ed. Gosselin
Pl. = *Fénelon: Œuvres*, ed. Le Brun

For complete bibliographical information for these editions, please see the Further Reading section. Finally, numbers in square brackets refer to pages in the Pléiade, and have been included to facilitate interested readers' efforts to reference the original in the most easily available French edition.

Further Reading

Readers of French have far more of Fénelon's writings (and writings on Fénelon) available to them than do readers of English. Three French editions of his writings are especially valuable: the two-volume Pléiade edition edited by Jacques Le Brun (Gallimard, 1983–1987), which includes an indispensable critical apparatus; the ten-volume Saint-Sulpice edition edited by Jean-Edmé-Auguste Gosselin (Lefort, 1848–1852), which includes many of Fénelon's contributions to the religious controversies in which he was engaged; and the eighteen-volume edition of his correspondence chiefly edited by Jean Orcibal (Klincksieck, 1972–1976; Droz, 1987–2007), which is distinguished by its magisterial commentaries.

Among English-language translations of Fénelon, most relevant to readers of this volume will be Patrick Riley's edition of *Telemachus* (Cambridge, 1994), a useful revision of Tobias Smollett's eighteenth-century English translation. Other complete texts of Fénelon's published in modern English translations include his *Dialogues on Eloquence*, edited by W. S. Howell (Princeton, 1951); his *Treatise on the Education of Girls*, edited by H. C. Barnard (Cambridge, 1966); and his *Letter to the French Academy*, edited by Barbara Warnick (University Press of America, 1984). Beyond these, Fénelon lives on in English only via several evangelical presses that have produced compilations of selections from his spiritual writings. These include, among others, *Fénelon: Selected Writings*, edited by Chad Helms (Paulist, 2006); and *The Complete Fénelon*, edited by Robert Edmonson and Hal Helms (Paraclete, 2008).

Several English-language biographies have surveyed Fénelon's life and thought. The best of these is also the most recent: Peter Gorday's *François Fénelon: A Biography—The Apostle of Pure Love* (Paraclete, 2012) offers an excellent and long-overdue introduction to Fénelon's life and ideas and is by far the best place for English-language readers to begin. Also still helpful in this vein is James Herbert Davis's intellectual biography *Fénelon* (Twayne, 1979), as well as Thomas Merton's short essay "Reflections on the Character and Genius of Fénelon," in *Fénelon: Letters of Love and Counsel*, edited by John McEwen (Harcourt Brace, 1964).

A helpful overview of the world in which Fénelon lived and wrote is offered in Robin Briggs, *Early Modern France, 1560–1715* (Oxford, 1998), which surveys the political, social, and economic context of seventeenth-century France. An overview of Fénelon's religious context can be found in Joseph Bergin, *The Politics of Religion in Early Modern France* (Yale, 2014). Overviews of his philosophical context include Desmond Clarke, *French Philosophy, 1572–1675* (Oxford, 2016), and Michael Moriarty, *Early Modern French Thought*, volumes 1 and 2 (Oxford, 2003–2006). Nannerl Keohane, *Philosophy and the State in France* (Princeton, 1980), remains the best survey of the context of late seventeenth-century French political thought available in English.

Fénelon's philosophical ideas have received helpful attention from several French scholars; especially valuable are Henri Gouhier, *Fénelon philosophe* (Vrin, 1977), and Laurence Devillairs, *Fénelon: Une philosophie de l'infini* (Cerf, 2007). Fénelon's religious thought and spirituality, and especially his concept of pure love, have also rightly received extensive attention; especially useful treatments include Denise Leduc-Fayette, *Fénelon et l'amour de Dieu* (PUF, 1996); Michel Terestchenko, *Amour et désespoir: De François de Sales à Fénelon* (Seuil, 2000); and Le Brun, *Le pur amour. De Platon à Lacan* (Seuil, 2002). Recent English-language studies of his ideas of pure love and disinterestedness include Benjamin Thompson and Robert Lamb, "Disinterestedness and Virtue: 'Pure Love' in Fénelon, Rousseau, and Godwin," *History of Political Thought* 32 (2011); and Charly Coleman, *The Virtues of Abandon: An Anti-Individualist History of the French Enlightenment* (Stanford, 2014).

Like his philosophical and religious ideas, Fénelon's political ideas have often been examined by French scholars; key studies include Roland Mousnier, "Les idées politiques de Fénelon," *Dix-septième siècle* 12–14 (1951–1952); Françoise Gallouédec-Genuys, *Le Prince selon Fénelon* (PUF, 1963); François Xavier-Cuche, *Une pensée sociale catholique: Fleury, La Bruyère, Fénelon* (Cerf, 1991); and Olivier Leplatre, *Fénelon ou l'inquiétude du politique* (Hermann, 2015). Riley's introductory essay in his edition of *Telemachus* offers a helpful introduction to Fénelon's political thought for English-language readers; I provide a book-length treatment of Fénelon's political ideas in *The Political Philosophy of Fénelon* (Oxford, 2020), meant as a companion to the present volume.

Several other studies of aspects of Fénelon's political ideas and activities will also be useful to English-language readers. Lionel Rothkrug, *Opposition to Louis XIV: The Political and Social Origins of the French Enlightenment*

(Princeton, 1965) masterfully surveys the reform efforts of Fénelon and his aristocratic circle. Fénelon's political economy and its influence have more recently become a focus of English-language scholarship; especially valuable on this front are Henry C. Clark, *Compass of Society: Commerce and Absolutism in Old-Regime France* (Lexington, 2006); Istvan Hont, "The Early Enlightenment Debate on Commerce and Luxury," in *The Cambridge History of Eighteenth-Century Political Thought*, edited by Mark Goldie and Robert Wokler (Cambridge, 2006); and Paul Schuurman, "Fénelon on Luxury, War and Trade in the *Telemachus*," *History of European Ideas* 38 (2012). The influence of Fénelon's thought has also received significant attention. Fénelon's influence on Ramsay and in Stuart England is insightfully examined in Andrew Mansfield, *Ideas of Monarchical Reform: Fénelon, Jacobitism and the Political Works of the Chevalier Ramsay* (Manchester, 2015); his influence in Enlightenment Europe is chronicled in the very welcome volume *Fénelon in the Enlightenment: Traditions, Adaptations, and Variations*, edited by Doohwan Ahn, Christoph Schmitt-Maass, and Stefanie Stockhorst (Rodopi, 2014); and the interesting story of his influence in America is told in Patricia A. Ward, *Experimental Theology in America: Madame Guyon, Fénelon, and Their Readers* (Baylor, 2009). Fénelon's influence on Rousseau has long been a subject of particular scholarly interest; among the best studies in English are Riley, "Rousseau, Fénelon, and the Quarrel between the Ancients and the Moderns," in *Cambridge Companion to Rousseau* (Cambridge, 2001), and Matthew D. Mendham, "Rousseau's Partial Reception of Fénelon: From the Corruptions of Luxury to the Contradictions of Society," in *Fénelon in the Enlightenment*.

Fénelon

Introduction

Fénelon may be the most neglected of the major moral and political thinkers of early modernity. His political masterwork was the most-read book in eighteenth-century France after the Bible.[1] Enlightenment philosophers from Leibniz to Bentham testified to his genius. In his own age, he was recognized as a key leader of the political resistance to the absolutism of Louis XIV, a pioneering theorist of education and rhetoric, a prescient student of economics, and an insightful commentator on international relations. Beyond politics, Fénelon played a central role in several of the most prominent debates of his age, including philosophical debates among Descartes's heirs, spiritual debates over the meaning of quietism, theological debates over Jansenism, and the literary debates that have come to be known as the Quarrel of the Ancients and the Moderns.

Fénelon can thus lay legitimate claim to our attention. Yet today English-language readers rarely engage his work, at least in part because of the relative scarcity of translations of his writings. This volume aims to remedy this by bringing to English-language audiences the first collection of his moral and political writings in translation. By so doing it hopes to make the riches of his moral and political thought available not only to students of French history but also to students and scholars in fields from political science and economics to philosophy, education, rhetoric, religion, and literature—as well as to those engaged in the debates over political resistance and reform today.

1. Fénelon's Life

The momentous life of François de Salignac de la Mothe-Fénelon can be divided into three stages.[2] Of the first, comprising his childhood, we know relatively little. Fénelon was born in Périgord in 1651. He was the second son of the second wife of his father, an impoverished aristocrat who died when his son was very young, but whose connections to various Church figures would prove useful to his son throughout his life. Sent to the university at Cahors,

Fénelon. Ryan Patrick Hanley, Oxford University Press (2020) © Oxford University Press.
DOI: 10.1093/oso/9780190079581.001.0001

Fénelon took his first degree in 1669, and afterward went to Paris to continue his education; by 1677 he had been ordained and had received his doctorate in theology. In Paris, Fénelon began his association with the mentors who would shape his career. These included Louis Tronson, director of the seminary at Saint-Sulpice at which Fénelon studied, and Jacques-Bénigne Bossuet, Bishop of Meaux and an influential figure in Louis XIV's court. The former would prove a revered source of comfort and wisdom for Fénelon in his later career; the latter would prove the power behind both Fénelon's rise and his later fall. In Paris, Fénelon also began his career as a young priest preaching at parishes associated with Saint-Sulpice; in 1679 he received his first full-time post as the director of the *Institution des Nouvelles Catholiques*, a school for Protestant girls converting to Catholicism. The talents Fénelon displayed in this delicate job earned him his next post. In late 1685, and in the immediate wake of Louis XIV's notorious revocation of the Edict of Nantes that had formerly guaranteed the religious freedom of French Protestants, Fénelon was appointed head of the mission to Saintonge charged with converting the Huguenots there. Saintonge was one of the most concentrated Protestant centers in France, and it is a testament to the faith the authorities had in Fénelon's abilities that he was assigned to this post. It is also a testament to Fénelon's talents on several fronts that he was able to fulfill these difficult duties in a reasonably gentle manner.[3] And his work did not go unnoticed. The governor of the region to which he was assigned was a son of the great Colbert, finance minister of Louis XIV, and Fénelon's services in his district led him to welcome Fénelon into his circle—a circle that included, among other noteworthy figures, the Duke of Beauvillier and the Duke of Chevreuse (each of whom had married daughters of Colbert), who would prove lifelong friends and key allies in Fénelon's later efforts at resistance and reform.

By the time Fénelon returned to Paris in 1687 he was well on his way to becoming an established figure across several spheres. In the Church, Bossuet had taken him as his protégé. Testifying to his rise in the wider intellectual world, within a few years he would be elected to the *Académie française*. And in 1689, he made his political debut when, on the strength of Beauvillier's recommendation, he was named preceptor (or tutor) to the Duke of Burgundy, grandson of Louis XIV and *Petit Dauphin*. It was a decisive event in Fénelon's professional career to that point, and made possible his development as a political thinker and political reformer. As tutor, Fénelon enjoyed access to the court and its machinations; observing them with care provided him a great deal of material on which his later political inquiries would draw. And as tutor to a potential heir to the throne, Fénelon was conscious that his efforts to shape the mind and soul of his young charge might potentially shape the nation. It was also a post in which he was clearly invested, and that allowed him to draw on his many diverse talents as an educator, author, spiritual advisor, and political observer. In time, Fénelon's duties would expand to include serving as preceptor to Burgundy's two brothers, the other *Enfants de France*: the Duke of Anjou (who would become Philip V, King of Spain) and the Duke of Berry. Yet these moments at the center of French politics were not to last, owing largely to what would become the defining episode of the next stage of Fénelon's career: his encounter with Madame Guyon.

Jeanne-Marie Bouvier de la Motte-Guyon was a self-taught spiritualist. A pioneer of the new form of mysticism that had been recently gaining ground in France, Guyon arrived in Paris in the mid-1680s and began to correspond with Fénelon. Many studies have been devoted to their relationship, but for our purposes what matters is their shared interest in the idea of "pure love" that would prove to be the downfall of each. Pure love was itself a controversial concept; only a year before the first meeting of Guyon and Fénelon, Rome had condemned the teachings of the Spanish priest and author Miguel de Molinos on the nature of the inner life and the role of love in it. Guyon, however, shared Molinos's intense interest in the inner life, and her explications of it—perhaps owing to what is generally agreed to be a lack of theological sophistication—soon brought her own writings under suspicion. This ultimately led to a comprehensive examination of her doctrines by the Church authorities at the request of Madame Maintenon, wife of Louis XIV. Fénelon himself initially supported the investigation, but it soon turned unfavorable for his associate; in 1694 Guyon's doctrines were condemned by the Archbishop of Paris, and in 1695 she was imprisoned at Vincennes, later to be transferred to the Bastille. Throughout the initial stages of this process, Fénelon stayed loyal to Guyon. But by August 1698 matters were different; by then he had concluded that Guyon had "deceived" him and that she was a "hypocrite."[4] Yet by that point matters had moved well beyond the question of Guyon and her fate, and the controversy had come to focus on the defense of the doctrine of pure love that Fénelon had taken it upon himself to advance, much to Bossuet's consternation. The result was a protracted and bitter and increasingly public and personal battle between Fénelon and his mentor. In its course, Fénelon wrote a host of works meant to demonstrate the orthodoxy of true love and its essential commensurability with the doctrines of the Church Fathers and Councils; by far the most important of these was Fénelon's *Explication of the Maxims of the Saints* of 1697. But for all his efforts Fénelon was ultimately outmaneuvered by Bossuet and came out on the losing side. At Bossuet's request, Louis XIV wrote directly to Pope Innocent XII to ask for his judgment on the *Maxims*. The result was the papal brief *Cum alias* released on March 12, 1699, formally condemning twenty-three propositions of the *Maxims*.

Fénelon's response has often been taken as evidence of his grace. Immediately on news of the condemnation he made a full public recantation of his offending propositions; the Pope was so taken with Fénelon's docility that he considered appointing him cardinal. But the greatest blow to Fénelon's career was still yet to come. As part of his education of Burgundy, Fénelon had drawn up a series of didactic texts, including fables and dialogues and histories. The longest of these was a book-length manuscript that told the story of the son of Odysseus in search of his lost father. But this text, written for a specific and single addressee, would prove to have a very different destiny. Stolen by an unknown someone, the manuscript was published without the author's approval and appeared in April 1699—a short six weeks after *Cum alias*—under the title *Les aventures de Télémaque*. The event determined the remainder of its author's career. The king, reading the lessons it sought to teach his grandson, immediately (and rightly) saw in it a repudiation of the sort of glory and grandeur to which he had dedicated his reign. The result was Fénelon's banishment from court—and thus the same text that would bring Fénelon fame in the Enlightenment was, in the short run, the cause of the end of his official political career.

Thus begins the third and final stage of Fénelon's life. Banished from Versailles and stripped of his position as tutor to Burgundy, Fénelon retreated to his diocese of Cambrai, of which he had been appointed bishop in 1695. It was, in one sense, political exile. But it was, in another sense, the beginning of a new stage in his career as both a political and a spiritual thinker. In Cambrai, Fénelon's chief concerns were management of his parish and ministry to the needs of his largely Flemish parishioners. It was a task that suited him well, as it allowed him to make the most of his gifts as a spiritual counselor and his experience as a teacher. It also provided him with a new perspective on politics. Cambrai lay in the heart of the northern borderlands that had long been contested in a series of bloody battles as a part of the War of Spanish Succession, and during his time there in the first decades of the eighteenth century Fénelon saw firsthand the personal costs and devastation of both war and famine. He also maintained his correspondence with his former student, himself called to fight in these wars. And for a brief time, it seemed that Fénelon's political influence may reemerge. April 1711 saw the death of Burgundy's father, the *Grand Dauphin*, which left the Duke next in line to the throne. Later that year, in conjunction with his allies, Fénelon completed a draft proposal for reform of the French state, and it seemed possible and even likely that he would be appointed prime minister of France on Burgundy's accession to the throne, and thus in a position to enact his envisioned reforms. But it was not to be. In early 1712, while ministering to his wife who had fallen ill with measles, the Duke contracted the disease himself and followed his wife in death. Burgundy's death brought Fénelon's time in politics to an end for good, and he devoted the remainder of his career mostly to theological debates, actively and extensively participating in the critique of Jansenism that reached its peak with the papal bull *Unigenitus* of 1713. Illness and death came for Fénelon himself in early 1715, only months before the death of Louis XIV.

2. Fénelon's Writings

Fénelon's writings span a remarkably wide range—rhetoric, education, literature, art, politics, philosophy, theology, and spirituality—and left a lasting mark on many of these fields. A brief introductory survey of these writings, focusing especially on those that have been translated for this volume, may thus also be helpful.[5]

Fénelon's earliest writings lie in the intertwined fields of rhetoric and education. This was largely the result of his employments in the first stages of his career; as a young priest preaching his first sermons, the mechanisms of pulpit eloquence would have been much on his mind, just as the methods and aims of education would have been much on his mind during his labors at both *Nouvelles Catholiques* and the mission to Saintonge. In any case, it was at the time of these employments that Fénelon began work on his *Dialogues on Eloquence*. Though not published until 1718, the *Dialogues* would have lasting influence on eighteenth-century conceptions of oratory and rhetoric, and provide a crucial window into his understanding of eloquence and its place in both pulpit oratory and education. Fénelon would return to questions of rhetoric and eloquence in one of his last literary productions, his *Letter to the Academy*. Written in 1714 in response to a solicitation for

suggestions on projects the Academy should pursue in the wake of completion of its landmark dictionary, Fénelon's *Letter* elaborates on the themes of
his *Dialogues*. But the two are also joined by a shared focus on education. As
such, they provide key insight into Fénelon's intentions and methods as an
educator, and introduce themes central to his educational writings proper.
And foremost among these is Fénelon's treatise *On the Education of Girls*,
composed in the mid-1680s for the Duke and Duchess of Beauvillier, who
sought Fénelon's advice on the education of their eight daughters.

Fénelon's professional career also shaped the development of another side
of his literary corpus: his contributions to philosophy, theology, and spirituality. On the first of these fronts, Fénelon's time under Bossuet in the 1680s
witnessed his composition of his two contributions to post-Cartesian philosophy. These included his *Demonstration of the Existence of God* (first
published in 1712), which used arguments both drawn from natural religion and from reason independent of experience to argue for God's existence; and his *Refutation of Malebranche* (first published in 1732), composed
at Bossuet's direct request, which offers insight into Fénelon's understanding
of providence via its several objections to Malebranche's positions on the nature and limits of God's freedom. These two works, in conjunction with his
metaphysical treatise on the nature of being entitled the *Nature of Man* (composed c. 1688 though not published until 1904) and numerous occasional
works—including an important letter that has been excerpted and separately
published under the title *Refutation of Spinoza*—constitute his principal
contributions to what we would today consider philosophy. In the 1690s,
with the Guyon affair in full bloom, Fénelon's energies refocused on theology. Many of the most important of his writings in this vein sought to provide defenses of the orthodoxy of his positions via a demonstration of their
consistency with the Church's positions. For us they are especially valuable
as sources of explication of his concepts of love and hope and self-interest
and as such demand attention for how they comport with and illuminate the
tenets of his political philosophy. The best-known of these writings remains
the *Explication of the Maxims of the Saints* (1697). Yet Fénelon's shorter occasional writings on matters of spirituality also remain of great interest, and especially the short essay "On Pure Love" that has been included in this volume
and that also likely dates to the period of the quietism controversy.

Fénelon's writings on philosophical and theological and spiritual subjects
were very extensive. Our principal interest however is his political writings.
The earliest of these are the didactic writings he composed for the moral and

political education of the young Duke. These include two works included here: the *Fables* and the *Dialogues of the Dead*. The first was a contribution to a genre that La Fontaine, among others, had recently revived; the second a contribution to a genre that Fontenelle, among others, had recently popularized. Both works date to the early period of Fénelon's preceptorship in the early 1690s, when the Duke (born 1682) was a young boy. Accordingly, they seek to employ the various literary devices at their author's disposal to charm their addressee and thereby lead the future prince to embrace the virtues and policies that Fénelon thought indispensable to effective rule. In total Fénelon wrote nearly forty fables and nearly eighty dialogues for the Duke; included here are a selection of these, including those which most directly address the core themes of his political thought.

Attending to the substance and the methods of the *Fables* and the *Dialogues* can help to clarify and bring into relief the political teachings of *Telemachus*—the work to which its author owed much of his later fame. The centerpiece of the education that Fénelon sought to provide to the Duke of Burgundy, *Telemachus* was originally conceived and composed for an audience of one. Fénelon laid out his intentions for the text in a frequently cited memoir.[6] Defending his work from the charge that it was meant as an attack on or satire of specific public figures, Fénelon insists that in it he sought "only to entertain the Duke of Burgundy with these adventures, and to instruct him while entertaining him, without ever wishing to give this work to the public." And the instruction he meant to convey is clear: *Telemachus*, he explains, "is a fictional narration in the form of an epic poem, like those of Homer and Virgil, in which I put the key teachings appropriate for a prince destined by birth to reign," including "all the truths necessary for government, and all the faults that sovereign power can have."[7] *Telemachus*, as has often been noted, was thus in many ways an anti-Machiavellian mirror-for-princes. That said, *Telemachus* is not a treatise, but a work of fiction—a literary effort that presents its teachings in a text that self-consciously sought to bring together the virtues of the ancient epic and the modern novel. The book itself tells the story of Telemachus, the son of Odysseus, following him around the Mediterranean in search of his father who has yet to return to Ithaca from the Trojan Wars. Its subtitle specifically presents it as a continuation of the fourth book of Homer's *Odyssey*. In Homer's epic, Telemachus is only present for the first four books, disappearing entirely from the story until his father's homecoming in the final book. Fénelon exploits this narrative silence, taking the essentially blank slate of Homer's treatment to develop a portrait of a young prince destined to rule, and guided in his search by his wise tutor, Mentor—in fact the disguised goddess Minerva. Together Mentor and Telemachus track across the Mediterranean in search of Odysseus for eighteen books of the text, with the tutor taking every opportunity to convey the essential lessons of good government and virtuous living to his young charge, lessons that include innovative proposals on questions ranging from free trade and taxation, international relations and just war, and the virtues of of statesmen and ministers as well as kings.

In addition to his didactic writings for the young Duke, Fénelon's political writings also include several other works written for specific addressees. The most striking of these is his *Letter to Louis XIV*. Generally thought to date to late 1693 or early 1694—and hence written in the immediate wake of one of the worst famines in French history—the *Letter* is a thorough and uncompromising excoriation of the Sun King.[8] It is so vehement that until a manuscript copy in his hand was discovered it was often doubted that Fénelon could have been the author. We still do not know whether the letter was in fact ever sent to the king, or was even intended to have been sent; many have hypothesized that it was in fact meant for Maintenon or Beauvillier, perhaps to assist in sharpening criticisms they might deliver to the king directly in their own name.[9] However this may be, the *Letter* is an enduring model of what it looks like to speak truth to power, one which particularly offers an uncompromising critique of the obsession with grandeur and glory that led Louis to privilege the image of himself and his court over the well-being of his people. Similarly important are two other pieces of correspondence included here: Fénelon's 1701 letter to the chief advisor of the newly crowned King Philip V of Spain—who was in fact Fénelon's own former pupil and brother to the Duke of Burgundy, the Duke of Anjou—and his 1709 letter to the Duke of Burgundy, which features a memorable sketch of "the King of England," James Edward Stuart.

Another political work meant for a specific addressee is the oration that Fénelon delivered at the consecration of Joseph-Clément of Bavaria, Elector and ultimately Archbishop of Cologne. The significance of this event was that Joseph-Clément, in addition to enjoying a long friendship with Fénelon, was born Elector though he pursued a career in the Church. Fénelon served as his *consécrateur* (the technical term for a bishop who ordains a priest to become a bishop) at his ceremony held on May 1, 1707, and he used the *Discourse* delivered on that occasion to set forth several of his key statements on the proper relationship of Church and state.

The relationship of politics to religion is also central to the work that follows, Fénelon's *Examination of Conscience Concerning the Duties of Kingship*. The addressee of the *Examination* was again the Duke of Burgundy—but not the young boy Fénelon had taught. Thought to date to early 1711, the *Examination* was written when the Duke was nearly thirty, by which time he had seen war firsthand. The essay is itself a contribution to a particular religious genre. Prior to receiving the sacrament of penance, Catholics have been traditionally expected to make an examination of their conscience. Fénelon's focus in this particular examination of conscience written for the prince is however not just sacramental but also political, and in it he draws on his understanding of moral psychology, his experiences as a spiritual director, and his skills at literary persuasion—all to focus the Duke's mind on the duties of a king and the arts of good governance, and particularly on the ways in which a ruler can transcend his pride to work for the well-being of the people he serves. The text is especially noteworthy for its concluding supplement, which sets forth what has been regarded as one of the first modern articulations of balance-of-power theory.

The final group of political writings included here dates also to Fénelon's Cambrai years. As noted earlier, Fénelon's time in Cambrai was one of tremendous military and political upheaval. Much of this owed to the War of Spanish Succession that had been waged to establish the Bourbon claim to the Spanish throne. But it was also a period of domestic turmoil owing in part to famines France suffered during the final decade of the seventeenth century and the first decade of the eighteenth. Fénelon chronicled his reflections on these events in a series of short writings that his modern editors have gathered together under the heading "Political Memoranda." Collectively these memoranda afforded Fénelon an opportunity to apply his political theory to practical political questions. The first memorandum included here was written in 1710 to detail domestic conditions in France at the height of the War of the Spanish Succession and particularly emphasizes the human cost of the war. The second memorandum, in contrast, offers a practical scheme for reform in France. Known as the "Plans of Government" or "Tables of Chaulnes"— Chaulnes being the location of the Duke of Chevreuse's estate at which Fénelon and his circle of aristocratic reformers met to develop these plans— the "Tables" were compiled in November 1711 in the wake of the death of the Duke of Burgundy's father, the *Grand Dauphin*. Their aim is to lay out a comprehensive scheme for reforming social and political institutions in France upon the Duke's expected accession to the throne as the successor to his grandfather, Louis XIV. Written mostly in Fénelon's hand, the "Tables" are not a treatise, but a set of notes. Yet their careful organization into bracketed headings and subheadings—evident on the folio pages of the manuscript (A.S.-S. Ms. 2027) and which this translation aims to replicate—attests to the degree to which these notes represent an organized and comprehensive vision of political reform. Of course, in the end, Fénelon's hopes for an opportunity to enact these reforms were dashed upon the Duke's death, only months after the drafting of the "Tables"—an event that gave occasion to another key memorandum, the "Memorandum on the Measures to Take after the Death of the Duke of Burgundy," dated March 15, 1712, which has also been included here.

The final text included here is not a political text at all. Over the course of his career Fénelon wrote a great number of short occasional pieces on religious and spiritual matters. "On Pure Love" is one of the most important of these. It is thought to date to the period of his quarrel with Bossuet over quietism, and is significant both for the explication it provides of his views on pure love, the central concept of Fénelon's spirituality, and for the contrast it provides to the ideas developed in his political writings.

3. Fénelon's Political Ideas

Fénelon's moral and political writings span a wide variety of literary genres: fables, dialogues, letters, sermons, memoranda, an epic, and writings of spiritual counsel. But for all these diverse methods of presentation, as a political thinker Fénelon returns again and again across his moral and political writings to a strikingly consistent set of themes. These themes might be roughly grouped into three categories: the virtues necessary for effective political rule, the organization of institutions within the state, and international relations.

Fénelon's teachings on the virtues of the good ruler are perhaps the most prominent and frequently emphasized of all his political teachings—as is perhaps hardly surprising in a thinker whose primary employment for some years concerned the education of a young prince. Across his works written for this prince one finds a series of portraits of kings and leaders both good and bad. In holding these various figures up for his pupil's emulation (or avoidance), Fénelon recommends three sorts of virtues. The first are the skills that enable kings and rulers to perform their functions with maximum effectiveness and efficiency. On this front Fénelon calls particular attention to the acumen and knowledge of men that enable kings to choose counselors well, the independence and self-sufficiency that enable kings to take advice from counselors without being manipulated by them, the farsighted vision that enables kings to foresee the long-term implications of their policies, and the even-temperedness that enables them to serve as supreme judges in their realm. A second class of virtues concerns what we might call virtues of character. On this front, Fénelon particularly emphasizes the courage that enables kings to lead effectively in times of both war and peace, the prudence that enables them to weigh and choose one course of action over another in light of the circumstances, and the moderation that enables them to temper their self-interested desires for wealth and power and pleasure. The third class of virtues is related to this last virtue and concerns a king's disposition or orientation toward his people. One of the most ubiquitous themes in Fénelon's political thought concerns the threats to the common good and to political stability posed by a ruler's self-interest or self-love. Ensuring that the king always puts the people first requires that he cultivate a host of dispositions: the fortitude that enables him to withstand the suffering that reminds him that he is a human being like other human beings, the piety that restrains his pride and induces in him a healthy humility, and, most importantly, the love of the people that leads the good king to seek to be the father rather than the master of those he leads.

A second prominent theme in Fénelon's political thought concerns the organization of the state. His development of this theme in many ways parallels his development of the theme of the virtues of political rule. Indeed just as Fénelon holds up for the emulation of individual princes a series of portraits of admirable kings, he similarly describes a series of admirable societies and regimes for our reflection. Some portraits are fictional, such as the bee republic of the *Fables* and the several cities and regimes described in *Telemachus*. Others are drawn from life, such as the descriptions of France in the letters and memoranda included in this collection. But what all of these portraits share is the conviction that the flourishing or corruption of a state depends on the particular arrangement of its social and political institutions, and in particular the way in which these institutions serve either to augment or diminish the general well-being and happiness of the citizens. A sense of the range of Fénelon's concerns on this front can be gleaned from the subheadings that he used to organize his reform proposals in the "Tables of Chaulnes." These subheadings—which include "Commerce" and

"Justice" and "Nobility" and "Church"—capture and help to clarify Fénelon's principal concerns as a theorist of institutions not only in the "Tables" but indeed across his works. Thus under the heading of "Commerce," the "Tables" sets forth a series of proposals for encouraging free trade—a theme especially prominent in the account of Tyre in *Telemachus*. Under the heading of "Church," the "Tables" lay out a comprehensive theory of the relationship of Church and state—a question central to the *Discourse Delivered at the Consecration of the Elector of Cologne*. Under the heading of "Nobility," Fénelon examines questions of social rank and equality—issues prominent in several of the *Dialogues* (and especially those in which Socrates is a character). Under the heading of "Justice" (and indeed throughout the "Tables"), Fénelon lays out a series of proposals for the reform of a range of institutions from the armed forces to the judiciary to the civil administration to the court and household of the king—themes that reemerge across his political writings, including especially (though hardly only) in his account of the reform of Salente in *Telemachus*.

A third theme central to Fénelon's political thought concerns international relations. Fénelon's life spanned a remarkably tumultuous period in the history of Europe. His vision of international politics and his proposals for its prosecution and reform accordingly reflect his experiences as a firsthand witness to the devastating effects of Louis XIV's military and diplomatic and commercial policies on France and its people as well as its neighbors. His experiences in Cambrai particularly sensitized him to the ways in which ordinary people are often compelled to bear the brunt of the costs of the policies determined by elites, and many of his reforms when it comes to issues of international relations are governed by his concern to reestablish the well-being of the people as the proper and primary concern in matters of international affairs. This is perhaps most evident in the way he treats war. As many readers have seen, Fénelon deplored war, and especially wars fought for selfish gain and glory. At the same time, Fénelon was hardly a pacifist; even in preferring peace to war he was well aware that it is sometimes necessary to preserve peace by preparing for war—a theme especially central to the *Examination of Conscience* and its teachings on just war. But Fénelon encourages not just military preparedness but also preemptive negotiation and diplomacy in an effort to stave off unnecessary wars before they began—another area he believed had been compromised by Louis's cynical approach to international law and diplomacy. But even as Fénelon draws on a rich tradition of thinking about just war and the laws of peoples to formulate nuanced positions of his own, his most important and far-seeing contributions as a commentator on international affairs comes on two other fronts. As a theorist of commerce, Fénelon recognized the ways in which international trade could promote mutual gains and peaceful bonds between nations: an idea that not only subverted the zero-sum mercantile assumptions prevalent in his day, but also anticipated many of the defenses of free trade set forth by later Enlightenment thinkers. And Fénelon was also one of the first thinkers in Europe to articulate a theory of balanced powers among the European states—an idea that he develops especially in the "Supplement" to the *Examination*.

Fénelon addressed a wide range of political issues across a wide range of texts, as will be clear by this point. One thus might wonder how—and indeed whether—his many discrete treatments of these issues hang together. Elsewhere I have argued that, taken together, his political ideas form a coherent whole, and that this whole deserves to be regarded as constituting a true political philosophy. But here it may be most useful just to note that the political writings that follow are, each in their own way, fundamentally efforts at practical political reform. Fénelon wrote in and for an age whose politics troubled him deeply. Yet he cherished the hope that through a certain type of responsible resistance and reform, agents of political change might be able to hasten the arrival of a brighter future.

This fact is important to keep in mind for several reasons, but especially for how recognition of it can help keep us from misconstruing his intentions as a writer on politics. Fénelon has sometimes been portrayed as a political idealist, especially by those who have focused on specific areas of his political thought abstracted from his claims elsewhere, and by those who have sought to make his political ideas conform to his spiritual teachings. In this latter vein, some have sought to read Fénelon's politics through the lens of his concept of pure love. But readers of this volume will need to determine for themselves how exactly his concept of pure love comports or does not comport with his political thought. Fénelon of course sincerely loved pure love, and genuinely believed it to represent the perfection of human beings rejoined to our creator. Yet my own sense is that Fénelon understood the political world to be a less-than-perfect world, a world driven by self-love, and indeed one that could never be fully transformed into a perfect world animated solely by pure love. In light of this, his hopes for reform take a specific and more moderate form. Far from seeking to substitute pure love for self-love and thereby render the political world perfect, Fénelon sought rather to make his political world better than it might otherwise be. To use terms made famous by Saint

Augustine (a thinker never far from Fénelon's mind, whether he is writing on political matters or spiritual matters), Fénelon understood well the profound divide separating the city of man from the city of God, and as a political thinker he made it his mission to reform and to improve the earthly city to the degree of which it is capable.

1

Fables (selections)

[Pl. 1:175–275]

1. The Bee and the Fly [206]

One day a bee spied a fly near her hive. "What are you doing here?" she demanded furiously. "Really, vile animal: you dare to mingle with the queens of the air?"

"You're right," the fly coolly replied. "One should never approach a nation so spirited as yours."

"None are so wise as we are," said the bee. "We alone have laws and a well-administered republic. We graze only on fragrant flowers; we make only a delicious honey that rivals nectar. Get out of my sight, you nasty intrusive fly. Buzz off and go back to making your living on the dung heaps!"

"We live as we can," the fly responded. "Poverty is not a vice, but anger is a great one. You may make sweet honey, but your heart is always bitter. You are wise in your laws, but carried away in your conduct. The anger that stings your enemies kills you, and your insane cruelty hurts you [207] more than it hurts anyone else. It is better to have less dazzling qualities, with more moderation."

2. The Pigeon Punished for Its Restlessness [215]

Two pigeons used to live together in a dovecote in profound peace. They sliced through the air on wings that beat so quickly they seemed to stay still. They playfully flew after each other, fleeing and chasing each other in turn. Then they searched for grain on the farmer's threshing floor or in the neighboring meadows. After that they used to go slake their thirst in the pure currents of a river flowing through fields of flowers. From there they returned to their dovecote, whitewashed and peppered with small holes, where they passed the time living happily together with their faithful companions. Their hearts were tender, and the shimmering plumage of their necks was more colorful than fickle Iris.[1] The sweet murmur of these happy pigeons

Fénelon. Ryan Patrick Hanley, Oxford University Press (2020) © Oxford University Press.
DOI: 10.1093/oso/9780190079581.001.0001

could be heard, and their life was delightful. Then one of them, tired of the pleasures of a peaceful life, allowed himself to be seduced by a mad ambition, and set his mind to politics. Abandoning his old friend, he left for the coast of the Levant, passing over the Mediterranean, floating through the air on his wings like a ship cleaving the waves of Tethys with its sails.[2] After reaching Alexandretta, he continued to make his way over land to Aleppo.[3] On arriving there, he greeted the other pigeons of the country who served as official couriers, and he envied their happiness. Immediately word spread among them that a stranger had arrived in their nation, crossing great lands, and he was enlisted into the ranks of the couriers. Week in and week out he carried attached to his feet the letters of a pasha, flying at least twenty-eight leagues a day.[4] He was proud to carry secrets of state, and he pitied his old companion, who lived without glory in the holes of his dovecote. But one day, while carrying the letters of the pasha—who was suspected of infidelity by the Great Lord—someone sought to discover [216] through his letters whether the pasha had some secret communication with the officers of the King of Persia.[5] A flying arrow pierced the poor pigeon, who managed to drag on for a bit on a struggling wing, even as his blood flowed. At last he fell, the shadows of death already covering his eyes. As the letters were taken from him to be read, he expired full of grief, condemning his vain ambition and longing for the sweet repose of his dovecote where he was able to live in security with his friend.

3. The Bees [229]

A young prince, at the moment of the return of the zephyr when all nature was reawakening, was strolling in a delightful garden when he heard a great noise and saw a beehive. This spectacle was new to him, and drawing near he saw with astonishment the order, the care, and the work of this little republic. The cells had begun to form and take on a regular appearance. One group of bees filled them with their sweet nectar; the others brought flowers that they had selected from all the riches of the spring. Idleness and laziness were banned from this little state; everything there was in movement, but without confusion and without disorder. The higher-ranking bees supervised the others, who obeyed their superiors without murmur and without jealousy. While the young prince admired this spectacle that was previously unfamiliar to him, a bee whom all the others recognized as their queen came before him and said to him: "The sight of our work and our conduct pleases you, but more importantly it must instruct you. We suffer neither disorder nor vice among us; one is eminent among us only by one's work, and by talents that can be useful to our republic. Merit is the sole path that can raise one to the highest ranks. We busy ourselves night and day with things useful to men. Would that you may be like us one day, bringing to the human race the order that you so admire here! By so doing you will promote its happiness and your own; you will fulfill the task that destiny has imposed on you, because you will be above others only [230] in order to protect them, only to divert those harms that threaten them, only to procure them all the goods that they have the right to expect from a vigilant and fatherly government."

4. The Adventures of Aristonoüs [248]

Sophronime, having lost the estate of his ancestors through shipwrecks and other misfortunes, consoled himself for this loss by his virtue in the island of Delos.[6] There he sang on his golden lyre the marvels of the god worshiped there; he cultivated the Muses, by whom he was loved; he eagerly sought out all the secrets of nature, the paths of the stars and the heavens, the order of the elements, the structure of the universe that he measured by his compass, the uses of plants, the anatomies of animals, but above all he studied himself and applied himself to the beautification of his soul by virtue. Thus fortune, in seeking to beat him down, had raised him to true glory, that of wisdom.

While he lived happily and simply in this [249] retreat, one day he spied on the seashore a venerable old man who was unknown to him; he was a stranger who had come to land on the island. This old man admired the shores of the seas, where he knew that this island had floated in days gone by; he considered this coast, where small hills ever covered with budding and flowering turf overlooked sand and rocks; he could not gaze enough on the pure fountains and the rapid rivers that watered this delightful countryside. He advanced toward the sacred woods that surrounded the temple of the god. He was astonished to see this verdure that the north winds never dared to tarnish, and he considered again the temple, made of a Parian marble whiter than snow and surrounded by tall columns of jasper. Sophronime was no less attentive in his contemplation of the old man: his white beard fell onto his chest, his wrinkled face had nothing deformed about it; it was still exempt from the injuries of an extreme old age; his eyes showed a sweet liveliness; his form was great and majestic, but a little bowed, and an ivory staff supported him. "O stranger," Sophronime said to him, "what do you seek in this island, which seems unknown to you? If it is the temple of the god, you see it from afar, and I offer myself to lead you to it, as I fear the gods, and I have learned what Jupiter wants us to do for the assistance of strangers."

"I accept," responded the old man, "the offer that you make me with such signs of kindness; I pray the gods will reward your love for strangers. Let us go to the temple." Along the way he recounted to Sophronime the story of his voyage. "I am," he said, "Aristonoüs, a native of Clazomenae, city of Ionia, situated on this agreeable coast that juts out into the sea and seems to go join the island of Chios, blessed fatherland of Homer.[7] I was born to poor but noble parents. My father, Polystrate, who was already burdened by a numerous family, did not want to raise me; he had me exposed by one of his friends from Teos. An old woman of Erythrae, who had land close by the place where I had been exposed, fed me on goat's milk in her house, but as she had difficulty enough making her own living, as soon as I was old enough to serve, [250] she sold me to a slave merchant, who took me to Lycia. He sold me, at Patara,[8] to a rich and virtuous man named Alcine: this Alcine took care of me in my youth.[9] To him I seemed docile, moderate, sincere, affectionate, and dedicated to all the honest things he wanted to teach me; he gave me to the arts favored by Apollo; he taught me music, bodily exercises, and above all the art of curing the wounds of men. I soon acquired a fairly decent reputation in this art, which is so necessary, and Apollo, who inspired me, revealed to me marvelous secrets. Alcine, who loved me more and more, and who was delighted to see the success of his cares for me, freed me and sent me to Damocles, King of Lycaonia,[10] who, given over to pleasures, loved life and feared its loss. This king, in order to hold on to me, showered me with riches. Some years later, Damocles died. His son, whom flatterers had inflamed against me, led me to become disgusted with all glittering things. At last I felt a powerful desire to return to Lycia, where I had passed my childhood so sweetly. I hoped to again find Alcine there, who had raised me and who was the first author of all my fortune. In arriving in this country, I learned that Alcine had died after having lost his property and suffering with great steadfastness the misfortunes of his old age. I went to scatter flowers and tears on his ashes; I put an honorable inscription on his grave, and I inquired as to what had become of his children. I was told that the only one remaining, named Orciloque, could not bear to be seen propertyless in his home country where his father had lived in such splendor, and had embarked on a foreign ship in order to go and lead an obscure life on some far-off island. I was further told that this Orciloque had been shipwrecked, a little time afterward, near the island of Karpathos, and that as a result there no longer remained any family of my benefactor Alcine.[11] I immediately thought to buy the house where he had lived, along with the fertile fields around it that he possessed. I was very glad to see these places again, which recalled to me the sweet memory of an age so agreeable, and a master so good: it seemed to me that I was again in this flower of my earliest youth [251] when I had served Alcine. No sooner had I purchased the rights to his property from his creditors than I was obliged to go to Clazomenae: my father Polystrate and my mother Phidile were dead. I had several brothers who did not get along; as soon as I had arrived at Clazomenae, I presented myself to them in simple dress, as a man deprived of property, and showing them the marks that you know we take care to make in exposing infants. They were shocked to see thus augmented the number of the successors of Polystrate, who were obliged to divide his little estate; they even wanted to contest my birth, and they refused to recognize me before the judges. Thus, in order to punish their inhumanity, I declared that I would agree to be like a stranger to them; and I requested that they would be likewise forever excluded from becoming my inheritors. The judges arranged it, and then I showed them the riches that I had carried in my ship. I revealed to them that I was that Aristonoüs who had acquired all the treasures of Damocles, King of Lycaonia, and that I had never married.

My brothers regretted having treated me so unjustly; and in the hopes of one day being able to be my heirs, they made extreme efforts to work their way back into my good graces, but in vain. Their division was the cause of the sale of our father's property; I bought it, and they had the unhappiness of seeing all our father's property pass into the hands of the one to whom they had not wanted to give the least part of it. Then they all fell into a frightful poverty. But once they had become sufficiently aware of the error of their ways, I desired to show them my good nature; I pardoned them, I received them in my house, and I gave each of them enough to engage profitably in commerce. I reunited all of them; they and their children lived together peacefully under my roof, and I became the common father of all these different families. By their union and their application to labor, they soon amassed considerable riches. However, old age, as you see, came to my doorstep; it bleached my hair and wrinkled my face; it warned me that I would not long enjoy such perfect prosperity. [252] Before dying, I wanted to see one last time again that land which is so dear to me, and which touched me more than even my

fatherland, this Lycia, where I learned to be good and wise under the conduct of the virtuous Alcine. While recrossing the sea, I met a merchant from
one of the Cyclades Islands, who assured me that a son of Orciloque who
exhibited the wisdom and the virtue of his grandfather Alcine was still living
at Delos.[12] At once I gave up heading for Lycia, and rushed to seek, under the
auspices of Apollo, in his island, this precious remnant of a family to whom
I owe everything. Little time remains for me to live: Fate, enemy of that sweet
repose that the gods so rarely grant to mortal men, will hurry to cut short my
days. But I would be content to die, so long as my eyes, before closing themselves to the light, had seen the grandson of my master. Speak then, O you
who live with him in this island, do you know him? Can you tell me where
I can find him? If you enable me to see him, may the gods reward you for it by
making you see on your knees the children of your children down to the fifth
generation! May the gods keep all of your house in peace and in abundance
as the fruit of your virtue!"

While Aristonoüs thus spoke, Sophronime poured forth tears mixed
of joy and sadness. Finally, unable to speak, he threw his arms around the
old man's neck, embraced him, held him tight, and in pain cried out these
words between sighs: "I am, O my father, the one you are looking for: you see
Sophronime, grandson of your friend Alcine. It is I, and in listening to you,
I cannot doubt that the gods have sent you here to ease my pains. Gratitude,
which seems lost to the earth, finds itself once again in you alone. In my
youth I heard it said that a celebrated and rich man, established in Lycaonia,
had been nourished at the home of my grandfather; but as Orciloque my father died young, leaving me at my cradle, I have known these things only
confusedly. I have not dared to go to Lycaonia in incertitude, and I have preferred to remain on this island, consoling myself in my miseries by contempt
for vain riches, and by the sweet work of cultivating the Muses [253] in the
sacred house of Apollo. Wisdom, which accustoms men to live on little and
to be tranquil, has for me taken the place of all other goods."

In finishing this speech, Sophronime, seeing that he had arrived at the
temple, proposed to Aristonoüs to make his prayer and offerings there. They
sacrificed to the god two sheep whiter than snow and a bull who had a cres-
cent on the front between his two horns; finally they sang verses in honor of
the god who illuminates the universe, who rules the seasons, who presides
over the sciences, and who gives life to the choir of the nine Muses. After
leaving the temple, Sophronime and Aristonoüs passed the rest of the day
recounting their adventures to each other. Sophronime received the old

man in his home, with the tenderness and respect he would have granted to Alcine himself, had he still been living. The next day they left together, setting sail for Lycia. Aristonoüs led Sophronime into a fertile countryside on the banks of the river Xanthe, into the waves in which Apollo, returning from the hunt covered in dust, had so often plunged his body and washed his beautiful blond hair. Alongside this river they found poplars and willows whose tender budding foliage concealed the nests of countless birds that sang day and night. The river, falling from a rock with much noise and foam, broke its stream in a canal full of little stones; all the plain was covered with golden harvest; the hills, which raised themselves into an amphitheater, were full of vineyards and orchards. All nature was cheerful and charming, the heavens were sweet and serene, and the land always ready to draw from its breast new riches in order to repay the pains of the laborers. In progressing along the river, Sophronime spied a house that was simple and unprepossessing, but of an agreeable architecture with just proportions. He found there neither marble, nor gold, nor silver, nor ivory, nor fine furnishings; everything there was proper and full of charm and convenience, without lavishness. A fountain flowed in the middle of the court, and formed a little canal bordered by a green carpet. The gardens were not immense; one saw there fruits and plants useful [254] for human nourishment; at the two sides of the garden stood two thickets, of which the trees were almost as old as the earth their mother, and of which the thick branches made darkness impenetrable to the rays of the sun. They entered into a banquet hall, where they enjoyed a pleasant meal of the dishes that nature furnished in the gardens, and one saw nothing there of what men in their weakness go seek so long and so dearly in the cities; there was milk as sweet as that which Apollo took care to draw when he was a shepherd in the land of King Admetus,[13] honey more exquisite than that of the bees of Hybla in Sicily, or of Mount Hymettus in Attica; there were vegetables from the garden, and fruits that had been gathered. A wine more delicious than nectar flowed from large vases into chiseled goblets. During this frugal but sweet and tranquil meal, Aristonoüs did not want to place himself at the table. At first he did all he could, under various pretexts, to hide his modesty; but finally, as Sophronime pressed him, he declared that he had resolved never to dine with the grandson of Alcine, whom he had so long served in this same hall. "There," he said to him, "is where this wise old man had been accustomed to dine; there is where he conversed with his friend; there is where he played various games; here is where he strolled while reading Hesiod and Homer, here is where he lay down for the night." In recalling these circumstances his heart filled with pity, and tears flowed from his eyes. After the meal, he took Sophronime to see the beautiful meadow where his great lowing herd roamed along the banks of the river; then they spied the flock of sheep returning from the green pastures; the mothers bleating and full of milk were followed by their little bounding sheep. Everywhere were bustling workers, who loved the work for the sake of their gentle and humane master, who rendered himself beloved of them, and who softened the pains of their bondage.

Aristonoüs, having shown Sophronime this house, these slaves, these herds, and these lands rendered so fertile by meticulous cultivation, spoke these words to him: "I am delighted to see you in the ancient estate of your ancestors; I am content, because I put you [255] in possession of the place where I served Alcine so long. Enjoy in peace what was his, live happily, and prepare yourself from afar by your vigilance an end sweeter than his." At the same time he made him a bequest of this property with all the solemnities prescribed by the laws, and he declared that it excluded his natural heirs from his succession, if ever they were so ungrateful as to contest the gift that he had made to the grandson of his benefactor Alcine. But this was not enough to satisfy the heart of Aristonoüs. Before giving over his house, he adorned it entirely with new furnishings, simple and modest in truth, but fitting and pleasant; he filled the haylofts with rich gifts of Ceres, and the cellar with a wine of Chio, worthy of being served by the hand of Hebe or of Ganymedes at the table of great Jupiter.[14] He put there also Pramnian wine, with an abundant provision of the honey of Hymettus and of Hybla, and the oil of Attica, almost as sweet as honey itself. Finally he added there countless fleeces of wool as fine and as white as snow, riches skinned from the tender sheep that graze on the mountains of Arcadia and in the rich pastures of Sicily. In such a state he left his house to Sophronime, and he also gave him fifty Euboean talents, and reserved to his relations the property that he possessed in the peninsula of Clazomenae, near Smyrna, of Lebedus and Colophon, which was tremendously valuable. The bequest being made, Aristonoüs reembarked in his ship to return to Ionia. Sophronime, astonished and moved to tears by such magnificent benefactions, accompanied him all the way to the vessel with tears in his eyes, declaring that he would forever be his father as he held him tightly in his arms. Aristonoüs soon arrived home by a fortunate navigation, and none of his relatives dared complain about what he had given to Sophronime. "I have left," he said to them, "for my last will and testament, this order: that all my goods will be sold and distributed to the poor of Ionia, if ever any of you should challenge the gift that I have made to the grandson of Alcine."

The wise old man lived in peace, enjoying the goods the gods had given him for his virtue. Every year, despite his old age, he made a voyage to [256] Lycia in order to see Sophronime again, and to make a sacrifice on the tomb of Alcine, which he had enriched with the most beautiful ornaments of architecture and sculpture. He had ordered that his own ashes, after his death, should be carried into the same tomb, so that they might rest with those of his dear master. Every year in the spring, Sophronime, impatient to see him again, turned his eyes constantly toward the seashore, in order to try to spy the boat of Aristonoüs, which arrived in this season. Every year he had the pleasure of seeing coming from afar, across the bitter waves, that boat which was so dear to him, and the arrival of that ship was infinitely sweeter to him than all the graces of nature being reborn in the spring after the rigors of dreadful winter.

One year he failed to see arriving, as in other years, that much-sought ship. He sighed bitterly; sadness and fear were evident on his face; sweet sleep eluded him; exquisite dishes lost their taste, he was restless, alarmed at the least noise, always turned toward the port; he asked constantly if some ship from Ionia had not been seen. And then he saw one, but alas! Aristonoüs was not there; it carried only his ashes in a silver urn. Amphiclès, long-time friend of the deceased, close to the same age, and faithful executor of his last will, sadly carried this urn. When he came up to Sophronime, speech failed both of them, and they could only express themselves by their sobs. Having kissed the urn and bathed it with his tears, Sophronime spoke thus: "O old man, you have made my life happy, and you cause me now the cruelest of all sadnesses. I will not see you again; death would be sweet as it would allow me to see you and follow you to the Elysian fields, where your shade enjoys the blessed peace that the just gods reserve for virtue. You restored justice to our times and piety and gratitude on the earth: in an age of iron you showed the goodness and innocence of the golden age. The gods, before crowning you in the dwelling place of the just, accorded to you here below a happy old age, long and pleasant; but, alas! [257] nothing lasts forever. I take no pleasure in enjoying your gifts, because I am reduced to enjoying them without you. O dear shade! When will I follow you? Precious ashes, if you could feel something again, you would surely feel the pleasure of being mixed with those of Alcine. Mine will mix themselves here too one day. Until that time, my entire consolation will be to preserve what remains of what I most loved.

O Aristonoüs! O Aristonoüs! No, you will not die, and you will live always in the depths of my heart. May I sooner forget myself than ever forget this so lovable man, who loved me entirely, who loved virtue entirely, to whom I owe everything!"

After these words, broken by deep sighs, Sophronime put the urn in the tomb of Alcine. He made several sacrifices, the blood of which flooded the altars of turf surrounding the tomb; he spilled abundant libations of wine and milk; he burned incense that came from the furthest regions of the East, raising a fragrant cloud to the skies. In the same season Sophronime established in perpetuity funeral games in honor of Alcine and Aristonoüs, drawing participants from Caria, that happy and fertile country; from the enchanted banks of the Meander, which flows with so many twists and turns, and which seems to regret leaving the country it waters; from the ever verdant banks of the Cayster; from the edges of the Pactolus, flowing over golden sands; from the Pamphylia that Ceres, Pomona, and Flora so marvelously adorn; finally from the vast plains of Sicily, watered like a garden by the torrents that fall from Mount Taurus, ever covered in snow.[15] During this solemn celebration, young boys and girls, clad in flowing robes of linen whiter than lilies, sang hymns in praise of Alcine and Aristonoüs, as one could not praise the one without praising the other as well, nor separate two men so closely united, even in death.

What was most wonderful there was that from the first day, as Sophronime made the libations of wine and milk, a myrtle of exquisite fragrance and foliage grew in the middle of the tomb, and [258] suddenly raised its tufted head to cover the two urns with the shade of its branches. All cried out that Aristonoüs, in reward for his virtue, had been changed by the gods into so beautiful a tree. Sophronime took care to water it himself, and to honor it as a divinity. This tree, far from growing old, renewed itself every decade, and by this marvel the gods sought to show that virtue, which throws such a sweet perfume over the memory of men, never dies.

5. Life of Plato [274]

Plato was of the highest birth an Athenian could be. Through his mother he was descended from Solon, and through his father from the ancient kings. In his youth he went off to war and showed great valor there. He was the disciple of Socrates, whose conversations he reported in his writings. As Socrates never wanted to write, we have nothing from him except the works of his two disciples Plato and Xenophon. These two disciples were jealous of each other. Afterward Plato had the curiosity to seek out the wisdom of foreigners. He traveled through Egypt and Phoenicia, where he took care to collect the traditions of the priests and the wise men. It cannot be doubted that he knew the books of Moses and the other works of the Jews. Dion, the son-in-law of the tyrant Dionysius and a great lover of letters and wisdom, brought him to Sicily. Dionysius himself saw him, admired him, and was at the point of renouncing his tyranny as a result of his counsels; but he was deterred by Philistus, a sophist and flatterer, who feared losing by this change the good fortune that he enjoyed. This false sage, jealous of Plato, gradually rendered him hateful to the tyrant. When Plato saw that the tyrant was incorrigible, he courageously showed him again the misery and indignity of a man who holds his fatherland in slavery. Irritated, the tyrant sold him as a slave to a man who took him to the island of Euboea, where his freedom was bought with Dion's money. After the death of the first Dionysius, he made the second of his two voyages to Syracuse, where Dion made him numerous considerable presents. The young Dionysius even wanted to give him a city where he might set up his laws and his republic, [275] but the wars did not allow for the execution of this project. Some time after, with Dion having twice driven out the young Dionysius, who was ultimately reduced to serving as a schoolmaster in Corinth in order to make a living, Plato did not want to return to Syracuse to enjoy the favor of his friend who had the supreme authority. On the contrary, he wrote him in order to persuade him to quit this odious power and to return liberty to his citizens after having cut down the tyrant following the example of Timoleon. Dion was harshly punished for not having profited from such wise counsel, because his own fellow-citizens assassinated him.

Plato remained peacefully in Athens, where he taught his followers in a grove near the city called Academy, from the name of Academus, who had given this place for public recreation. He was well built, of good appearance, eloquent, adept at exercises, and neat in his dress and in his furnishings, which irritated many of the other philosophers of his time, who affected to be wretched and filthy like Diogenes. He had broad shoulders, which gave him the name of Plato. His disciples were called academicians, after the place where he taught them. Later on they came to be divided into three sects. The ancients conserved Plato's principles. The moderns fell into the skepticism of the Pyrrhonians. Plato lived to the age of eighty-one, in full health, and in the highest repute.

2

Dialogues of the Dead Composed for the Education of a Prince (selections)

[Pl. 1:279–510]

1. Achilles and Homer [285]

ACHILLES: I'm delighted, great poet, to have served to immortalize you. My quarrel with Agamemnon, my sadness over the death of Patroclus, my wars against [286] the Trojans, the victory I won over Hector: these have given you the finest subject for poetry the world has ever seen.

HOMER: I admit that the subject is fine. But I surely would have been able to find others. A proof that others exist is that I indeed found others. The adventures of the wise and patient Ulysses are surely worth as much as the anger of the impetuous Achilles.

ACHILLES: What! You compare the crafty and deceitful Ulysses to the son of Thetis, more terrible than Mars! Go, ungrateful poet. You will feel . . .

HOMER: You have forgotten that shades must never work themselves into a state of anger. The anger of a ghost is hardly to be feared. You have no other arms to employ beyond good arguments.

ACHILLES: Why can't you admit that you owe to me the glory of your most beautiful poem? The other is only a heap of old wives' tales. The whole thing drags and proclaims itself as the work of an old man whose fire has gone out, and who doesn't know when to hang it up.

HOMER: You're like those men who, ignorant of the different genres of literature, think an author contradicts himself when he passes from a lively and fast-moving genre to a gentler and more moderate one. They would need to know that perfection lies in always observing diverse characters, varying one's style according to the subjects, raising and lowering oneself at the right moment, and thus offering, by this contrast, characters more pronounced and more agreeable. It is necessary to know how to sound the trumpet, to strum the lyre, and even to play the flute. I bet you would

Fénelon. Ryan Patrick Hanley, Oxford University Press (2020) © Oxford University Press.
DOI: 10.1093/oso/9780190079581.001.0001

have liked me to have painted Calypso with her nymphs in her grotto, or Nausicaa on the seashore, like the heroes and gods fighting at the gates of Troy. Stick to talking about war—that's your thing—and never get mixed up trying to judge poetry in my presence.

ACHILLES: O, you are proud, blind old man! You availed yourself of my death.

HOMER: I availed myself of my own as well. You're now just the shade of Achilles, and I'm only the shade of Homer.

ACHILLES: Ah! That I cannot make this ungrateful shade feel my former power! [287]

HOMER: Since you accuse me of ingratitude, I want to disabuse you once and for all. You merely furnished me a subject that I could have found anywhere. But I gave you a glory that another could not have given you and that will never fade.

ACHILLES: What! You really suppose that without your verses the great Achilles would not be admired by all nations and in all ages?

HOMER: Ridiculous vanity! For having spilled more blood than another at the siege of a city that was only taken after your death? Ha! How many heroes are there who have vanquished great peoples and conquered great realms? And yet they're forgotten in the shadows. We don't even know their names. The Muses alone can immortalize great actions. A king who loves glory must seek it in these two things: first he must merit it by virtue, and then make himself loved by the children of the Muses, who can sing his deeds to all posterity.

ACHILLES: But princes cannot always depend on having great poets: it is by chance that long after my death you conceived the project of making your *Iliad*.

HOMER: It's true. But when a prince loves letters, he forms many poets during his reign. His rewards and his esteem excite a noble emulation among them, and taste becomes perfected. He has only to love and to favor the Muses. They soon bring forth men of inspiration to praise all that is praiseworthy in him. When a prince lacks a Homer, it's because he is not worthy of having one. His lack of taste attracts ignorance, coarseness, and barbarism. Barbarism dishonors the nation as a whole, and takes away all hope of lasting glory from the prince who reigns. Do you not know that Alexander, who only a short while ago came here below, despaired of not having a poet who could do for him what I have done for you? He had a proper taste for glory. As for you, you owe everything to me, and yet you are not ashamed to treat me ungratefully. Now is hardly the time to get angry. Your anger before Troy furnished me the subject of a poem, but I can no longer sing of the tantrums you would have here, and they would not do you any honor. [288] Just remember that with Fate having stripped you of all other advantages, all that remains to you is the great name you draw from my verses. Goodbye. When you are in a better mood, I will come to sing to you in these woods certain passages from the *Iliad*—for example the death of the Greeks in your absence, the consternation of the Trojans on seeing you appear in order to avenge Patroclus, the gods themselves astonished to see you as devastating as Jupiter. After this, say, if you dare, that Achilles does not owe his glory to Homer.

2. Confucius and Socrates [295]

CONFUCIUS: I hear that your Europeans often come to us in the East, and that they call me the Socrates of China. I'm honored by this name.

SOCRATES: Let's leave off the compliments; they're not suitable here. On what is this resemblance between us founded?

CONFUCIUS: On the fact that we lived at nearly the same time, and that we have both been poor, moderate, and eager to make men virtuous.

SOCRATES: For my part, I didn't train, as you did, excellent men, in order to go into all the provinces to sow the seeds of virtue, fight against vice, and instruct men.

CONFUCIUS: You formed a school of philosophers that greatly enlightened the world.

SOCRATES: My aim has never been to render the people philosophical; I have not dared to hope for this. I abandoned the crude and corrupted vulgar to all their errors; I limited myself to the instruction of a small set of followers of a cultivated mind who sought the principles of good morals. I never wanted to write anything, and I found speech best for teaching. A book is a dead thing that does not respond to the diverse and unexpected difficulties of each reader; a book passes through the hands of men incapable of making good use of it; a book is susceptible to several interpretations contrary to the author's intent. I preferred to choose certain men, and confide in them a doctrine that I could make them understand through conversation.

CONFUCIUS: This plan is fine; it attests to a way of thinking that is entirely straightforward, entirely solid, and entirely free from vanity. But has it succeeded in avoiding differences [296] of opinions among your followers? As for me, I avoided subtle reasoning and limited myself to maxims suitable for the practice of the virtues in society.

SOCRATES: As for me, I believed that true maxims can only be established in ascending to the first principles that can demonstrate them, and in refuting all the other prejudices of men.

CONFUCIUS: But in the end, did your first principles enable you to avoid differences of opinion among your followers?

SOCRATES: Not in the least. Plato and Xenophon, my principal followers, had entirely different views. The Academicians trained by Plato divided themselves between them; this experience disabused me of my hopes for mankind. One man can do almost nothing for other men. Men can do almost nothing for themselves, owing to the weakness in which their pride or their passions hold them; all the more can men do almost nothing for each other. Examples and artfully insinuated reasons only have some effect on a small number of men born better than others. In the end, a general reform of a republic seems to me impossible, so disillusioned am I with the human race.

CONFUCIUS: As for me, I wrote, and I sent out my followers in order to try to bring good morals to all the provinces of our empire.

SOCRATES: You wrote short and simple things, if what has been published under your name is indeed yours. These are merely maxims that have perhaps been gleaned from your conversations, in the same way that Plato transcribed mine in his dialogues. Maxims thus cut and pasted have an edge that, I suspect, was not to be found in your discussions. Moreover you were descended from a royal house and had great authority throughout your country: you could do things that were not permitted to me, an artisan's son. As for me, I had no use for writing, and I spoke only too much: I even removed myself from all positions in my republic in order to lessen envy; and I couldn't thrive there insofar as it is impossible to make anything good of men. [297]

CONFUCIUS: I was happier among the Chinese. I left them laws that were wise and quite well administered.

SOCRATES: Given what I have heard reported by our Europeans, it was a good thing that China had such good laws and rigorous administration.[1] There is a good likelihood that the Chinese have been better than they are. I don't want to deny that a people, when it has a good and constant form of government, can become wholly superior to other people less well governed. For example, we Greeks, who had wise legislators and certain disinterested citizens who dreamt only of the good of the republic, we were far more cultivated and virtuous than the peoples that we labeled Barbarians. The Egyptians, before us, likewise had wise men governing them, and it was from them that we received our good laws. Among the Greek republics, ours excelled in the liberal arts, in the sciences, in arms, but it was Lacedaemonia that displayed a pure and austere discipline for a longer time. Thus I admit that a people governed by a long line of good legislators, and who have upheld virtuous customs, can be better administered than others who have not had the same culture. A people well led will be more sensitive to honor, firmer in the face of danger, less susceptible to pleasure, more accustomed to getting by with little, more just, and thus able to prevent the usurpations and frauds of citizen on citizen. It is thus that the Lacedaemonians were disciplined; it is thus that the Chinese were able to be in distant ages. But I still believe that an entire people is not capable of ascending to the principles of true wisdom. They can attend to certain useful and commendable rules, but this is owing rather to the authority of education, respect for the laws, zeal for the fatherland, the emulation that comes from examples, the force of custom, often even the fear of dishonor and the hope of being rewarded. But to be a philosopher—to follow the good and the beautiful in itself out of simple persuasion and the true and free love of the good and the beautiful—this [298] can never be spread among an entire people; this is reserved to certain chosen souls that the heavens wanted to separate from others. The people are capable only of certain virtues of habit and opinion, on the authority of those who have won its trust. Once again, I believe that such was the virtue of your ancient Chinese. Such men are just in matters in which one has accustomed them to impose a rule of justice, and not in other, more important affairs in which they are not in the habit of passing judgment. One will be just toward one's fellow citizen, and inhumane toward one's slave; zealous for one's fatherland, and unjust when conquering a neighboring people, never considering that the whole world is but a common fatherland, where all the peoples of different nations ought to live as a single family. Such virtues, founded on the custom and prejudices of a people, are always crooked, as they fail to ascend to the first principles that give the full scope of the true idea of justice and virtue. These same peoples, who appeared so virtuous in certain sentiments and in certain discrete acts, had a religion full of fraud, injustice, and impurity, though their laws were just and austere. What a muddle! What a contradiction! And yet this is what was best in these so greatly celebrated peoples; this is humanity with its best foot forward.

CONFUCIUS: It may be that we have been happier than you, owing to our great virtue.

SOCRATES: So it's said, but in order to be truly sure, Europeans would need to know your history as well as they know their own. When commerce is entirely free and frequent, when the European critics have passed into China in order to examine with rigor all the ancient manuscripts of your history, when they have distinguished fables and doubtful things from certain ones, when they have seen the strengths and weaknesses of the ancient morals in all particulars, perhaps then one will find that the majority of men have always been weak, vain, and corrupt among you like everywhere else, and that men have been men in all countries and in all times. [299]

CONFUCIUS: But why do you not believe our historians and your chroniclers?[2]

SOCRATES: Your historians are unknown to us; we have from them only bits extracted and reported by uncritical transcribers. It would be necessary to master your language, to read all your books, to see especially the originals, and to wait for a great number of wise men to have done this work in depth so that, by the great number of examiners, the matter could be fully clarified. Until then, your nation seems to me a spectacle that is fine and great from afar, but very dubious and questionable.

CONFUCIUS: You don't want to believe anything, merely because Ferdinand Mendez Pinto exaggerated a lot?[3] Do you doubt that China is a great and mighty empire, well populated and well governed—that the arts flourish there, that advanced sciences are cultivated there, that respect for the laws is exemplary there?

SOCRATES: How would you have me convince myself of all these things?

CONFUCIUS: Through your own chroniclers.

SOCRATES: It is necessary then that I believe them, these chroniclers?

CONFUCIUS: Why not?

SOCRATES: And that I believe what they say about both the bad and the good? Answer, please.

CONFUCIUS: Let it be so.

SOCRATES: According to these chroniclers, the vainest, most superstitious, most self-interested, most unjust, most dishonest people of the earth are the Chinese.

CONFUCIUS: There are vain and dishonest men everywhere.

SOCRATES: I agree, but in China the principles of the entire nation, to which no dishonor is attached, are lying and boasting of lies. What can one expect from such a people when it comes to distant truths that are difficult to shed light on? All their histories attest to their magnificence: how could they not, as they are so vain and prone to exaggeration even in contemporary matters one can see with one's own eyes, and in which they are guilty of having sought to deceive foreigners? The Chinese, from what I've heard, seem quite similar to the Egyptians. They are a tranquil and peaceful people, in a beautiful and rich [300] country; a vain people that despises all the other peoples of the world; a people that prides itself on its extraordinary antiquity, and puts its glory in the number of centuries it has lasted; a people that despite its politeness is superstitious to the most vulgar and ridiculous extremes; a people that puts all its wisdom in preserving its laws, without daring to examine what might be good in them; a solemn, mysterious, composed people, rigid observers of all its ancient customs with regard to appearances, without seeking there justice, sincerity, and the other inner virtues; a people that has made great mysteries of several very superficial things, the simple explication of which much diminishes the value. The arts there are quite mediocre, and the sciences were almost nonexistent there when our Europeans first became acquainted with them.

CONFUCIUS: Did we not have printing, gunpowder, geometry, painting, architecture, porcelain making, and even a method of reading and writing far superior to those of your Westerners? As for the antiquity of our histories, it is proven by our astronomical observations. Your Westerners claim that our calculations are faulty; but they do not doubt the observations themselves, and they admit that they correspond correctly with the revolutions of the heavens.

SOCRATES: You lump these things together in order to bring together all the things that are most estimable in China. But let's examine each of them more closely in turn.

CONFUCIUS: Certainly.

SOCRATES: Printing is merely a convenience for men of letters, and does not merit great glory. A mediocre artisan could make such an invention; it is even imperfect in your hands, because you only use plates, while the Westerners use not only plates but also movable type, by which they make all the compositions they please in very little time. Moreover it is not so much a question of having an art to facilitate studies, as of the use to which one puts them. The Athenians of my time did not have printing, [301] and nevertheless the fine arts and advanced sciences flourished among them; on the other hand, the Westerners, who invented printing superior to that of the Chinese, were vulgar, ignorant, and barbaric men. Gunpowder is a pernicious invention; it destroys the human race; it harms all men, and truly serves none; one soon imitates what others use against them. In the West, where firearms have been much better improved than in China, such arms decide nothing on one side or the other; the means of defense are proportional to the arms of the attackers; all of this ends up in a kind of balance, after which each is no more advanced than when one had only towers and simple walls, with pikes, javelins, swords, bows, testudo formations, and battering rams. If both sides had agreed to renounce firearms, countless superfluous and useless things could be dispensed with; valor, discipline, vigilance, and genius would play a greater part in the decisions of all wars. Here then is an invention that it is hardly permissible to admire.

CONFUCIUS: Do you despise our mathematicians as well?

SOCRATES: Have you not established that I should, as a rule, believe the facts reported by our chroniclers?

CONFUCIUS: It's true. But they admit that our mathematicians are clever.

SOCRATES: They say that they have made definite progress, and that they know well how to do several operations; but they add that they lack method, that they make certain demonstrations poorly, that they deceive themselves in calculations, that there are several very important things of which they have discovered nothing. That's what I hear said. These men, so intoxicated by the knowledge of the stars, and who limit their main study to them, found themselves even in this field of study very inferior to the Westerners who traveled in China, and who, it appears, are not the West's best astronomers. All this hardly corresponds to this marvelous idea of a people superior to all other nations. I say nothing of your [302] porcelain; it is your soil rather than your people who deserve the credit; or at least insofar as it owes to human merit, it is only the merit of a lowly artisan. Your architecture lacks fine proportions; everything in it is low and squashed; everything is jumbled, and littered with small ornaments that are neither noble nor natural. Your painting has some life and indefinable grace, but it has neither correct design, nor organization, nor nobility in the figures, nor truth in its representations. One sees there neither natural landscapes, nor histories, nor reasonable and developed concepts; one is merely dazzled by the beauty of the colors and the enamel.

CONFUCIUS: This same enamel is a marvel inimitable in all the West.

SOCRATES: It's true: but you have this in common with the most barbaric people, who have sometimes the secret of making in their country, by the help of nature, things that the most industrious nations would not know how to execute by themselves.

CONFUCIUS: Let's go on to writing.

SOCRATES: I agree that you have in your writing a great advantage insofar as it can be put into use among all the neighboring people who speak languages other than Chinese. Each character signifies an object, just as our entire words do, and a foreigner can read your writings without knowing your language, and he can reply to you by the same characters, even though his language may be entirely unknown to you. Such characters, if they were used everywhere, would be like a common language for the entire human race, and the convenience of it for commerce would be inestimable from one end of the world to the other. If all nations could agree to teach these characters to their children, the diversity of languages would not impede travelers, and there would exist a universal bond of society. But nothing is more impracticable than such a universal employment of your characters; there are such an overwhelming number of them that in order to signify all the objects to which one refers in human language, your wise men take a great number of years to learn how to write. What nation will subject itself to so tiresome a study? There is no science so thorny that isn't learned more quickly. What does one know, in [303] truth, when one only knows how to read and write? Moreover, can one hope that all nations will agree to teach this writing to their children? As soon as you establish this art in a single country it becomes very incommodious: from then on you no longer have the advantage of making yourself understood to nations of an unknown language, and you have the extreme disadvantage of miserably passing the best part of your life trying to learn how to write. Thus you throw yourself into two inconveniences: one of vainly admiring a fruitless and tiresome art, the other of consuming your entire youth in this dry study, which excludes you from making any progress in more solid knowledge.

CONFUCIUS: But our antiquity—are you honestly not convinced of it?

SOCRATES: Not at all. The reasons that persuade Western astronomers that your observations must be true can have struck your astronomers as well, and have furnished them a plausibility in order to authorize your vain fictions concerning the antiquity of China. Your astronomers would have seen that such things have come to arrive in such and such a time, by the same rules that persuade our astronomers in the West; they would not have failed to base their alleged observations on these rules in order to give them an appearance of truth. A people so powerfully vain and jealous of the glory of its antiquity, as little as it might be intelligent in astronomy, does not fail to color thus its fictions; chance even may have helped a little. In the end it would be necessary for the wisest astronomers of the West to have had the opportunity of examining in the originals all this train of observations. The Egyptians were great observers of the stars, and at the same time lovers of their fables in order to go back thousands of centuries. We need not doubt that they worked to harmonize these two passions.

CONFUCIUS: So what then would you conclude about our empire? It was beyond the reach of all commerce with your nations, where sciences reigned; it was surrounded on all sides by vulgar nations; it has certainly had, for several centuries since my [304] time, laws, administration, and arts that other Eastern peoples have not had. The origin of our nation is unknown, hidden in the obscurity of the most distant centuries. So you clearly see that I have neither stubbornness nor vanity on this. Honestly, what do you think about the origin of such a people?

SOCRATES: It is difficult to determine what really happened, among all that has come and gone in the course of populating the earth. But here's what seems likely to me. The most ancient peoples of our histories, the strongest and most civilized peoples, are those of Asia and Egypt; this is in a sense the source of the colonies. We see that the Egyptians established colonies in Greece, and have formed their morals. Some Asians, like the Phoenicians and the Phrygians, have done the same on all the Mediterranean coasts. Other Asians of these realms who were on the banks of the Tigris and of the Euphrates have been able to penetrate as far as into the Indies in order to people them. The peoples, in multiplying themselves, will have crossed the rivers and the mountains, and will have gradually spread their colonies even as far as into China: nothing in this vast and almost entirely unified continent will have stopped them. There is hardly any indication that men might have come up to China by way of the extreme north that we today call Tartary, as the Chinese since the most distant antiquity seem to have been peoples gentle, peaceful, orderly, and wisdom-loving—the opposite of the violent and wild nations that were nourished in the savage countries of the North. There is hardly any indication either that men might have reached China by sea; great sea voyages were then neither common nor possible. Moreover, the morals, the arts, the sciences, and the religion of the Chinese accord very well with the morals, the arts, the sciences, and the religion of the Babylonians and of these other peoples that our histories depict. I thus would be inclined to believe that some centuries before yours these Asiatic peoples penetrated as far as China; that they founded your empire there, that you had clever kings and virtuous legislators; that China once was more estimable for arts and morals than it is now; [305] that your historians flattered the pride of the nation; that things which would merit some praise have been exaggerated; that fable has been mixed with truth; and that one has wanted to hide from posterity the origin of the nation in order to render it more marvelous to all other peoples.

CONFUCIUS: Your Greeks, have they not done as much?

SOCRATES: Still worse: they have their fabled times, which come close to yours. I lived, following the common supposition, around three hundred years after you. However, when one tries to search with care before my time, one finds no historian other than Herodotus, who wrote immediately after the Persian Wars—that is to say around sixty years before my death. This historian established nothing else, and posits no dates that can be verified by contemporary authors, for all that which is much more ancient than this war. The times of the Trojan War, which are only around six hundred years before me, are still times acknowledged as fabulous. Judge for yourself whether it's necessary to be surprised by the idea that China might not have existed for centuries before you, as suggested in its histories.

CONFUCIUS: But why would you be inclined to believe that we are descended from the Babylonians?

SOCRATES: For this reason. There is much that indicates that you come from some people of upper Asia who gradually spread as far as China, and perhaps even in the time of some conquest of the Indies, which brought the conquering people all the way into the countries that today constitute your empire. Your antiquity is great; your sort of colony must then have been made of one of these ancient peoples, such as those of Nineveh or Babylonia. You must come from some powerful and magnificent people, because this is still the character of your nation. You are alone of this sort in all your countries, and the neighboring peoples, who have nothing similar, could not have given you morals. Like the ancient Babylonians, you have astronomy, and even judicial astrology, superstition, the art of divination, an architecture more sumptuous than proportioned, a life of pleasure and splendor, of great [306] cities, an empire where the prince has an absolute authority, laws greatly revered, temples in abundance, and a multitude of gods of all shapes. All this is only a conjecture, but it could be correct.

CONFUCIUS: I'm going to ask King Yao about this, who walks, it is said, with your ancient kings of Argos and Athens in this myrtle grove.[4]

SOCRATES: As for me, I trust neither Cecrops, nor Inachus, nor Pelops, nor even the heroes of Homer, on the subject of our antiquity.[5]

3. Solon and Justinian [317]

JUSTINIAN: Nothing compares to the majesty of the Roman laws. Among the Greeks you had a reputation for being a great legislator; but if you had lived among us, your glory would have been entirely obscured.

SOLON: Why would I have been despised in your country?

JUSTINIAN: Because the Romans looked to the Greeks for most of their laws and for their perfection.

SOLON: What did they find that was of such benefit to them?

JUSTINIAN: We have countless marvelous laws that have been made at different times. I will have, for centuries to come, the glory of having compiled all this grand body of laws in my Code.[6]

SOLON: Indeed I have often heard Cicero say here below that the laws of the Twelve Tables were the most perfect that the Romans could have had. You will be pleased if I note in passing that these laws went from Greece to Rome, and that they came principally from Lacedaemonia.

JUSTINIAN: They could come from wherever you please. But they were too simple and too short to compare to our laws, which anticipated everything, decided everything, and put everything in order to the last detail.

SOLON: As for me I believed that laws, in order to be good, would need to be clear, straightforward, short, well suited to the people who have to interpret them, and capable of being easily upheld, loved, and followed at every hour and every moment.

JUSTINIAN: But straightforward and short laws do not fully exercise the science and the genius of the legal experts;[7] they would not go to the depths of delicate questions.

SOLON: I admit that it seemed to me that the laws were made in order to avoid thorny questions, and [318] to preserve a people's good morals, order, and peace, but you tell me that they should exercise subtle minds, and furnish them what they need to make their cases.

JUSTINIAN: Rome produced wise legal experts; Sparta had only ignorant soldiers.

SOLON: I would have thought that good laws are those which enable one to dispense with legal experts, and that even the unlearned could live in peace under the shelter of such simple and clear laws, without being reduced to consulting vain sophists on the meanings of various texts, or on how to reconcile them. I would conclude that laws are hardly good when it takes all the wise men to explain them, and that they never agree among themselves.

JUSTINIAN: In order to make everything agree, I made my compilation.

SOLON: Tribonianus told me yesterday that he made it.[8]

JUSTINIAN: It's true, but he made it by my orders. An emperor does not execute such a work himself.

SOLON: As for me, I reigned in the belief that the principal duty of the one who governs the people is to give them laws that reconcile the king and the people in order to make them good and happy. To command armies and carry home victories is nothing compared to the glory of a legislator. But getting back to your Tribonianus, he merely made a compilation of laws from different times that have often varied, and you have never had a true body of laws all made with the same design of forming the morals and the entire government of a nation. Yours is a collection of individual laws made to judge the reciprocal claims of individuals. The Greeks alone have the glory of having made fundamental laws in order to conduct a people on philosophical principles, and in order to regulate all its policies and all its government. As for the multitude of your laws that you so extol, they make me think that you haven't had good ones, or that you haven't known how to preserve them in their simplicity. In order to govern a people well, it is necessary to have few judges and few [319] laws. There are few men capable of being judges; a multitude of judges corrupts everything. A multitude of laws is no less dangerous; they are not more understood, and they are not more protected. As soon as there is a multitude of them, men become accustomed to revere them in appearance, and to violate them under specious pretexts. Vanity makes them, bringing them forth with pomp; avarice and the other passions lead them to be despised. They are mocked by the subtlety of the sophists, who for money interpret them as anyone requests: from this is born chicanery, a monster born to devour the human race. I judge of causes by their effects. The laws only appear to me good in the country where lawsuits are not brought, and where short and straightforward laws have prevented all disputes from arising. I would like to see neither dispositions by will, nor adoptions, nor disinheritances, nor substitutions of one heir for another, nor loans, nor sales, nor exchanges. I would like to see only a very limited area of land in each family, that this property be inalienable, and that the magistrate divide it equally among the children according to the law after the death of the father. Were families to multiply themselves too much beyond the proportion of the extent of their lands, I would send a party of people to form a colony on some deserted island. In return for this short and simple rule, I would trade your entire jumble of laws, and I would hope merely to order morals, to teach youth sobriety, work, patience, contempt of softness, and courage in the face of both pain and death. This would be better than all that sly and subtle reasoning over contracts or trusteeships.

JUSTINIAN: Laws so sterile and austere would overturn everything that is the most ingenious in jurisprudence.

SOLON: I prefer straightforward, tough, and rude laws to an ingenious art of troubling the peace of men, and corrupting the foundations of morals. There has never been an age that has seen more laws than yours; there has never been an empire so cowardly, so effeminate, so degenerate, so unworthy of the ancient Romans who so resembled the Spartans. You yourself have been only a cheat, a blasphemer, a rogue, a destroyer of good laws, a man vain and fake in everything. Your Tribonianus was just as evil and [320] dissolute. Procopius unmasked you.[9] Getting back to the laws: they are laws only insofar as they are easily known, believed, loved, and followed, and they are good only insofar as they work to render the people good and happy. You have made nobody good and happy by your ostentatious compilation: from which I conclude that it deserves to be burned. But I see that you are angry. His Imperial Majesty believes himself to be above the truth; but his shade is now only a shade to which one speaks the truth with impunity. Nevertheless I'm leaving so that you can calm down your awakened anger.

4. Socrates and Alcibiades (1) [324]

SOCRATES: Here you are, agreeable as ever! Who will you charm here below?

ALCIBIADES: And you, here you are, always the teaser. Who will you persuade here, you who always want to persuade somebody?

SOCRATES: I stopped wanting to persuade men after the experience of seeing how my discourses succeeded so poorly at persuading you to virtue.

ALCIBIADES: Would you have wanted me to have lived in poverty, like you, without entering into public affairs?

SOCRATES: Which would have been better: not entering into them, or making a mess of them and becoming the enemy of the fatherland?

ALCIBIADES: I prefer my character to yours. I was beautiful, magnificent, all covered in glory, living in pleasure, the terror of the Lacedaemonians and Persians. The Athenians were only able to save their city by recalling me. If they had believed me, Lysander would never have entered their port.[10] As for you, you were only a poor man—ugly, bald, pug-nosed, passing his life talking in order to blame men for all they did. Aristophanes portrayed you on stage; you passed for a blasphemer, and were killed.[11]

SOCRATES: Well, that's quite a list of things you've put together. Let's examine them in detail. You were beautiful, but disparaged for having put your beauty to shameful uses. Pleasures corrupted your beautiful nature. You rendered great services to your fatherland, but you did it great harms as well. In the goods and the harms that you did to it, it was ambition and not the love of virtue that made you act, with the consequence that it brought you no true glory. The enemies of Greece to whom you were delivered could not trust you, and you could not trust them. Would it not have been better to live in poverty in your fatherland, and to suffer there patiently all that the vicious typically do [325] in order to stifle virtue? It's better to be ugly and wise like me than beautiful and dissolute like you were. The only thing for which one can reproach me is for having loved you too much, and for having allowed myself to be dazzled by a disposition as insubstantial as yours. Your vices dishonored the philosophical education Socrates gave you. That's my error.

ALCIBIADES: But your death shows that you were a blasphemer.

SOCRATES: The blasphemers are those who shattered the herms.[12] I preferred swallowing the poison for having taught the truth, and vexing the men who cannot bear it, to meeting death in the arms of a courtesan as you did.

ALCIBIADES: Your raillery is always barbed.

SOCRATES: Ha! A man fit for doing good and who only did evil—how can he be endured? You still insult virtue.

ALCIBIADES: What? So the shade of Socrates and virtue are the same thing? Now we see how presumptuous you are.

SOCRATES: Forget Socrates, if you want; I'm fine with that. But after having betrayed my hopes for the virtue that I tried to inspire in you, don't go on to mock philosophy and boast to me of all your deeds. They had glamour, but no focus. You don't have anything to laugh about. Death made you as ugly and pug-nosed as me. What's left now of all your pleasures?

ALCIBIADES: Ah! It's true: all that remains of them now is shame and remorse. But where are you going? Why do you want to leave me?

SOCRATES: Goodbye. I did not follow you in your ambitious voyages, not to Sicily, or to Sparta, or in Asia. It's not right that you follow me in the Elysian Fields, where I go to lead a peaceful and blessed life with Solon, Lycurgus, and the other wise men.

ALCIBIADES: Ah! My dear Socrates, must I be separated from you! Alas! Where then am I to go?

SOCRATES: To those vain and weak souls whose life was a perpetual mix of good and evil, and who have never loved the ways of pure virtue. You were born to follow it. You preferred your passions. Now [326] it abandons you in its turn, and you will regret it eternally.

ALCIBIADES: Alas! My dear Socrates, have you not loved me? Do you no longer want to have any pity on me? You cannot deny it, because you know better than any that my nature was good at its core.

SOCRATES: This is what renders you all the more inexcusable. You were born good, and you lived badly. My friendship for you, as much as your beautiful nature, only contributes to your condemnation. I loved you for virtue's sake, but in the end I loved you to the point of risking my reputation. For the love of you I suffered being unjustly suspected of monstrous vices that my entire doctrine condemned. I sacrificed to you my life as well as my honor. Have you forgotten the expedition of Potidaea, where I lodged with you the whole time?[13] A father couldn't have been more attached to his son than I was to you. In every military engagement I was always at your side. One day, with the result of combat in doubt, you were injured; immediately I threw myself in front of you in order to cover you with my body, like a shield. I saved your life, your liberty, your arms. The crown was due to me for this deed; I begged the heads of the army to give it to you. I cared for your glory alone. I would never have thought that you could have been capable of becoming the shame of your fatherland and the cause of all its misfortunes.

ALCIBIADES: For my part, I imagine, my dear Socrates, that you haven't forgotten this other occasion as well, where, our troops having been defeated, you withdrew on foot in great pain, and finding myself mounted on horseback I stopped in order to hold off the enemies who would have taken you. Let's be fair.

SOCRATES: I agree. If I recall what I did for you, it's not to reproach you for it, or to bring credit to me; it's to show the care that I took to make you good, and how poorly you repaid me for all my pains.

ALCIBIADES: You have nothing to say against my early youth. Often, while listening to your lessons, I was so touched that I was almost brought to tears. If sometimes I gave you the slip when I was swept away by groups of friends, you ran after me, like a master after his runaway slave. I never dared resist you. I listened only to [327] you; I feared only your displeasure. It is true that I once challenged Hipponicus by giving him a slap. I gave it to him, and then I went to ask forgiveness of him and stripped myself before him, so that he might punish me with the rod. But he pardoned me, seeing that I had offended him only by the thoughtlessness of my playful and whimsical nature.[14]

SOCRATES: So you only committed the fault of a young fool; but later you committed the crimes of a villain who had no respect for the gods, who deceived virtue and good faith, who reduced his fatherland to ashes in order to gratify his ambition, who carried dissolute morals to all foreign nations. Go—you arouse horror and pity in me. You were made to be good, but it pleased you to be evil; I cannot console myself for it. Let's part ways. The three judges will decide your fate; but there can no longer be any union between us two here below.

5. Socrates and Alcibiades (2) [327]

SOCRATES: Well, you've become quite wise at your own expense, and at the expense of those you deceived. You could have been the worthy hero of a second *Odyssey*, as you saw the morals of a greater number of people in your travels than Ulysses saw in his.

ALCIBIADES: It's not experience that eluded me, but wisdom. And even though you mock me, you know better than to deny that a man learns much when he travels and when he carefully studies the morals of so many peoples.

SOCRATES: It's true that this study, if done well, could do much to enlarge the mind, but it would require a true philosopher, someone tranquil and industrious, who, unlike you, wasn't dominated by ambition and by pleasure—a man with neither passion nor prejudice, who sought out all that was good in each people, and who might discover [328] the advantages and disadvantages of the laws of each country. On returning from such a voyage, this philosopher would be an excellent legislator. But you have never had what it takes to be a man who gives laws; your talent lay in violating them. Barely more than a child, you counseled your uncle Pericles to wage war in order to avoid having to account for the public funds. I even believe that in death you would still be a dangerous guard of the laws.

ALCIBIADES: Let it go, please. The river of forgetfulness must efface all my sins. Let us speak of the morals of peoples. I found everywhere only customs, and very few laws. All the barbarians have no other rules than habit and the examples of their fathers. Even the Persians, whose morals in the times of Cyrus have been so praised, have no trace of this virtue. Their valor and magnificence attest to a thoroughly beautiful nature, but it is corrupted by softness and by the most vulgar splendor. Their kings, worshiped like idols, could know neither the truth nor how to be upright men; humanity cannot bear with moderation a power so disordered as theirs. They imagine that everything is made for them; they toy with the property, the honor, and the lives of other men. Nothing attests to barbarianism in a nation as much as this form of government; here there are no longer laws, and the will of a single man, all of whose passions are flattered, is the only law.

SOCRATES: That country was hardly suited to a genius so free and so daring as your own. But do you not find also that the freedom of Athens is another extreme?

ALCIBIADES: Sparta is the best that I've seen.

SOCRATES: The servitude of the helots didn't appear to you contrary to humanity?[15] Go straight up to first principles, cast aside all your prejudices: you have to admit that on this front the Greeks were somewhat barbarian themselves. Is it really permissible for one group of men to treat another like pack animals?

ALCIBIADES: Why not, if it is a subjugated people?

SOCRATES: Subjugated peoples are yet people; [329] the right of conquest is less strong than the rights of humanity. What goes by the name of conquest comes to be the epitome of tyranny and the execration of the human race if the conqueror has failed to make his conquest by a just war, and make the conquered people happy in giving them good laws. It is thus not permissible for the Lacedaemonians to treat the Helots, who are men like them, so disgracefully. What horrible barbarity, to see one people toying with the life of another, indifferent to their morals and peace! Just as the head of a family must never, for the sake of the greatness of his house, go so far as to seek to disturb the peace and freedom of all the people, of which he and his family are only a part, so too it would be insane, brutal, and pernicious for the head of a nation to put his glory in augmenting the power of his people by troubling the peace and liberty of neighboring peoples. A people is no less a member of the human race, which forms a general society, than a family is a member of a particular nation. Each owes infinitely more to the human race, which is the great fatherland, than to the particular fatherland into which he is born: it is thus infinitely more pernicious to violate justice by pitting people against people than to violate it by pitting families against family and against their republic. To give up all feeling is not only to lack politeness and to fall into barbarism, but it is the most unnatural blindness of brigands and savages. It is to be no longer a man; it is to be a cannibal.

ALCIBIADES: You are getting angry! You used to strike me as having a better disposition than anyone. Your barbed ironies had something playful in them.

SOCRATES: I wouldn't know how to be playful on such serious matters. The Lacedaemonians have abandoned all the peaceable arts in order to save themselves for war alone. And as war is the greatest of evils, they know only how to do evil; they take pride in it; they disdain everything but the destruction of the human race, and anything that fails to serve the brutal glory of a handful of men called Spartans. Other men must cultivate the [330] earth in order to feed them, while they save their energy for ravaging and depopulating the neighboring lands. They are not sober and austere toward themselves in order to be just and moderate toward others; on the contrary, they are hard and fierce against everything but the fatherland—as if the human race was not more their fatherland than Sparta. War is an evil that dishonors the human race. If one could bury all the histories and forget them forever, it would be necessary to hide from posterity that men have been capable of killing other men. All wars are civil wars, as it is always man against man, spilling his own blood, tearing his own entrails. The more war is extended, the more it is evil; thus the wars between peoples who compose the human race are still worse than those between families that trouble a nation. It is thus permissible only to wage war against one's will, and as a last resort, in order to fend off the violence of an enemy. How is it that Lycurgus wasn't horrified at having formed a people who were lazy and ignorant of all the sweet and innocent occupations of peace, and of having given to it no other exercises of mind and body than those of harming humanity by war!

ALCIBIADES: You're right to be angry. But would you prefer a people like the Athenians, who have perfected to the fullest all the arts dedicated to pleasure? It's better still to bear fierce and violent dispositions, like those of Lacedaemonia.

SOCRATES: Well, you've changed! You're no longer that disparaged fellow from a disparaged city: the banks of the Styx work fine changes! But maybe you speak this way to us out of obligingness, since all your life you've been a Proteus as far as morality goes.[16] In any event, I admit that a people who via the contagion of its morals carries sumptuousness, softness, injustice and fraud home to other peoples, does still more evil than those who have no other occupation or any other merit than spilling blood, as virtue is more precious to men than life. Lycurgus is thus praiseworthy for having banished from his republic all the arts that serve only to promote sumptuousness and [331] pleasure, but he is inexcusable for having deprived it of agriculture and the other arts necessary for a simple and frugal life. Is it not shameful that a people cannot suffice to itself, and that it takes recourse to another people forced into agriculture in order to feed itself?

ALCIBIADES: Oh well, I won't bother blaming them on this front. But do you not prefer the severe discipline of Sparta, and the inviolable subordination that there renders the young subservient to the old, to the unbridled license of Athens?

SOCRATES: A people spoiled by an excessive freedom is the most insupportable of all tyrants; thus anarchy is the greatest of evils only insofar as it is the most extreme despotism: the populace risen up against the laws is the most insolent of all masters. But it is necessary to find a middle ground. This middle would consist in a people having written laws, forever immutable, consecrated by the entire nation; that these laws would be above everything; that those who govern would only have authority through them; that they could do all for the good, in following the laws; that they could do nothing against the laws in order to authorize evil. This is what men, were they not blind and enemies to themselves, would unanimously establish in order to be happy. But some, like the Athenians, overturn the laws, out of fear of giving too much authority to magistrates, by whom the laws ought to reign; and others, like the Persians, by a superstitious respect for the laws, place themselves in a sort of slavery under those who ought to make the laws reign, such that these men rule in such a way that the only law left in reality is their absolute will. By such means neither comes closer to their goal, which is a freedom limited solely by the authority of the laws, of which those who govern must be merely the simple defenders. The one who governs must be the most obedient to the law. His person is nothing if separated from the law, and it is consecrated only as long as he is himself, free of passion and free of interest, the living law given for the good of men. Judge by this how much the Greeks, who despise all barbarians, are still in barbarianism. The Peloponnesian War, in which the ambitious jealousy of two republics set the whole world on fire for twenty-eight years, is fatal proof of this. [332] And even you with whom I am speaking here, did you not sometimes flatter the unhappy and implacable ambition of the Lacedaemonians, and sometimes the more vain and more cheerful ambition of the Athenians? Athens with less strength launched greater projects and long triumphed over all Greece. But in the end it fell all at once, because the despotism of the people is a foolish and blind force, which turns itself against itself, and which is superior to the laws only in order to succeed at destroying itself.

ALCIBIADES: I see well that Anytus wasn't wrong to make you drink a little hemlock, and that your politics deserve to be feared still more than your new religion.

6. Alexander and Aristotle [358]

ARISTOTLE: I'm delighted to see my disciple. What glory it is for me to have taught the conqueror of Asia!

ALEXANDER: My dear Aristotle, I see you again with pleasure. I haven't seen you since I left Macedonia. But I never forgot you during my conquests, as you know well.

ARISTOTLE: Do you remember your youth, which was so pleasant?

ALEXANDER: Yes, it seems to me that I am again at Pella or at Pynde, and that you are coming from Stagira to teach me philosophy.

ARISTOTLE: But you neglected my precepts a little when your heart came to be intoxicated by excessive prosperity.

ALEXANDER: I admit it. You know well that I am sincere. Now that I am only the shade of Alexander, I admit that Alexander was too haughty, and too proud for a mortal.

ARISTOTLE: You didn't take my great-souled man for your model.[17]

ALEXANDER: I didn't try. Your magnanimous man is simply pretentious. There's nothing true or natural about him; he's stilted and exaggerated in everything.

ARISTOTLE: But were you not exaggerated in your heroism? Crying for not having yet conquered one world, when told there were several; running through immense kingdoms in order to return them to their kings after having conquered them, ravaging the universe in order to make yourself talked about, throwing yourself alone onto the ramparts of an enemy town, wanting to pass for a divinity! You're more exaggerated than my great-souled man.

ALEXANDER: It feels like I'm back at your school. You tell me all my truths as if we were still at Pella. It would not have been very safe to speak to me so freely on the banks of the Euphrates, but on the banks of the Styx, one listens to a critic more patiently. [359] Tell me then, my poor Aristotle, you who know everything: how is it that certain princes are so happy in their childhood, and that in what follows they forget all the good maxims they learned when it comes time to put them to use? To what does it serve that they talk like parrots in their youth, approving everything that is good, given that the reason which should develop in them with age seems to flee them as soon as they enter into the world?

ARISTOTLE: Your youth was indeed marvelous. You spoke with elegance to the ambassadors who came to Phillip; you loved letters; you read the poets, you were charmed by Homer; your heart was enflamed at the recitation of the virtues and the great actions of the heroes. When you took Thebes, you respected the house of Pindar; then you went, entering into Asia, to see the grave of Achilles and the ruins of Troy. All this showed a humane nature, sensitive to beautiful things. This beautiful nature showed itself again when you entrusted your life to the doctor Phillip, but above all when you treated so well the family of Darius, such that this king, in dying, might console himself in his misfortunes, thinking that you would be the father of his family. This is what philosophy and a good nature had instilled in you. But the rest, I dare not say it . . .

ALEXANDER: Say, say, my dear Aristotle; spare nothing.

ARISTOTLE: This sumptuousness, this softness, these suspicions, these cruelties, these tantrums, these fits of anger against your friends, this credulity in the cowardly flatterers who called you a god.

ALEXANDER: Ah, you speak the truth. I wanted to be dead after having conquered Darius.

ARISTOTLE: What! You didn't want to have subjugated the rest of the East?

ALEXANDER: This conquest is less glorious to me, as it is shameful to me to have succumbed to my prosperity, and to have forgotten the human condition. But, tell me then, how does it come to be that one is so wise in childhood, and so little reasonable when one needs to be?

ARISTOTLE: Because in youth one is instructed, encouraged, corrected by good men. In what follows, one [360] abandons oneself to three sorts of enemies: one's presumption, one's passions, and one's flatterers.

7. Coriolanus and Camillus [376]

CORIOLANUS: So, like me, you've felt the ingratitude of the fatherland. It's a strange thing, serving a foolish people. Admit it honestly, and excuse a little those who lack patience.[18]

CAMILLUS: For my part I find that there is never an excuse for those who rise up against their fatherland. One can withdraw, succumb to injustice, wait for less difficult times. But it is an act of impiety to take up arms against the mother who gave birth to us.

CORIOLANUS: These great names of mother and of fatherland are only names. Men are born free and independent. Societies, with all their [377] subordinations and regulations, are human institutions that can never destroy the liberty essential to man. If the society of men into which we are born lacks justice and good faith, we owe it nothing, we return to the natural rights of our liberty, and we can go seek some other more reasonable society in order to live there in peace, as a traveler passes from town to town according to his taste and comfort. All these fine ideas of the fatherland were given out by deceitful minds, full of ambition, in order to dominate us. The legislators have deceived us by them. But it is necessary always to return to the natural right that renders every man free and independent. Each man, being born in this state of independence with respect to others, commits his freedom in putting himself in the society of a people, only on the condition that he will be treated fairly. As soon as the society abandons this condition, the individual recovers his rights and the entire earth belongs to him as much as it does to others. He need only protect himself from a force superior to his own and to enjoy his freedom.

CAMILLUS: You've become quite the subtle philosopher here below. You were said to be less devoted to reasoning while you were living. But do you not see your error? This pact with a society can have some plausibility when a man chooses a country in which to live. Even still there is the right of punishing him according to the laws of the nation, if he has been incorporated into the nation, and he fails to live in accord with the customs of the republic. But children who are born in a country cannot choose their fatherland; the gods give it to them, or rather give them to this society of men which is their fatherland, such that this fatherland possesses them, governs them, rewards them, and punishes them as its children. It is not choice, administration, art, or arbitrary institutions that subjugate children to a father. It is nature that has decided it. The fathers joining together make the fatherland, and have complete authority over the children that they have put into the world. Would you dare to doubt this?

CORIOLANUS: Yes I do. Though a man may be my father, I am a man as much as he, and as [378] free as him by the essential rule of humanity. I owe him recognition and respect. But in the end nature has not made me dependent on him.

CAMILLUS: You're establishing fine rules for virtue here. Each will believe he has the right to live according to his own ideas. The world will no longer have regulation, or security, or subordination, or social order, or sure principles of good morals.[19]

CORIOLANUS: Reason and virtue will always be impressed on the hearts of men by nature. If they abuse their freedom, too bad for them. But though their freedom poorly held can turn into license, it is yet the case that they are free by their nature.

CAMILLUS: I accept it. But it is necessary also to admit that all the wisest men, having felt the inconvenience of this freedom which would make as many bizarre governments as there are muddle-headed men, have concluded that nothing was so crucial to the peace of the human race, as subjecting the multitude to laws established in each place. Isn't it true that this is

the rule that wise men have in all countries made the foundation of all
society?

CORIOLANUS: It's true.

CAMILLUS: This regulation was necessary.

CORIOLANUS: That's true too.

CAMILLUS: Not only is it wise, just, and necessary in itself, but it's also authorized by almost universal consent, or at least the consent of the majority.
If it is necessary for human life, it is only the indocile and irrational who
reject it.

CORIOLANUS: I agree. But it is merely arbitrary.

CAMILLUS: That which is essential to society, to peace, to the security of men,
that which reason demands, must necessarily be founded in rational nature itself, and is not arbitrary. Thus this subordination is not an invention
made to lead weak minds, it is, on the contrary, a necessary bond that
reason furnishes in order to order, to pacify, to unite men with each other.
Thus it is true that reason, which is the true nature of rational animals,
[379] demands that they subject themselves to laws and to certain men
who are in the place of the first legislators, who in a word they obey, that
they see all together to the needs and the common interests, that they use
their freedom only according to reason in order to strengthen and perfect
society. This is what I call being a good citizen: loving the fatherland, and
devoting oneself to the republic.

CORIOLANUS: You accuse me of subtlety, but you're more subtle than I am.

CAMILLUS: Not at all. Let's go into the details if you want. What proposition of
mine has surprised you? Reason is natural to man. Is this true?

CORIOLANUS: Yes, undoubtedly.

CAMILLUS: Man is not free to go against reason. What do you say to that?

CORIOLANUS: There is no way to prevent reason from acting.

CAMILLUS: Reason wants us to live in society and thus under subordination.
Respond.

CORIOLANUS: I believe it like you.

CAMILLUS: Thus it is necessary that there be inviolable rules of society that
one calls laws, and men who guard the laws, called magistrates, in order
to punish those who will violate them. Otherwise there would be as many
arbitrary governments as people, and the most muddle-headed people
would be those who would most wish to overturn morals and laws in
order to govern, or at least to govern themselves according to their
caprices.

CORIOLANUS: All this is clear.

CAMILLUS: Thus it is characteristic of a being naturally rational to subject its freedom to the laws and to the magistrates of the society in which it lives.

CORIOLANUS: This is certain. But one is free to leave this society.

CAMILLUS: If everyone is free to leave the society in which they are born, soon there will be no social order anywhere.

CORIOLANUS: Why?

CAMILLUS: For this reason. It's that as the number of muddle-heads grows, the more the muddle-heads would believe themselves able to cast off the yoke of their fatherland, [380] and go live elsewhere without order and without constraint. The majority would come to be independent, and would soon destroy all authority everywhere. They will even go out of their fatherland to take up arms against the fatherland itself. From this moment on there is no longer a constant and stable society of people. Thus you would overturn the laws and the society that reason according to you requires, in order to flatter an unbridled freedom or rather the license of the foolish and evil who only believe themselves free when they can scorn reason and the laws with impunity.

CORIOLANUS: Now I see clearly the train of your reasoning, and it's beginning to grow on me.

CAMILLUS: Add that this establishment of republics and of laws being thus authorized by the consent and the universal practice of the human race, some brutal and savage peoples excepted, all of humanity has been living under law for innumerable centuries, by an absolute necessity. Even the foolish and the evil, so long as they are not entirely so, feel and recognize this need to live together, and to be subject to the laws.

CORIOLANUS: I understand well, and you want to say that the fatherland having this sacred and inviolable right, one cannot take up arms against it.

CAMILLUS: It's not just me who wants it: nature demands it. When your mother Volumnia and your wife Veturia spoke to you for Rome, what did they say to you? What did you feel at the bottom of your heart?

CORIOLANUS: It's true that nature spoke to me for my mother. But she did not speak to me likewise for Rome.

CAMILLUS: Well, your mother did speak to you for Rome, and nature spoke to you through the lips of your mother. Thus the natural bonds that attach you to the fatherland. Could you attack the city of your mother, of all your relations, of all your friends, without violating the rights of nature? And now I'm not speaking to your reason. It's your sentiment free from reflection that I'm consulting.

CORIOLANUS: It's true. One acts against nature [381] whenever one fights against one's fatherland. But if it's not permissible to attack it, at least admit that it's permissible to abandon it, when it is unjust and ungrateful.

CAMILLUS: No, I'll never admit it. If she exiles you, if she rejects you, you can go seek out refuge elsewhere. To leave her breast when she chases you out is to obey her. But it's necessary still to respect her from afar, to desire her well-being, to be ready to return there, to defend her, and to die for her.

CORIOLANUS: Where do you get all these fine ideas of heroism? When my fatherland renounced me and sought to reduce me to nothing, the contract between us was over; I renounced her in turn, and no longer owe her anything.

CAMILLUS: You've already forgotten that we have put the fatherland in the place of our parents, and that over us it has the authority of the laws, without which there would be no fixed and ordered society anywhere.

CORIOLANUS: It's true. I figure that one must regard as a true mother this society which gave us birth, morals, and nourishment, which acquired such great rights over us by our relations and by our friends that it carries in its breast. I'd like it if one were to owe it what one owes to a mother, but . . .

CAMILLUS: If my mother had abandoned and mistreated me, could I refuse to recognize her and fight against her?

CORIOLANUS: No, but you could . . .

CAMILLUS: Could I despise and abandon her, if she were to return to me and show genuine remorse for having mistreated me?

CORIOLANUS: No.

CAMILLUS: It's necessary then to be always entirely ready to take up again our natural sentiments for the fatherland, or rather never to lose them, and to return to its service whenever it opens the way to it for you.

CORIOLANUS: I admit that this way seems to me the best. But the pride and vexation of a man who has been pushed to the limit does not allow him to make every reflection. The insolent Roman people trampled the patricians underfoot. I would not suffer this indignity. The furious people compelled me to retire to the land of the Volsci. When I was there, my resentment and the [382] desire of rendering myself worthy of those people, enemies of the Romans, led me to take up arms against my country. You made me see, my dear Furius, that it would have been necessary to remain passive amid my misfortunes.

CAMILLUS: We have here below the shades of several great men who have done what I'm describing to you. Themistocles, having made the error of going into Persia, preferred to die by drinking the bull's poisonous blood rather than to serve the king of Persia against the Athenians. Scipio, vanquisher of Africa, having been treated unworthily at Rome because one accused his brother of having taken money in his war against Antiochus, retired to Liternum, where he passed the rest of his days in solitude, unable to reconcile himself either to living in the midst of his ungrateful fatherland or to neglecting the fidelity that he owed it.[20] Thus what we learned from him since he descended into Pluto's realm.

CORIOLANUS: You cite other examples and you say nothing of yours, which is the most beautiful of all.

CAMILLUS: It's true that the injustice that was done to me rendered me useless. Even the other captains had lost all authority; all they did was to try to flatter the people, and you know how fatal it is to a state when those who govern it feed themselves always on vain and flattering hopes. All at once the Gauls, who had been shown bad faith, won the battle of Allia; this is what would have come of Rome if they had pursued the Romans.[21] You know that the youth withdrew into the Capitol, and that the senators planted themselves in their curule seats, where they were killed. It is not necessary to recount the rest, which you have heard retold a hundred times. If I hadn't stifled my resentment in order to save my fatherland, everything would have been lost without recourse. I was at Ardea when I learned of Rome's misfortunes. I armed the Ardeates. I learned by spies that the Gauls, believing themselves the masters of all, lost themselves in the pleasures of the table. I surprised them at night. In so doing I made a great slaughter. At this stroke the Romans, like men brought back from the dead leaving the grave, sent for me, begging me to be their chief. I responded that they could not represent the fatherland, [383] nor could I recognize them, and that I would await the orders of the patrician youth who had defended the Capitol, because they were the true body of the republic, they were the only ones I had to obey in order to put myself at the head of their troops. Those who were in the Capitol elected me dictator. Nevertheless the Gauls were consumed by contagious diseases after a siege of seven months before the Capitol. Peace was made, and at the moment that they were weighing out the funds which they had promised to withdraw, I arrived and gave the gold back to the Romans: "We do not defend our city," I said to the Gauls, "with gold but with iron; withdraw yourselves."[22] They were surprised, and they withdrew. The next day, I attacked them in their retreat, and I cut them to pieces.

8. Caesar and Cato [402]

CAESAR: Alas my dear Cato, you look like you're in a pitiful state! What a horrible wound!

CATO: I stabbed myself at Utica after the battle of Thapsus so as not to outlive freedom.[23] But you who so pity me, how did it happen that you should follow me so closely? What do I see? How many wounds there are on your body! Wait while I count them ... twenty-three in all.

CAESAR: You'll be quite surprised to know that I was pierced by all these blows in the middle of the senate by my best friends. What treason!

CATO: No, I'm not surprised by it. Did you not tyrannize [403] your friends as much as the rest of the citizens? Must they not take up their arms in vengeance for their oppressed fatherland? It would be necessary not only to sacrifice our friend, but even our own brother, as Timoleon did, and our own children, as did the elder Brutus.[24]

CAESAR: One of his descendants has only too well followed this fine lesson. It was Brutus, who I always loved, and who passed for my son, who was the head of the conspiracy to butcher me.

CATO: O fortunate Brutus, who set Rome free, and who consecrated his hands in the blood of a new Tarquin more impious and proud than the one who was chased out by Junius.[25]

CAESAR: You have always been prejudiced against me, and exaggerated in your maxims of virtue.

CATO: Who prejudiced me against you? Your life—dissolute, extravagant, artificial, effeminate—your debts, your intrigues, your audacity. That's what prejudiced Cato against this man whose flowing robe and air of softness promised nothing that was worthy of the ancient morals. You haven't fooled me. I've known you from your youth. O if I had been believed ...

CAESAR: You would have gotten me caught up in the conspiracy of Catiline in order to lose me.[26]

CATO: Well you lived like a woman, and you were only a man when it came to opposing your fatherland. What did I not do to convince you? But Rome ran to its destruction, and it did not want to know its enemies.

CAESAR: Your eloquence alarmed me, I admit it, and I had recourse to authority. But you cannot deny that I conducted myself in business like a clever man.

CATO: Or rather a clever villain. You dazzled the most wise by your moderate and insinuating discourse. You favored the conspirators under the pretext of not pushing rigor too far. I alone resisted in vain. From then on the gods were angry with Rome.

CAESAR: Tell me the truth. After the battle of Thapsus you were afraid of falling into my hands; you would have been embarrassed to appear before me. Ha! Didn't you know that I only wanted to conquer and to pardon? [404]

CATO: It is the pardon of the tyrant, it is life itself—yes, the life of Cato owed to Caesar—that I feared. It was better to die than to see you.

CAESAR: I would have treated you generously, as I treated your son. Wouldn't it have been better to come again to the aid of the republic?

CATO: There is no longer a republic as soon as there is no longer freedom.

CAESAR: But why then turn your fury on your own self?

CATO: My own hands brought me to freedom despite the tyrant, and I despised the life he would have offered to me. As for you, your own friends had to tear you apart as a monster.

CAESAR: But if life was so shameful for a Roman after my victory, why send me your son? Did you want to corrupt him?

CATO: Each makes his decision to live or to die according to his heart. Cato could only die. His son, less great than he, could still bear life, and because of his youth hope for freer and happier times. Alas, what did I not suffer when I let my son go to the tyrant!

CAESAR: But why do you label me a tyrant? I never took the title of king.

CATO: It is a question of the thing and not the name. Moreover, how many times did one see you take various twists and turns in order to accustom the senate and the people to your royalty! Even Anthony, in the festival of the Lupercalia, was so impudent as to place a crown on your head, pretending it was a joke. This game seemed too serious and horrified people. You felt the public indignation, and returned to Jupiter an honor that you dared not accept. This is what served to determine the conspirators to your destruction. Anyway, we know the news pretty well here below, don't we?

CAESAR: Too well. But you aren't doing me justice. My government was gentle. I comported myself like a true father of the fatherland. The sadness that the people displayed after my death attests to this. That is a time where you know that flattery is no longer in season. Alas, these poor men, when presented with my bloodied robe, wanted to avenge me. What regrets! [405] What pomp on the field of Mars at my funeral! What do you say to that?

CATO: That the people are always people: credulous, vulgar, capricious, blind, enemies of their own interests. In order to have promoted the successors of the tyrant, and to have persecuted his liberators, what have the people not suffered? Innumerable proscriptions have made the purest blood of the citizens flow. The triumvirs have been more barbarous than even the Gauls who took Rome. Happy are those who have not seen these days of desolation! But finally tell me, O tyrant, why did you tear out the entrails of Rome your mother? What fruit remains from having put your fatherland in chains? Is this the glory you sought? Would you not have found a purer and more dazzling glory in preserving the freedom and greatness of this city, queen of the universe, as had the Fabricii, the Fabii, the Marcellii, the Scipios? Did it get you a sweet and happy life? Did you find it amid the horrors inseparable from tyranny? All the days of your life were as perilous for you as those where all the good citizens immortalized their virtue in butchering you. You never saw a true Roman without going pale out of dread of his courage. So is this the tranquil and happy life that you have bought by so many struggles and crimes? But what am I saying? You have not even had the time to enjoy the fruits of your impiety. Speak, speak, tyrant. Now it takes you as much effort to endure my gaze as I would have had in suffering your odious presence when I killed myself at Utica. Say, if you dare, that you have been happy.

CAESAR: I admit that I wasn't. But it was men like you who disturbed my happiness.

CATO: Or rather you disturbed it yourself. If you had loved the fatherland, the fatherland would have loved you. The one the fatherland loves has no need of protection; the entire fatherland watches over him. True security lies only in doing good, and in making the entire world desire its preservation. You wanted to reign and to make yourself feared. Well, you reigned, and you were feared. But your men delivered themselves from the tyrant and from fear together. Thus die those who, wanting to be feared by all men, themselves have everything to [406] fear from all those interested in forestalling them and delivering themselves from them.

CAESAR: But this strength that you call tyrannical had become necessary. Rome no longer could bear its freedom; it needed a master. Pompey began to be it; I could not allow him to be it to my disadvantage.

CATO: What was needed was to strike down the tyrant without aspiring to tyranny. After all, if Rome was so cowardly as not to be able to live without a master, it would be better to leave it to another to do this crime. When a traveler falls into the hands of villains who prepare to rob him, is it necessary to thwart them by rushing to act in an equally horrible way? But Pompey's excessive authority served as a pretext for you. Does one not know what you said, in going into a small city in Spain where several citizens craved the magistracy? Do you believe that people have forgotten that Greek verse which was so often on your lips?[27] Even more, if you knew the misery and the infamy of tyranny, why didn't you quit it?

CAESAR: Ha! How was I supposed to quit it? The path by which one ascends to tyranny is rough and steep, but there's no place where one can get off it and go back down; one leaves it only by falling off the precipice.

CATO: Unhappy one! Why then aspire to this? Why overturn everything in order to attain it? Why shed so much blood, sparing not even your own, which was still spilled too late? You look for excuses in vain.

CAESAR: And you haven't answered me. I asked you how one can safely quit tyranny.

CATO: Go ask Sulla, and shut up.[28] Consult that monster starved for blood. His example will make you blush. Goodbye. I fear that the shade of Brutus would be shocked if it saw me speaking with you.

9. Louis XI and Cardinal Balue [448]

LOUIS XI: How dare you, villain, present yourself again before me after all your treasons![29]

BALUE: Where then do you want me to go hide myself? Am I not hidden enough in the crowd of the shades? We are all equal here below.

LOUIS XI: It's all well for you to speak like this, you who were only the son of a Verdun miller!

BALUE: Ha! With you, it was an asset to be of low birth. Your stooge Provost Tristan, your doctor Coctier, your barber Olivier le Diable—they were your favorites and your ministers. Janfredy, before me, obtained the crimson by your favor.[30] My birth was about as worthy as these men's.

LOUIS XI: None of them committed treasons so black as yours.

BALUE: I don't believe it. If they hadn't been dishonest men, you wouldn't have employed them or treated them so well.

LOUIS XI: Why do you insist that I didn't choose them for their merit?

BALUE: Because merit was always suspect and hateful to you, because virtue frightened you and you had no idea how to make use of it, because you wanted for your servants only base and venal souls who were ready to enter into your intrigues, your deceptions, and your cruelties. An upright man, who would have felt horror at the thought of deceiving and doing evil, would have been good for nothing to you, who want only to deceive and to harm in order to satisfy your limitless ambition. Since it is necessary to speak frankly in the land of truth, I admit that I was a dishonest man; but this was the reason you preferred me to others. Did I not serve you well and readily in order to deceive the great and the common? Have you found a cheat more adaptable than I for all these people? [449]

LOUIS XI: It's true. But in deceiving others in order to obey me, it wasn't necessary to fool me also. You conspired with the Pope to make me abolish the Pragmatic Sanction, against the true interests of France.[31]

BALUE: Ha! Were you ever concerned for France or its true interests? You have only ever been concerned with your own. You sought to take advantage of the Pope and sacrifice the canons to him to serve your interest; I merely served you in your own fashion.

LOUIS XI: But you put all these visions in my head, against the true interest of even my crown, to which my true greatness was attached.

BALUE: No. I would have liked you to have sold dearly this miserable document at the court of Rome.[32] But let's go further. Even if I had deceived you, what would you have said to me?

LOUIS XI: Sorry, say to you? I find you wholly ridiculous. If I were still alive, I'd have you locked in a cage.

BALUE: Ho! I was there long enough. If you get angry with me I won't say a single word. Don't you know that I hardly fear the bad mood of the shade of a king? What then! Do you think you're still at Plessis-lez-Tours with your assassins?[33]

LOUIS XI: No, I know that I'm not there, and this must make you happy. But in the end I'm willing to listen to you for the singularity of the experience. So, prove to me by good reasoning that you were compelled to commit treason against your master.

BALUE: This paradox surprises you, but I'll prove it entirely to you.

LOUIS XI: Let's see what he wants to say.

BALUE: Is it not true that a poor miller's son, who never had any other education than that of the court of a great king, was compelled to follow the maxims that are there accepted as the best and most convenient as a matter of common consent?

LOUIS XI: What you say has some plausibility.

BALUE: Just respond yes or no without getting upset.

LOUIS XI: I dare not deny a thing that appears so well founded, nor admit what can burden me by its consequences. [450]

BALUE: I see that it's necessary that I take your silence for a forced consent. The fundamental maxim of all your counsels, which you spread throughout your court, was of doing everything for yourself alone. You put no value on either the princes of your blood, or the queen, whom you held captive and distant, or the dauphin, whom you brought up in ignorance and in prison, or the realm, which you ravaged by your harsh and cruel policies. All this was nothing compared to the interests that led you always to privilege jealousy for tyrannical authority; you even counted for nothing the favorites and the most trustworthy ministers who you used in order to deceive others. You never loved any of them; you never confided in any of them except in cases of need. You sought to dupe them in their turn, like the rest; you were ready to sacrifice them on the least suspicion or for the smallest advantage. One never had a single moment of security with you; you toyed with the lives of men. You loved nobody: who would have wanted to love you? You wanted to deceive everyone: who would have wanted to confide in you out of good faith and good friendship, and without interest? This disinterested fidelity, where would one have learned it? Did you deserve it? Did you hope for it? Could one have practiced it before you and in your court? Could one have lasted a week in your company with an upright and sincere heart? Was one not forced to be a rogue just in order to approach you? Was not one declared a villain in order to earn your favor, since it could only be earned by villainy? Was this not a given? If one had wanted to preserve some honor and some conscience, one would have done well to have taken care never to have been known by you, and go off to the ends of the earth sooner than live in your service. As soon as one is a rogue, one is so for everyone. Would you desire that a soul that you had corrupted, and in which you had inspired only evil toward all the human race, never had that pure and unstained virtue, that disinterested and heroic fidelity to you alone? Were you such a dupe as to think this? Did you not count on everyone acting toward you as you did to them? Even if [451] one had been good and sincere toward all other men, one would have been forced to become false and evil with you. Thus in betraying you I merely followed your lessons, merely marched in the trail you had blazed, merely rendered to you that which you always gave, merely did what you expected of me, merely took for the principle of my conduct the principle that you yourself regarded as the only one which necessarily animates all men. You would have despised a man who would have known other interests than his own. I didn't want to deserve your hatred, and I preferred to dupe you than to be a fool according to your own principles.

LOUIS XI: I admit that your reasoning challenges and piques me. But why conspire with my brother the Duke of Guyenne, and the Duke of Burgundy, my cruelest enemy?[34]

BALUE: It's because they were your most dangerous enemies that I aligned with them, in order to have a resource against you, if your touchy jealousy carried you against me. I knew that you would count on my treasons and that you could believe them without foundation. I preferred betraying you in order to save myself from falling into your hands, rather than perishing in your hands merely for suspicions and without having actually betrayed you. In the end I was quite pleased, according to your maxims, with making myself wanted by both parties, and drawing from you, in the tumult of affairs, the reward for my services that you would never have willingly accorded me in peacetime. Thus that which necessarily awaits the ministers of an ungrateful, defiant, deceitful prince, who loves only himself.

LOUIS XI: But so too this is what necessarily awaits a traitor who sells out his king. He isn't killed while he is cardinal, but he is held eleven years in prison, and stripped of his great wealth.[35]

BALUE: I admit my sole error: it was of not being careful enough in deceiving you, and allowing my letters to be intercepted. Give me another chance, and I will dupe you again according to your standards, but I would dupe you more subtly, out of fear of getting caught.

10. Louis XI and Louis XII [454]

LOUIS XI: Well, if I'm not mistaken, it's one of my successors.[36] Although the shades can have no majesty here below, it seems to me that this one here could well be some king of France, because I see that these other [455] shades respect him and speak French to him. Who are you? Tell me, I beg you.

LOUIS XII: I am the Duke of Orleans, become king under the name of Louis XII.

LOUIS XI: How did you govern my realm?

LOUIS XII: The opposite of how you did. You made yourself feared, I made myself loved. You began by burdening the people, I relieved them, and I preferred their peace to the glory of conquering my enemies.

LOUIS XI: You didn't know the art of ruling then. I was the one who gave my successors unlimited authority. I was the one who broke up the leagues of the lords and princes. I was the one who raised immense sums. I discovered the secrets of others. I knew how to hide my own. Finesse, haughtiness, and severity are the true maxims of government. I have a great fear that you will have spoiled everything, and that your weakness will have destroyed all my work.

LOUIS XII: I showed by the success of my maxims that yours were false and pernicious. I made myself loved. I lived in peace without going back on my word, without spilling blood, without ruining my people. Your memory is hateful; mine is respected. During my life, men were faithful to me; after my death, I was mourned, and one feared of never again having so good a king. When one benefits from being generous and of good faith, one does well to despise cruelty and finesse.

LOUIS XI: That's a fine philosophy that you no doubt learned in that long imprisonment where, I've been told, you languished before occupying the throne.

LOUIS XII: This imprisonment was less shameful than yours in Péronne.[37] Thus the ends served by finesse and duplicity. One gets himself taken by his enemy. Good faith is not so exposed to such great perils.

LOUIS XI: But I was clever enough to escape from the hands of the Duke of Burgundy.

LOUIS XII: Yes, by dint of money, by which you corrupted his servants, and in following him shamefully to the ruining of your allies the Liégeois, that he made you to go see die.

LOUIS XI: Did you extend the kingdom as I did? [456] I reunited the crown of the duchy of Burgundy, the countship of Provence, even Guyenne.

LOUIS XII: I get it: you knew the art of ridding yourself of a brother in order to have his share. You profited from the misfortunes of the Duke of Burgundy, who ran to his ruin. You won the counselor of the count of Provence in order to capture his succession.[38] As for me, I was content to have Brittany by a legitimate alliance with the heiress of this house, whom I loved and married after the death of her son. Moreover I dreamed less of having new subjects than of rendering faithful and happy those I already had. The wars of Naples and Milan taught me how much distant conquests harm a state.[39]

LOUIS XI: I see well that you lacked ambition and genius.

LOUIS XII: I lacked that false and duplicitous genius that made you so criticized, and that ambition that finds honor in counting sincerity and justice for nothing.

LOUIS XI: You talk too much.

LOUIS XII: You're the one who often talked too much. Have you forgotten the merchant of Bordeaux, established in England, and King Edward, whom you invited to come to Paris?[40] Goodbye.

11. Henry VII and Henry VIII [459]

HENRY VII: So, my son, how did you reign after me?[41]

HENRY VIII: Happily and with glory for thirty-eight years.

HENRY VII: That's wonderful! But were others as content with you as you seem to be with yourself?

HENRY VIII: I speak only the truth. It's true that you rose to the throne through your courage and your skill; you left it to me in peace. But what haven't I done! I held the balance between the two greatest powers of Europe, Francis I and Charles V.[42] That was my work abroad. As for domestic affairs, I delivered England from papal tyranny and I changed its religion, without anybody daring to resist.[43] After having made such a reversal, to die in peace in one's bed—this is a beautiful and glorious end.

HENRY VII: But I heard that the pope had given you the title of Defender of the Church, because of a book that you had made against Luther's ideas.[44] So how did this change come about?

HENRY VIII: I saw how unjust and superstitious the Roman Church was.

HENRY VII: Had she crossed you in some scheme?

HENRY VIII: Yes. I wanted to divorce. That Aragonaise displeased me; I wanted to marry Anne Boleyn. Pope Clement VII appointed Cardinal Campége for this case. But afraid of angering the emperor, nephew of Catherine, he only wanted to sport with me. Campége took nearly a year to get from Italy to France.[45] [460]

HENRY VII: So what did you do?

HENRY VIII: I broke with Rome; I mocked its censures; I married Anne Boleyn, and I made myself the head of the Anglican Church.

HENRY VII: I am no longer surprised to have seen so many people departed from the world strongly discontent with you.

HENRY VIII: Such great changes cannot be made without some severity.

HENRY VII: I hear from all sides that you were thoughtless, inconstant, lustful, cruel, and bloodthirsty.

HENRY VIII: It's the papists who described me that way.

HENRY VII: Let's leave aside the papists and get to the heart of the matter. Have you not had six wives, of whom you repudiated the first without justification, killed the second, split the stomach of the third to save her child, killed the fourth, repudiated the fifth, and chosen so poorly the last that she remarried an admiral a few days after your death?

HENRY VIII: All that's true. But if you knew what these women were, you would pity me instead of condemning me: the Aragonaise was ugly and boring in her virtue; Anne Boleyn was a scandalous coquette; Jane Seymour was hardly any better; N. Howard was extremely corrupt; the princess of Cleves was a charmless statue; the last seemed wise, but she showed after my death that I was fooled.[46] I admit that I have been the dupe of these women.

HENRY VII: If you had remained married to your wife, all these misfortunes would never have befallen you; it is evident that God punished you. But how much blood have you spilled! They say you murdered several thousand people for the sake of religion, including numerous well-born prelates and clergy.

HENRY VIII: It was necessary in order to be free from Rome's yoke.

HENRY VII: What? Merely to keep a challenge going, merely to marry this Anne Boleyn, whom you yourself deemed worthy of torture!

HENRY VIII: But I had taken the property of the churches, which I couldn't return. [461]

HENRY VII: Wonderful! So that's how you justify your schism—by your ridiculous marriages and your pillaging of the churches!

HENRY VIII: Since you press me so much, I'll tell you everything. I was crazy for women, and fickle in my romances; I was as quick to lose interest, as I was to take interest. Moreover I was by nature jealous, suspicious, inconstant, fierce in pursuing my interests. I found that the heads of the Anglican Church flattered my passions and authorized whatever I wanted to do: Cardinal Wolsey, Archbishop of York, encouraged me to repudiate Catherine of Aragon; Cranmer, Archbishop of Canterbury, made me do all that I did for Anne Boleyn and against the Roman Church.[47] Put yourself in the place of a poor prince violently tempted by his passions and flattered by the prelates.

HENRY VII: Well, don't you know that there is nothing so cowardly or so prostituted as the ambitious prelates who attach themselves to the court? You should have sent them off into their dioceses and consulted good men instead. The wise laymen and the politically astute would never have advised you, even for the sake of the security of your realm, to change the ancient religion, and to divide your subjects into several opposed communions. Is it not ridiculous that you complained of the tyranny of the Pope, and then made yourself Pope in his place? That you wanted to reform the Anglican Church, and that this reform served to authorize all your monstrous marriages and plunder all the sacred property? You achieved this horrible work only by dipping your hands in the blood of the most virtuous people. You rendered your memory forever hateful, and you left in the State a source of eternal division. That's what comes from listening to evil priests. I don't say this out of piety. You know that this is not my character; I speak only in terms of politics, as if religion didn't matter at all. But as far as I can see, you have always only done evil.

HENRY VIII: I couldn't avoid doing so. Cardinal Pole and the papists together conspired against me.[48] It was necessary to punish the conspirators in order to protect my life. [462]

HENRY VII: Ha! It's an unhappy wretch who undertakes unjust things. Once begun, it's hard not to continue with them. One passes for a tyrant; one is exposed to plots. One suspects the innocents that one executes; one finds them guilty, and one makes them such, because the prince who governs poorly puts his subjects in temptation of being unfaithful to him. In such a state, the king is unhappy, and deservedly so; he has everything to fear; he has not a moment of freedom or security; it is necessary for him to spill blood; the more he spills of it, the more he is odious and exposed to plots. But before we finish, let's see what praiseworthy things you did.

HENRY VIII: I maintained an equal balance between Francis I and Charles V.

HENRY VII: A very difficult thing, indeed! Yet you didn't know how to deal with these characters. Wolsey played you in order to pander to Charles V, of whom he was the dupe, and who promised to make him pope. You tried to invade France, but lacked the diligence to succeed. You followed through on no negotiation; you knew neither how to make peace nor war. All you had to do was be the arbiter of Europe, and to give places on two sides; but you were incapable of hard work, patience, moderation, or firmness. The only things needful to you were your mistresses, favorites, and amusements; you showed vigor only against religion, and in exercising your cruelty in order to satisfy your shameful passions. Alas! My son, you are a strange lesson for all the kings who will come after you.

12. Henry III and Henry IV [474]

HENRY III: Ah! My poor cousin, you've fallen into the same misfortunes as me.[49]

HENRY IV: My death was as violent as yours. But no one other than your minions missed you owing to the immense goods that you showered on them with profusion.[50] As for me, all France mourned me as the father of all families. I will be held up for centuries to come as the model of a good and wise king. I began to put the realm into a state of calm, abundance, and good order.

HENRY III: When I was killed at St. Cloud, I had already demolished the League, and Paris was ready to surrender. I would have soon reestablished my authority.

HENRY IV: But how could you have rehabilitated so black a reputation? You passed for a cheat, a hypocrite, a blasphemer, an effeminate and dissolute man. When a reputation for probity and good faith has been lost, there is no longer a quiet and assured authority. You defeated the two Guises at Blois, but you could never defeat all those who were horrified by your treacheries.[51]

HENRY III: Ha! Do you not know that the art of dissimulation is the art of ruling?

HENRY IV: Thus the fine maxims of de Guast and some others that inspired you. The Abbé of Elbène and the other Italians put into your head the politics of Machiavelli.[52] The queen your mother nourished you on these sentiments. But she had good cause to repent of having done so. She got what she deserved. She taught you to become unnatural. You used it against her.

HENRY III: But how can one act sincerely and trust in men? They're all disguised and corrupt.

HENRY IV: You think this because you have never seen honest men, and don't believe that such can exist on earth. But you didn't seek them [475] out. On the contrary, you avoided them, and they avoided you; they were suspicious and inconvenient to you. It was necessary for the wicked to invent new pleasures for you, who were capable of the blackest crimes, and before which you remembered neither religion nor modesty violated. With such morals you didn't bother trying to find good men. As for me, I found some. I knew they served me in my council, in foreign negotiations, in several duties: for example Sully, Jeannin, d'Ossat, etc.[53]

HENRY III: To listen to you speak, one would take you for a Cato. Your youth was as disordered as mine.

HENRY IV: It's true: I was inexcusable in my shameful passion for women. But in my disorders I was never a deceiver, nor an evil man, nor a blasphemer—I've just been weak. Misfortune served me well, because I was naturally soft and too given to pleasures. If I had been born king, I would perhaps be dishonored, but having misfortune to overcome and my kingdom to conquer made it necessary for me to rise above myself.

HENRY III: How many opportunities of vanquishing your enemies did you lose as you amused yourself on the banks of the Garonne, sighing after the Countess of Guiche?[54] You were like Hercules running after Omphale.

HENRY IV: I can't deny it. But Coutras, Ivry, Arques, Fontaine-Française did a little to make up for it.[55]

HENRY III: Did I not win the battles of Jarnac and of Moncontour?[56]

HENRY IV: Yes, but King Henry III failed to live up to the high hopes held for the Duke of Anjou. Henry IV, on the contrary, was better than the King of Navarre.[57]

HENRY III: So you think that I haven't heard the talk about the Duchess of Beaufort, of the Marquise of Verneuil, of . . . But I can't even count them all.[58]

HENRY IV: I deny none of it, and I deserve blame. But I made myself loved and feared. I hated this cruel and deceitful politics that infected you, and which caused all your [476] misfortunes. I made war with vigor. In foreign affairs, I concluded a solid peace. In domestic affairs, I ordered the state and made it flourish. I recalled the great to their duty, and even the most insolent favorites, and all this without deceiving or assassinating or doing injustice, and trusting in good men and finding all my glory in relieving the people.

13. Cardinal Richelieu and Cardinal Mazarin [490]

RICHELIEU: Ah! It's you, Lord Jules![59] They say you governed France after me. How did you do? Did you succeed in reuniting all Europe against the house of Austria? Did you topple the Huguenot party that I had weakened? And did you succeed in cutting down the great?

MAZARIN: You began all this. But I had other things to attend to. It was necessary for me to prop up a turbulent regency.

RICHELIEU: A king who is inconsistent and jealous even of the minister who serves him creates more confusion in office than the weakness and confusion of a regency. You had a fairly steady queen under whom one could more easily conduct affairs than under a prickly king who was always embittered against me by some emerging favorite. Such a prince neither governs nor allows governing. It is necessary to serve him despite him, which can be done only by risking death. My life was troubled by those to whom I owed all my authority. You know that of all the kings who went through the siege of La Rochelle, the King my master was the one who gave me the most trouble.[60] I wasn't free to give the fatal blow to the party of the Huguenots, who had all the places of safety and all the formidable leaders. I carried the war almost into the heart of the house of Austria. We will never forget the revolt of Catalonia, the impenetrable secret with which Portugal prepared itself to shake off the unjust yoke of the Spanish, the Dutch supported by our alliance in a long war against the same power, all our allies of the North, of the Empire and of Italy, attached to me personally, like a man incapable of failing them, finally, within the state, the great lined up to do their duty.[61] I found them uncompromising, finding honor in incessantly caballing [491] against all those in whom the king entrusted his authority and not believing it necessary to obey the king even despite the fact that he had enlisted them in flattering their ambition, and giving them in their administrations a power without limits.

MAZARIN: As for me, I was a foreigner. Everyone was against me. I was only useful through my industry. I began by insinuating myself into the queen's mind. I knew to divide the men who had her confidence, I defended myself against the cabals of the courtiers, against the uncontrolled Parlement, against the Fronde, a party animated by an audacious cardinal jealous of my fortune, finally against a prince who constantly covered himself with new laurels, and who only used the reputation of his victories to ruin me with more authority.[62] I warded off all my enemies. Twice driven out from the realm, I twice returned triumphant. Even in my absence, it was I who governed the State. I drove Cardinal de Retz all the way to Rome. I reduced the Prince de Condé to having to save himself in Flanders. Finally I concluded a glorious peace, and in dying I left a young king in position to give the law to all of Europe.[63] All this I did by means of my ingeniousness for machinations, the flexibility of my negotiations, and by the art that I had of always holding men in a state of hopefulness. Note that I never spilled a single drop of blood.

RICHELIEU: You had no compunctions about spilling it; you were just too weak and too cowardly.

MAZARIN: Cowardly! Ha! Did I not send three princes to Vincennes? Monsieur the Prince had plenty of time to grow bored in prison.[64]

RICHELIEU: To which I respond that you dared neither to hold him in prison nor to deliver him, and that your perplexity was the true cause of the length of his term. But let's come to what matters. As for me, I did indeed spill blood; it was necessary in order to cut down the pride of the great who are always ready to rise up. It's not surprising that a man who let all the courtiers and all the army officers assume anew their old haughtiness killed nobody in so weak a government.

MAZARIN: A government is not weak [492] when it concludes business by skill and without cruelty. It's better to be a fox than a lion or a tiger.[65]

RICHELIEU: It's not cruelty to punish the guilty whose bad example inspires others. Impunity brings endless civil wars, it destroyed the authority of the king, ruined the State, and cost the blood of who knows how many thousands of men, whereas I reestablished peace and authority in sacrificing a small number of guilty heads. Moreover I never had any enemies other than those of the state.

MAZARIN: But you thought yourself the state personified. You supposed that one could not be a good Frenchman without being in your pay.

RICHELIEU: Did you spare the first prince of the blood when you judged him an obstacle to your interests? In order to be in good position at court was it not necessary to be a Mazarin? I never pushed suspicions and defiance further than you. We both served the state. In serving it we both wanted to govern. You tried to vanquish your enemies through ruses and cowardly artifice. As for me, I struck at mine with open force, and I believed in good faith that they sought my ruin only in order to throw France back into the calamities and confusion out of which I had taken such pains to draw it. But in the end I kept my word, I was friend and enemy in good faith, I supported the authority of my master with courage and dignity. He was only attached to those whose graces I pushed to such great lengths. I loved and sought out merit as soon as I recognized it. I only wanted them not to impede my government, which I believed necessary to the salvation of France. If they had wanted to serve the king according to their talents, on my orders they would have been my friends.

MAZARIN: Say rather that they would have been your valets, and well-paid valets, to tell the truth. But it was necessary for them to accommodate themselves to a jealous, imperious, implacable master with regard to everything that injured his envy.

RICHELIEU: Well, when I may have been too jealous and too imperious, this is a grand vice, it's true; but how many qualities did I have that attested to an [493] extensive genius and noble soul! As for you, Lord Jules, you showed only finesse and avarice. You did worse to the French than spilling their blood; you corrupted the foundations of their morals; you rendered probity low and ridiculous. I only punished the insolence of the great. You struck down their courage, degraded their nobility, overturned all ranks, rendered all their graces venal. You feared merit, one gained your favor only by showing oneself to be of bad character—low-minded, supple, and capable of evil intrigues. You never even had true knowledge of men. You were capable of believing only in evil; all the rest seemed to you just a fairy-tale. All you needed were deceitful minds who duped those you had to negotiate with, or traffickers who could get you money by all possible means. And your name lives on as debased and shameful, whereas on the contrary I am assured that mine grows ever more glorious within the French nation.

MAZARIN: You had nobler inclinations than me, and a little more haughtiness and pride. But you also have a certain vain and false something about you. As for me, I avoided this crooked grandeur as a ridiculous vanity: always poets, orators, actors! You were yourself an orator, rival poet of Corneille, you wrote books of devotion without being devout—always the gallant, excelling in every genre.[66] You ate up the flattery of all the other authors. Is there a single door or window in the Sorbonne where you didn't put up your crest?

RICHELIEU: Your mockery stings, but it's not unjustified. I see well that true glory steers clear of certain honors that vulgar vanity seeks out, and that wanting honor too much disgraces one. But in the end I loved letters. I excited emulation in order to reestablish them. As for you, you never attended to the Church or to letters or to the arts or to virtue. Is it really so surprising that a conduct so despicable served to arouse all the great of the state and all upright men against a foreigner?

MAZARIN: You speak only out of [494] false magnanimity. But governing a state well isn't a question of generosity or good faith or good heart; it's a question of having a mind full of expedients, whose plans are impenetrable, which squanders nothing on its passions but focuses entirely on its interests, and which is never lacking resources to overcome difficulties.

RICHELIEU: True acumen consists in never having need of deceiving, and succeeding always by upright means. It is only out of weakness and ignorance of the right way that one takes twists and turns and has recourse to ruse. True acumen consists in not occupying oneself with so many expedients, but in choosing from the start by a clear and precise view the best one compared to the others. This flurry of expedients comes less from the extent and force of one's genius, than from lack of power and precision in knowing how to choose. True acumen consists in understanding that ultimately the greatest of all resources in affairs is a universal reputation for probity. You are always in danger when you can trust your interests only to dupes or rogues. But when people count on your probity, the good and the evil alike trust you; your enemies fear you just as your friends love you. As for you, for all your protean personalities, you knew how to make yourself neither loved nor esteemed nor feared. I agree that you were a great actor, but not a great man.

MAZARIN: You speak of me as if I lacked heart. I showed by carrying arms in Spain that I didn't fear death. One saw it again in the dangers to which I was exposed during the civil wars of France. As for you, you were known to be afraid of your own shadow, and to have always thought you saw under your bed some assassin ready to stab you. But it is necessary to believe that you had these panic attacks only in certain hours?

RICHELIEU: Ridicule me as much as you please. As for me, I will always do you justice for your good qualities. You did not lack valor in war, but you lacked courage, firmness, [495] and greatness of soul in business. You were supple only out of weakness, and because you had no fixed principles of mind. You dared not resist forthrightly. It is that which made you promise too easily, and then elude all your promises by a hundred subtle excuses. These reversals were above all vulgar and useless; they sheltered you only because you had authority. An upright man would have preferred that you had simply said to him, "I did wrong to make promises to you and I lack the power to make good on what I promised," than of adding to the breach of promise the hypocrisy with which you toyed with the unfortunate. It matters little if one is brave in battle if one is weak in negotiation. Many princes capable of dying with glory disgraced themselves like the lowest of men by their weakness in everyday business.

MAZARIN: It's easy to talk like that. But when you have to satisfy everyone, you divert them as well as you can. There aren't enough favors to go around for everybody. Each of them is quite far from doing themselves justice. Not having anything else to give them, it is necessary at least to leave them vain hopes.

RICHELIEU: I accept that it is necessary to leave many men to hope. This is not to dupe them because each can find his reward in his rank, and even advance on certain occasions beyond what one would have expected. As for disproportionate and ridiculous hopes, if they have them, too bad for them. In that case you do not fool them; they fool themselves, and can only blame themselves for their own folly. But to give them in public promises that you laugh about in private is something that is unworthy of an upright man and pernicious to reputation in business. As for me, I supported and increased the authority of the king without having recourse to such contemptible methods. This is a conclusive fact, and you argue against a man who offers a decisive example against your maxims.

3

The Adventures of Telemachus (selections)

1. Egypt [Pl. 2:16–19]

"If the sorrow of our captivity had not rendered us insensible to all pleasures, our eyes would have been charmed on seeing this fertile land of Egypt, which seemed like a delightful garden watered by an infinite number of canals. We could not cast our eyes on the two riverbanks without seeing opulent cities, country houses agreeably situated, lands covered year in and year out by an endless golden harvest that never subsided, prairies full of flocks, laborers bent under the weight of fruits that the earth had discharged from her breast, and shepherds who made the sweet sounds of their flutes and pipes echo throughout the countryside."

" 'Happy,' said Mentor, 'the people led by a wise king! They enjoy abundance; they live happily, and they love the one to whom they owe all their happiness. It is thus,' he added, 'O Telemachus, that you must reign and bring joy to your people, if ever the gods allow you to possess the kingdom of your father. Love your people as your children; savor the pleasure of being loved by them, and make it such that they can never feel peace and joy without remembering that it is a good king who made them these rich presents. Kings who dream only of making themselves feared, and of beating down their subjects in order to render them more submissive, are the curse of the human race. They are feared as they desire to be; but they are hated, detested, and have still more to fear from their subjects than their subjects have to fear from them . . . .' "

[17] " . . . Then Mentor made me take note of the joy and abundance spread across all the countryside of Egypt, where as many as 2,200 cities lay. He admired the good administration of these cities,[1] the justice exercised in favor of the poor against the rich, the good education of children—who were accustomed to obedience, work, sobriety, love of arts and letters, attentiveness in all the ceremonies of religion, disinterestedness, desire for honor, faithfulness to men, and the fear of the gods that each father inspired in his children—and he did not fail to admire this beautiful order. 'Happy,' he said

Fénelon. Ryan Patrick Hanley, Oxford University Press (2020) © Oxford University Press.
DOI: 10.1093/oso/9780190079581.001.0001

to me without pausing, 'the people that a wise king leads thusly! But happier still the king who establishes the happiness of all peoples, and who finds his own happiness in his virtue! He is more than feared, for he is loved. Not only is he obeyed, but still more he is the king of all hearts. Each, so far from wanting to rid themselves of him, fears losing him and would give his life for him.' I took note of what Mentor said, and I felt my courage reborn in the depths of my heart as this wise friend spoke to me. As soon as we arrived at Memphis, that opulent and magnificent city, the governor ordered us to go up to Thebes in order to be presented to King Sesostris, who liked to examine things firsthand and who was strongly predisposed against the Tyrians.[2] We thus went again up along the Nile, up to this famous hundred-gated Thebes, where this great king lived. This city seemed to us of immense extent and more populated than the most flourishing cities of Greece. The administration there is perfect with regard to the cleanliness of the streets, the flow of the waters, the convenience of the baths, the cultivation of the arts, and the security of the public. Fountains and obelisks ornament the squares. The temples are of marble, and an architecture [18] simple but majestic. The palace of the prince is like a great city unto itself, in which one sees only marble columns, pyramids and obelisks, enormous statues, and furnishings of solid gold and silver. Those who had brought us told the king that we had been found in a Phoenician ship. Every day he heard, at certain appointed hours, all of his subjects who had either complaints to make to him, or opinions to give to him. He neither despised nor rebuffed anyone, and he believed himself to be king only to do good to all his subjects, whom he loved as his children. As for foreigners, he received them with kindness, and wanted to see them, because he believed that one could always learn something useful in instructing oneself in the morals and manners of distant peoples. This curiosity of the king led us to be presented to him. He was on a throne of ivory, holding in his hand a scepter of gold. He was already old, but pleasant, full of gentleness and majesty; he judged the people every day with a patience and wisdom that were admired without flattery. After having worked all day ordering business and rendering exact justice, he spent the evenings listening to wise men or conversing with the most upright men, whom he knew how to choose in order to admit them into his familiarity. In all his life one could reproach him only for having triumphed with too much pomp over the kings he had vanquished and of being too confident in one of his subjects whom I will sketch for you in a bit."

2. Tyre [Pl. 2:35–39]

"I profited from this stay by getting to know the morals of the Phoenicians, so celebrated by all the nations of the known world. I admired the happy situation of this great city, situated on an island in the middle of the sea.[3] The neighboring coast is delightful for its fertility, the exquisite fruits that it brings forth, the number of cities and villages that almost touch each other, and finally the gentleness of its climate, as the mountains shelter this coast from the burning winds of the south. It is refreshed by northerly winds that blow from the sea. This country is at the foot of Mount Lebanon, the summit of which cleaves the clouds on its way to touching the stars. A perpetual ice covers its face. Rivers full of snow fall like torrents from points of rocks that surround its head. Underneath one sees a vast forest of ancient cedars that seem as old as the earth where they are planted, and which carry their thick branches almost up to the clouds. Thick pastures lie under the forest on the slopes of the mountain. There one sees the lowing cattle roaming, as well as the bleating sheep, with their tender lambs bounding on the cool grass. Here too flow a thousand different streams of clear water, which distribute water everywhere. Finally one sees below these pastures the foot of the mountain, which is like a garden; spring and autumn reign there together, joining their flowers and fruits. Never do the tempestuous southern winds, which dry out and burn up everything, nor the harsh northern winds, ever dare to efface the lively [36] colors that ornament this garden. Near this beautiful coast that raises itself out of the sea is the island where the city of Tyre is built. This great city seems to float above the waters and to be the queen of all the sea. Merchants come there from all parts of the world, and its inhabitants are themselves the most famous merchants that the world has ever seen. When one enters this city, it first seems that it belongs to no one specific people, but is common to all peoples, and the center of their commerce. It has two great breakwaters, similar to two arms, which extend out into the sea and surround a vast port where the winds cannot enter. In this port one sees a forest of ship masts, and these ships are so numerous that the sea that carries them is difficult to spot. All the citizens apply themselves to commerce, and their great riches never render them averse to the work necessary to augment them. One sees on all sides there the fine linen of Egypt and the twice-dyed Tyrenian purple of a marvelous vividness; this double dye is so bright that time cannot efface it; it is used like fine wool that one enhances with embroidery of gold and silver. The Phoenicians have established trade with all the peoples up to the strait of

Gades, and they have even penetrated into the vast ocean that surrounds all the earth.[4] They have also made long navigations on the Red Sea, and it is by this route that they go to seek out in unknown islands gold, perfumes, and various animals found nowhere else."

"I could not raise my eyes from the magnificent spectacle of this great city, where everything was in motion. Unlike in the cities of Greece, I didn't see there any of those lazy and curious men who go to seek out the news in the public square, or watch strangers who arrive at the port. The men there are busy unloading their ships, transporting their merchandise or selling it, organizing their storehouses, and taking an exact account of what is owed them by foreign traders. The women never cease either spinning wool, or making embroidered designs, or folding the rich fabrics. 'How did it come about,' I said to Narbal, 'that the Phoenicians have rendered themselves the masters of the commerce of all the world and thus enrich themselves by the expenses of all other peoples?' 'You can see,' he replied to me, 'that the situation of Tyre is [37] fortunate for navigation. It is our fatherland that has the glory of having invented navigation. The Tyrians were the first (if we can trust the records of the most obscure antiquity) who mastered the floods, long before the age of Typhis and of the Argonauts so famous in Greece; they were, I say, the first who dared to put themselves into frail boats at the mercy of the waves and storms, who sounded the depths of the sea, who observed the distant stars, following the science of the Egyptians and the Babylonians, and finally the first who gathered together all the peoples that the sea had separated. The Tyrians are industrious, patient, hard-working, orderly, sober, and prudent. They have an exact administration. They are perfectly in accord with one another. No people has been more constant, more sincere, more faithful, more sure, more open to all strangers. This, to say nothing of other causes, is what gives them their empire over the sea, and allows so useful a commerce to flourish in their ports. If division and jealousy were to emerge among them; if they were to begin to go soft amid pleasures and laziness, if the leaders of the nation were to despise work and thrift, if the arts were to stop being esteemed in their city, if they were to lose good faith toward strangers, if they were to change in even the least respect the rules of free commerce, if they were to neglect their manufactures, and if they were to cease making the great advances necessary to render their goods perfect, each in its own way, you would soon see fall this power that you admire.'"

" 'But explain to me,' I said to him, 'the true means of one day establishing a similar commerce at Ithaca.' 'Do,' he responded to me, 'as one does

here: receive all foreigners well and easily. Make them find security, convenience, and total freedom in your ports. Never allow yourself to succumb to
avarice or pride. The true means of winning much is never wanting to win
too much, and knowing how to lose as appropriate. Make yourself loved
by all foreigners. Be tolerant of their small faults; be afraid of exciting their
jealousy by your haughtiness. Be consistent in the regulation of commerce,
ensure that the regulations are short and simple, accustom your peoples to
follow them inviolably, punish severely both fraud and the negligence or
sumptuousness of the merchants that ruins commerce by ruining the men
engaged in it. Above all [38] make sure never to hinder commerce in order
to turn it to your interests. It is necessary that the prince does not mix himself up in commerce, for fear of hindering it, and that he leaves all the profit
to his subjects who have taken the pains of it. Otherwise he will discourage
them. He will draw from it sufficient advantages by the great riches that will
enter into his States. Commerce is like certain springs: if you try to redirect
their course, you dry them up. It is only profit and convenience that attract
foreigners to your land. If you make commerce less convenient and less
useful to them, they will gradually withdraw and not return, because other
peoples, profiting from your imprudence, will attract them and lead them
away from you. It is even necessary to admit to you that the glory of Tyre
has been waning for some time. O if you had seen it, my dear Telemachus,
before the reign of Pygmalion, you would have been even more astonished!
You now find here only the sad remains of a grandeur that threatens to soon
end. O unfortunate Tyre, into what hands have you fallen! In other times
the sea carried to you the tribute of all the peoples of the earth. Pygmalion
fears everything, from foreigners and his subjects alike. Instead of opening
his ports in complete freedom to all the most distant nations, in accord with
our ancient custom, he wants to know the number of ships that arrive, their
countries, the names of the men on them, the type of their commerce, the
price of their merchandise, and the time they need to stay here. He does even
worse, because he uses deceptions in order to surprise the merchants and
to confiscate their merchandise. He harasses the merchants that he thinks
most opulent, he establishes new taxes under various pretexts. He himself
wants to enter into commerce, and everyone dreads having any business with
him. Thus commerce languishes. Little by little foreigners forget the route to
Tyre that was in other times so dear to them, and thus if Pygmalion does not
change his conduct, our glory and our strength will be soon carried to some
other people better governed than we are.'"

"I then asked Narbal how the Tyrians had rendered themselves so strong on the sea, because I wanted not to be ignorant of anything that contributes to the good government of a kingdom. 'We have,' he responded, 'the forests of Lebanon which furnish wood for ships, and we take care to save them for this use, never cutting them for any reason but [39] public need. For the construction of ships, we have the advantage of having skillful workers.' 'How,' I said to him, 'have you been able to form or find these workers?' He responded to me, 'They are formed little by little in the countryside. When those who excel in the arts are well rewarded, men who take them to their highest perfection are sure to be had, because the men who have more wisdom and talent do not fail to devote themselves to the arts to which great rewards are attached. Here we honor all those who succeed in the arts and in the sciences useful to navigation. A good geometer is respected, a good astronomer is highly esteemed, a pilot who surpasses others in his duties is showered with goods, a good carpenter is not despised—on the contrary, he is well paid and well treated. Good rowers even have steady rewards proportionate to their services. They are well fed; they are cared for when they are sick; in their absence, their wives and children are cared for; if they die in a shipwreck, their families are compensated; when they have served a certain time they are sent back to their homes. As a result, we have as many of them as we desire. The father is delighted to raise his son to so good a trade, and from his earliest childhood he hastens to teach him how to handle the oar, to tend to the lines, and to brave storms. It is thus that men are led without compulsion by reward, and by good order. Authority alone does nothing well; the submission of inferiors does not suffice: it is necessary to win hearts, and to show men their advantage in matters in which you hope to avail yourself of their industry.'"

3. Crete [Pl. 2:57–60 and 65–70]

"After we had admired this spectacle, we began to catch a glimpse of the mountains of Crete, which we still had trouble entirely distinguishing from the clouds of the sky and the waves of the sea. Soon we saw the summit of Mount Ida above the other mountains of the island, as an old stag in a forest carries its treelike antlers over the heads of the young fauns that follow it. Little by little we saw more distinctly the coasts of this island, which presented themselves to our eyes like an amphitheater. As much as the island of Cyprus had seemed to us neglected and uncultivated did that of Crete show itself to be fertile, and ornamented with every fruit by the inhabitants. On all sides, we noted villages well built, towns equal to cities, and cities simply magnificent. We saw no field where the hand of the diligent laborer had not left its mark; everywhere the plow had left hollow furrows: the bramble and thorns and other plants that elsewhere uselessly clutter the land are unknown in this country. We gazed with pleasure on cavernous valleys where herds of cattle lowed in verdant pastures; along rivers, where sheep grazed on the side of a small hill; on the vast countryside covered with yellow tufts, rich gifts of the fecund Ceres, finally on the mountains ornamented by vines and clusters of already ripened grapes, which promised to the harvesters the sweet presents of Bacchus in order to charm away the cares of men."

"Mentor told us that he had been in Crete previously, and he [58] recounted to us what he had seen of it. 'This island,' he said, 'admired by all foreigners, and famous for its hundred cities, effortlessly feeds all its inhabitants, however innumerable they might be. The earth never fails to spread its goods on those who cultivate it. Its fertile breast cannot be exhausted. The more men there are in a country—provided they are hard-working—the greater abundance they enjoy. They have no need to be jealous of each other. The earth, this good mother, multiplies its fruits according to the number of her children who have earned her fruits by their work. The ambition and avarice of men are the sole sources of their unhappiness. Men want to have everything, and they render themselves unhappy by the desire for the superfluous. If they had wanted to live simply and content themselves with satisfying their true needs, then abundance, joy, peace, and union would be seen everywhere. This is what Minos, the wisest and best of all kings, understood. All the most wonderful things that you see on this island are the fruit of his laws. The education that he gave the children renders the body healthy and robust. They are accustomed early on to a simple, frugal, and laborious life. It is assumed that all pleasure weakens the body and the mind. No other pleasure is ever proposed to them than that of being invincible by virtue, and of acquiring great glory. Courage here is thought to consist not merely in despising death amid the dangers of war, but still more in repugnance for excessive riches and shameful pleasures. Here three vices are punished that go unpunished among other peoples: ingratitude, dissimulation, and avarice. As for sumptuousness and softness, there is never any need to reprove them, because they are unknown in Crete. Everyone there works and no one dreams of enriching himself. Each believes himself wholly rewarded for his work by a sweet and orderly life in which one enjoys in peace and abundance all that is truly necessary for life. Neither precious furnishings, nor magnificent clothing, nor delicious banquets, nor gilded palaces are permitted there. Clothing is of fine wool, and beautiful colors, but all of a piece, and without embroidery. The meals there are sober; little wine is drunk there. Good bread makes up the principal part, along with the fruits that the trees offer up as if of their own volition, and the milk of the herds. At most is eaten a little plain meat without sauce. Even so care is taken to save the best amid the [59] great herds of cattle in order to make agriculture flourish. Houses there are tidy, commodious, and pleasant, but without ornament. Magnificent architecture is not unknown there, but it is reserved for the temples of the gods; men would not dare to have houses similar to those of the immortals. The great goods of the Cretans are health, strength, courage, peace and union of families, freedom of all citizens, abundance of necessary things, contempt for superfluities, habit of work and horror of laziness, emulation of virtue, submission to the laws, and fear of the just gods.'"

"I asked him in what the authority of the king consisted, and he replied to me: 'He has supremacy over his people, but the laws have supremacy over him. He has absolute power to do good, and hands bound as soon as he wants to do evil. The laws compel him to regard his people as the most precious of all trusts, on the condition that he will be the father of his subjects. They desire that a single man serves, by his wisdom and by his moderation, the happiness of all men; and not that all men serve, by their misery and cowardly servitude, to flatter the pride and softness of a single man. The king must never be above others, except in that which is necessary in order to relieve his difficult functions, or in order to impress on the people respect for the one who must support the laws. Moreover, the king must be more sober, more opposed to softness, and more exempt from sumptuousness and haughtiness than any other. He must not have more riches and pleasures but more wisdom, virtue, and glory than the rest of men. Beyond the state's borders he must be the defender of the fatherland in commanding the armies, and within, he must be the judge of the people in order to render them good, wise, and happy. It is not for his own sake that the gods made him king. He is only king in order to be the man of the people. It is to the people that he owes all his time, all his cares, all his affection, and he is not worthy of royalty as soon as he forgets to sacrifice himself to the public good. Minos desired his children to reign after him only on the condition that they would reign in accord with these maxims. He loved his people still more than his family. It is by such wisdom that he rendered Crete so strong and so happy. It is by this moderation that he outshone the glory of all the conquerors who wanted to make the people the instruments of their own greatness, that is to say their [60] vanity. Finally, it is by his justice that he merited to be the sovereign judge of the dead in the Underworld . . . .' "

[65] " . . . The first of these wise old men opened the book of the laws of Minos.[5] This was a great book, ordinarily shut up in a casket of gold with perfumes. All these old men kissed it with respect; because they say that after the gods from whom wise laws come, nothing must be more sacred to men than the laws destined to render them good, wise, and happy. Those who have the laws in their hands in order to govern peoples must always take care to govern themselves by the laws. It is law, and not man, which must reign. Such is the discourse of these sages. Then, the one who presided proposed three questions to be decided by the maxims of [66] Minos. The first question concerned who is the freest of all men. Some responded that it was a king who had an absolute empire over his people and who was victorious over all his enemies. Others maintained that it was a man so wealthy that he could satisfy all his desires. Others said that it was a man who never married, and who traveled all his life through different countries, without being ever subject to the laws of any one nation. Others imagined it was a barbarian who, living off the hunt in the middle of the woods, was independent of all civilization and all need.[6] Others believed it was a man newly set free, because in leaving all the rigors of servitude he enjoyed more than any other the sweetness of freedom. Others finally dared to say that it was a dying man, because his death delivered him from everything, and all men together had no power over him. When my turn came, I had no trouble responding, because I had never forgotten what Mentor had often said to me. 'The freest of all men,' I responded, 'is the one who can be free even in slavery. In whatever country and whatever condition one might be, one is entirely free, so long as one fears the gods, and fears only them. In a word, the truly free man is the one who, released from all fear and desire, is submissive only to the gods and to his reason.' The old men smilingly looked at each other, and were surprised to see that my response was precisely that of Minos."

"The second question was then posed in these terms: 'Who is the unhappiest of all men?' Each said what came to his mind. One said: 'It is a man who has neither property, nor health, nor honor.' Another said: 'It is a man who has no friends.' Others insisted that it is a man who has ungrateful children unworthy of him. A man of the Isle of Lesbos said, 'The unhappiest of all men is the one who believes he is. Because unhappiness depends less on the things that one suffers than the anxiousness with which one augments one's unhappiness.' At these words, all the assembly cried out. All applauded, and believed that the wise man of Lesbos would carry the prize on this question. But I was asked my thoughts, and I responded, following the maxims of Mentor: 'The unhappiest of all [67] men is a king who thinks himself happy in rendering other men miserable. He is doubly unhappy by his blindness: not knowing his unhappiness, he cannot cure himself of it; he even is afraid to know it. The truth cannot pierce the crowd of flatterers in order to reach him. He is tyrannized by his passions: he does not know his duties. He has never tasted the pleasure of doing good, nor felt the charms of pure virtue. He is unhappy and deserves to be so: his unhappiness grows daily, he runs to his ruin, and the gods prepare to confound him by an eternal punishment.' All the assembly agreed that I had beaten the wise man of Lesbos, and the old men declared that I had struck on Minos's true meaning."

"For the third question, it was asked which the gods prefer: a conquering king, invincible in war; or a king without the experience of war, but fit to govern the people wisely in peace. The majority replied that the king invincible in war was preferable. 'To what does it serve,' they said, 'to have a king who knows how to govern well in peace, if he does not know how to defend the country when war comes? The enemies will vanquish him and reduce his people to servitude.' Others insisted, on the contrary, that the peaceful king would be better, because he would fear war and take care to avoid it. Others said that a conquering king would work for the glory of his people as much as his own and would render his subjects masters of other nations, whereas a peaceful king would hold them in a shameful cowardice. I was asked for my thoughts. I responded thus: 'A king who knows how to govern only in peace or in war and who is not capable of conducting his people in both of these two states, is only half a king. But if you would compare a king who knows only war to a wise king, who, without knowing war, is capable of supporting it if necessary by his generals, I find him preferable to the other. A king entirely turned to war would always want to wage it. In order to extend his domination and his own glory he would ruin his people. What good is it to a people for its king to subjugate other nations, if they themselves are unhappy under his reign? Moreover, long wars are always followed by many disorders. Even the victors themselves unravel during these confused times. See what it cost Greece to have triumphed over Troy: she was deprived of [68] her kings for more than ten years. When everything is aflame because of war, laws, agriculture, arts languish. Even the best princes, as long as they

have to support a war, are compelled to do the greatest of evils, namely to tolerate license and avail themselves of the wicked. How many scoundrels are
there whom one would punish in times of peace, but whose audacity needs
to be rewarded in the disorders of war. No people has ever had a conquering
king without having much to suffer from his ambition. A conqueror, drunk
on his glory, ruins his own victorious nation as much as the vanquished nations. A prince who does not have the qualities necessary for peace cannot
make his subjects taste the fruits of a war happily concluded. He is like a man
who would defend his field against his neighbor and who would even usurp
his neighbor's, but who would not know how to labor or sow in order to
enjoy a harvest. Such a man seems born to destroy, to ravage, to overturn the
world, and not to make a people happy by a wise government. Let us come
now to the peaceful king. It is true that he is not fit for great conquests; that
is to say, he is not born to trouble the happiness of his people in desiring to
vanquish other peoples that justice has not rendered submissive to him. But
if he is truly fit to govern in peace, he has all the qualities necessary to secure
his people against his enemies. This is how: he is just, moderate, and easy
with regard to his neighbors. He never undertakes against them any scheme
that can trouble their peace. He is faithful in his alliances. His allies love
him, do not fear him, and have an entire confidence in him. If there is some
restless neighbor, haughty and ambitious, all the other neighboring kings,
who fear this restless neighbor and who are not jealous of the peaceful king,
join themselves to this good king in order to avoid being oppressed. His
probity, good faith, and moderation render him the arbiter of all the states
surrounding his own. While the enterprising king is hateful to all the others
and constantly exposed to their leagues, this one has the glory of being like
the father and the tutor of all the other kings. Thus the advantages that he
has outside his state. Those he enjoys within are even more solid. Since he is
fit to govern in peace, I must assume that he governs by the wisest laws. He
uproots sumptuousness, softness, and all the arts that serve only to flatter
the vices. [69] He makes the arts flourish that are useful to the true needs of
life. Above all he applies his subjects to agriculture. By this, he ensures them
of an abundance of necessary things. This hard-working people—simple in
its morals, accustomed to living on little, winning its life easily by the cultivation of the land—multiplies itself endlessly. One finds in his realm an
innumerable people, who are yet healthy, vigorous, and robust, who are not
weakened by pleasures, who are practiced in virtue, who are not attached
to the sweetness of a cowardly and pleasure-filled life, who know to despise

death, and who would sooner die than lose the freedom it enjoys under a wise king who dedicates himself to making reason alone reign. Were a conquering neighbor to attack them, he may not find them sufficiently accustomed to the rigors of camp, to ordering itself in battle, or to erecting machines in order to lay siege to a city. But he will find it invincible in its multitude, its courage, its patience amid trials, its habits of suffering poverty, its vigor in battle, and a virtue that failure itself cannot defeat. Moreover, if the king is not sufficiently experienced to command the armies himself, he will ensure that they are commanded by capable men, and he will know how to avail himself of them without losing his authority. Meanwhile he will draw on the aid of his allies. His subjects will prefer to die than to pass under the domination of another violent and unjust king. The gods themselves will fight for him. See what resources he will have amidst the greatest dangers. I conclude therefore that the peaceful king who has no experience with war is very imperfect, since he does not know how to fulfill one of his greatest functions, which is vanquishing his enemies. But I add that he is nevertheless infinitely superior to the conquering king who lacks the qualities necessary for peace, and who is fit only for war.' "

"I perceived in the assembly many men who could not share this opinion; because the majority of men, puffed up by empty things like victories and conquests, prefer them to that which is simple, tranquil, and solid, like peace and the good administration of peoples. But all the old wise men declared that I had spoken like Minos. The leader of these old men cried out: 'I see the fulfillment of an oracle of Apollo, known throughout our island. Minos consulted the god, in order to know how [70] long his race would reign, following the laws that he had come to establish. The god replied to him: "Your line will cease to reign when a foreigner will enter into our island in order to make your laws reign there." We have feared that some foreigner would come to conquer the island of Crete. But the unhappiness of Idomeneus, and the wisdom of the son of Ulysses, who understands the laws of Minos better than any other mortal, reveal to us the meaning of the oracle. Why do we delay crowning the one the fates give us for our king?' "

4. Bétique [Pl. 2:106–112]

But then Telemachus said to Adoam: "I remember that you told me of a voyage that you made to Bétique after we had left Egypt. Bétique is a country of which such marvelous things are recounted that one can hardly believe them. Please tell me, if you will, if everything that is said about it is really true."

"I'd be delighted," responded Adoam, "to sketch for you this famous country, so worthy of your curiosity, and which surpasses all its renown." Immediately he began thus:

"The river Bétis flows through a fertile country and under a gentle sky that is always calm. The country has taken its name from the river, which empties into the great Ocean, near the Pillars of Hercules, this place where the furious sea, bursting over its breakwaters, in former times separated the land of Tartessus from great Africa.[7] This country seems to have preserved the delights of the golden age. The winters there are mild, and the harsh north winds never blow. The summer's heat is always tempered by refreshing zephyrs, which come to cool the air toward the middle of the day. Thus the whole year is merely a happy marriage of spring and fall, which seem to join together. The earth, in the valleys and neighboring countryside, every year brings forth a double harvest. Its paths are bordered by laurels, pomegranates, jasmines, and other trees, always green and always blooming. The mountains are covered by flocks that furnish fine wool sought out by the entire known world. There are several mines of silver and gold in this beautiful country. But the inhabitants, easy and [107] happy in their simplicity, do not deign to count gold and silver among their riches. They value only that which truly serves the needs of men. When we began to conduct commerce among these people, we found gold and silver used by them like iron—for plowshares, for example. As they did not engage in any foreign commerce, they had no need of money. They are almost all shepherds or laborers. Few artisans are to be found in this country, as they tolerate only the arts that serve the true needs of men. Yet even as the majority of men in this country are devoted to agriculture or shepherding, they do not neglect the arts necessary for their simple and frugal life. The women spin this fine wool, and make from it fabrics of a marvelous whiteness; they make bread, prepare food, and find this labor easy, because in this country one lives off fruit or milk, and rarely meat. They use the skins of their sheep to make lightweight shoes for themselves, their husbands, and their children; they make tents, some of tanned hides and others of tree bark; they make and wash all the clothing of the family, and keep the houses in an admirable neatness and tidiness. Their clothes are simple to make, because in this mild climate only a piece of fine light wool is worn, which is not sized, and which each puts with long pleats around his body for the sake of modesty, giving it the shape that he wants. Beyond the cultivation of land and the watching of flocks, the men have no other arts to exercise than woodworking and ironworking. Even still they hardly use iron, except for instruments necessary for labor. All the arts related to architecture are useless to them, because they never build houses. 'To build dwellings that last longer than we do,' they say, 'is to attach one's self too much to the land. It is enough to protect ourselves from the injuries of the air.' As for all the other arts esteemed by the Greeks, the Egyptians, and all other civilized peoples, they detest them as inventions of vanity and softness. When told of peoples who know the art of making magnificent buildings, furniture of gold and silver, textiles ornamented with embroidery and precious stones, exquisite perfumes, [108] delicious dishes, instruments whose harmony charms, they respond in these terms: 'These peoples are very unfortunate to have employed so much work and industry in corrupting themselves! Such superfluities weaken, intoxicate, torment those who possess them. They tempt those who are deprived of them to want to acquire them by injustice and violence. Can a superfluity that serves only to render men bad really be called good? The men of these countries: are they healthier and more robust than us? Do they live longer? Are they more unified? Do they lead lives more free, more tranquil, more cheerful? On the contrary, they come to be jealous of each other, gnawed at by an enervating and black envy, always agitated by ambition, by fear, by avarice, incapable of pure and simple pleasures, since they are slaves of so many false necessities on which they make their happiness depend.'"

"It is thus," Adoam continued, "that these wise men speak, who have learned wisdom merely by studying nature in its simplicity. They are horrified by our politeness, and in truth it seems excessive to them next to their amiable lack of affectation. They live all together without dividing the land. Each family is governed by its head, who is its true king. The father of the family has the right to punish each of his children or grandchildren for their misdoings. But before punishing them, he takes the opinion of the rest of the family. These punishments almost never come about however, as this happy land abounds with innocence of morals, good faith, obedience, and horror of vice. It seems that Astraea, who is said to have retired to heaven, is again here below, hidden among these men.[8] Judges are unnecessary among them, because their own consciences judge them. All goods are common. The fruit of the trees, the vegetables of the earth, the milk of the flocks are riches so abundant, that a people so sober and so moderate has no need of dividing them up. Each family, wandering in this beautiful country, transports its tents from one place to another when it has consumed the fruits and exhausted the pastures of the place where it had placed itself. Thus, they have no interests to defend against one another, and they are all bound by a brotherly love that nothing troubles. It is their curtailment of vain riches and deceitful pleasures that preserves their peace, union, and freedom. They are all free and all equal. One sees among them no distinction other than [109] that which comes from the experience of the wise elders or from the extraordinary wisdom of some young men who equal in virtue the greatest of the elders. Fraud, violence, perjury, lawsuits, wars, never make their cruel and repugnant voices heard in this country so precious to the gods. Human blood has never stained this earth red. The blood of lambs hardly flows either. When one speaks to these peoples of bloody battles, rapid conquests, and the overturning of states that one sees in other nations, they could not be more astonished. 'What!' they say, 'men are not mortal enough, without rushing to kill each other? Life is so short! And it seems that it's too long to them! Have they been put on the earth to tear each other apart and make themselves mutually miserable?' In addition, these peoples of Bétique cannot understand how one can admire all the conquerors who subjugate great empires. 'What madness,' they say, 'to put one's happiness in governing other men, of whom the government is so difficult, if one wants to govern them with reason and in accord with justice! But how could it be pleasurable to govern them involuntarily? All that a wise man can do is desire to submit himself to governing a docile people whom the gods have charged him with, or a people who begs him to be its father and its pastor. But to govern people against their will—this is to render oneself completely miserable, in order to have the false honor of holding them in slavery. A conqueror is a man that the gods, angry with the human race, have given to the earth in their anger, in order to ravage kingdoms, in order to spread terror and misery and hopelessness everywhere, and in order to make as many slaves as there are free men. A man who seeks glory: does he not find enough in conducting with wisdom that which the gods have placed in his hands! Does he believe himself worthy of praise only in becoming violent, unjust, haughty, usurping, tyrannical over all his neighbors? One must never dream of war except to defend one's freedom. Happy the one who is neither the slave of others nor has the mad ambition of making others his slaves! These great conquerors, who are depicted to us with so much glory, resemble those overflowing rivers that seem majestic, but which ravage all the fertile countryside which they were merely meant to water.' " [110]

After Adoam had made this sketch of Bétique, Telemachus, charmed, asked him several questions in his curiosity. "These people," he asked him, "do they drink wine?"

"They don't think about drinking it," Adoam replied, "because they never wanted to make any in the first place. It's not that they lack grapes. No land brings forth grapes more delicious. But they are content to eat grapes as they do other fruit, and they fear wine as the corruptor of men. 'Wine is a species of poison,' they say, 'which puts men in a furor. It does not kill them but it renders them wild. Men can preserve their health and their strength without wine. With wine, they run the risk of ruining their health and losing good morals.'"

Telemachus then said, "I would like very much to know what laws regulate marriages in this nation."

"Each man," Adoam responded, "can have only one woman, and is required to keep her as long as she lives. In this country the honor of men depends as much on their faithfulness to their wives, as the honor of women in other countries depends on their fidelity to their husbands. No people are more honest, or so jealous of chastity. The women there are beautiful and pleasant, but simple, modest, and hard-working. Marriages there are peaceful, prolific, without blemish. Husband and wife appear to be only a single person in two separate bodies. The husband and wife together share all domestic cares. The husband rules all the affairs without, and the wife withdraws into her household, she supports her husband, she appears to be made only to please him, she wins his confidence and charms him less by her beauty than by her virtue. This genuine charm of their society lasts as long as their lives. Sobriety, moderation, and the pure morals of this people give them a long life, free from illnesses. Old men of one hundred and of one hundred and twenty years, who are still cheerful and vigorous, are seen there."

"It remains for me," Telemachus added, "to know how they manage to avoid war with their neighbors."

"Nature," said Adoam, "separated them from other peoples on one side by the sea, and on the other by the high mountains of the north. Moreover, the neighboring peoples respect them for their virtue. Often the other peoples, not being able to reach agreements among themselves, have appealed to them to judge their disputes and have conferred on them the lands and cities that they disputed over. As this wise nation [111] has never done any violence, no one distrusts it. They laugh when told of kings who cannot between them arrange the borders of their states. 'Is it to be feared,' they say, 'that the earth will fail men? There will be always more of it than they can cultivate. So long as there remain lands free and uncultivated, we would not wish even to defend our own against the neighbors who would come to seize it.' Among all the inhabitants of Bétique, neither pride, nor haughtiness, nor bad faith, nor a desire to extend their domination is to be found. Thus their neighbors have never had anything to fear from such a people, and they cannot hope to make themselves feared; this is why they leave them in peace. These people would abandon their country, or deliver themselves up to death, sooner than accept servitude. Thus they are as difficult to subjugate, as they are incapable of wanting to subjugate others. This is what establishes a deep peace between them and their neighbors."

Adoam finished this discourse in recounting the manner in which the Phoenicians conducted their commerce in Bétique. "These peoples," he said," were astonished when they saw arriving, across the waves of the sea, foreigners who came from so far away. They left us free to found a city in the island of Gades;[9] they even received us among them with kindness and gave us part of all they had, without wanting any payment from us. Moreover, they offered to give us for free all their extra wool, beyond what they needed for their own use; and in fact sent us a rich present of it. It is a pleasure for them to give their superfluous goods to foreigners. As for their mines, they had no trouble abandoning them to us; they were useless to them. It appeared to them that men were hardly wise to go seek out, by so many labors, in the bowels of the earth, that which can neither render them happy nor satisfy any true need. 'Do not dig,' they told us, 'so far below the earth: content yourself with working it; it will give you genuine goods that will nourish you; you will draw from it fruits more valuable than gold and silver, since men want gold and silver only to buy the food that would support their life.' We often wanted to teach them navigation and draw the young men from their country to Phoenicia. But they never wanted their [112] children to learn to live like us. 'They would learn,' they would say to us, 'to need all the things that have become necessary for you. They would want to have them. They would abandon virtue in order to obtain them through evil acts. They would become like a man who has good limbs, who, losing the habit of walking, accustoms himself in the end to needing to be always carried like an invalid.' As for navigation, they admire this art for its industry. But they believe it to be a pernicious art. 'If these men there,' they say, 'have in their country sufficient amounts of what is necessary for life, what do they go to seek for in another? That which satisfies nature's needs—is it not sufficient for them? They would deserve to be shipwrecked, since they seek death in the middle of storms, in order to assuage the avarice of the merchants and flatter the passions of other men.'"

Telemachus was delighted to hear this discourse of Adoam and he rejoiced that there was still in the world a people who, following nature's way, was both so wise and so happy. "O how far these morals are," he said, "from the vain and ambitious morals of the peoples who are thought to be the wisest! We are so spoiled that we can hardly believe that so natural a simplicity could be true. The morals of this people seem to us like a pretty fable, and ours must seem to them a monstrous nightmare."

5. Manduria [Pl. 2:127–129]

Idomeneus responded to [Mentor]: "When we arrived on this coast, we found there a savage people who wandered in the forests, living off its hunting and the fruits that the trees bore naturally. These peoples, called [128] the Mandurians, were terrified, seeing our boats and arms. They withdrew into the mountains. But, as our soldiers were eager to see the country and hunt stags, they ran into these fugitive savages. Then the chiefs of these savages said to them: 'We abandoned the pleasant seashores in order to cede them to you. There remain to us only the almost inaccessible mountains. At the very least it is just that you leave us there in peace and freedom. We find you wandering, dispersed, and weaker than us. It would be easy for us to slit your throats, and thereby deprive your companions of even the knowledge of your ill fate. But we do not want to dip our hands in the blood of those who are men just as much as we are. Go, and remember that you owe your lives to our sentiments of humanity. Never forget that it is from a people that you call crude and savage that you receive this lesson of moderation and generosity.'"

"The men of ours who were sent back by these barbarians returned to camp and recounted what had happened to them. Our soldiers were disturbed by it. They were ashamed to see that Cretans owed their lives to this band of fugitive men, who seemed to them more like bears than men. They went out to hunt in greater numbers than before, and with all sorts of arms. Soon they met the savages and attacked them. The combat was cruel. Spears flew from one side to the other, as hail falls on the countryside during a storm. The savages were constrained to withdraw into their steep mountains, where our men dared not engage them. A little later, these peoples sent to me two of their elder sages, who came to request peace. They approached me with presents: skins of wild beasts that they had killed and fruits of the country. After having given me their presents, they spoke thusly: 'O king, we hold, as you see, in one hand the sword, and in the other an olive branch.' (And indeed they held the one and the other in their hands.) 'Thus peace and war. Choose. We would prefer peace. It is for love of it that we have not been ashamed to cede to you the pleasant seashore, where the sun renders the land fertile and produces so many delicious fruits. Peace is sweeter than all these fruits. It is for its sake that we withdrew ourselves into these high mountains ever [129] covered with ice and snow, where neither the flowers of spring nor the rich fruits of autumn are ever seen. We are horrified by this brutality, which, under the fine names of ambition and glory, comes foolishly to ravage the provinces and spill the blood of men, who are all brothers. If this false glory touches you, we are unable to envy you for it, we beg you and we pray to the gods to preserve us from a similar fury. If the sciences that Greeks learn with so much care, and if the politeness of which they so pride themselves inspire in them only this detestable injustice, we believe ourselves too happy for never having had these advantages. We find glory in being always ignorant and barbarous, but just, humane, faithful, disinterested, accustomed to content ourselves on little, and in despising the vain delicacy that makes one need to have much. What we esteem is health, frugality, freedom, vigor of body and mind, love of virtue, fear of the gods, good-naturedness toward our neighbors, attachment to our friends, fidelity to everyone, moderation in prosperity, firmness before evils, courage always to speak the truth boldly, and horror of flattery. Thus the people we offer to you for neighbors and allies. If the gods in their irritation blind you to the point of making you refuse peace, you will learn, but too late, that the men who love peace by moderation are the most formidable in war.' "

"While these old men spoke thusly to me, I could only gaze at them. They had long unkempt beards, shorter white hair, thick eyebrows, lively eyes, countenances that were firm, voices grave and full of authority, manners simple and ingenuous. The furs that served as their clothing were tied at the shoulder, leaving visible their sinewy arms with muscles better developed than those of our athletes. I replied to these two emissaries that I desired peace. We together and in good faith fixed several conditions, we appealed to all the gods to be our witness, and I sent these men back to their home with presents."

6. Salente I [Pl. 2:158–170]

After the army had departed, Idomeneus led Mentor into all the quarters of the city. "Let us see," Mentor said, "how many people you have in the city and in the neighboring countryside. Let us make a count of them. Let us examine also how many laborers there are among these men. Let us see how much your lands produce, in middling years, of grain, wine, oil, and other useful things. We will know by this study if the land supplies enough to feed all its inhabitants, and if it also produces enough to sustain a useful commerce of its superfluities with foreign countries. Let us examine too how many ships and sailors you have. It is by this that your strength can be judged." He went to visit the port and entered each ship. He informed himself of the countries to which each went to trade, what merchandise it [159] carried there, what it took in returning, what was the expense of the boat during the trip, the loans that the merchants made to each other, the companies that they formed among themselves, in order to know if they were fair and faithfully observed, and finally the dangers of shipwrecks and the other misfortunes of commerce, in order to prevent the ruin of the merchants, who, by the avidity of gain, often undertake things which are beyond their power. He desired that all bankruptcies be severely punished, because those who are exempt from bad faith are almost never free from temerity. At the same time, he made rules to ensure that it was easy not to become bankrupt: he established magistrates to whom the merchants rendered account of their goods, their profits, their expenses, and their undertakings. They were never permitted to risk the property of others, and they could even risk only half of their own. In addition, they joined together for the undertakings they could not do alone, and the administration of these companies was inviolable by the rigor of the pains imposed on those who would not follow them. Moreover, freedom of commerce was absolute. So far from impeding it by taxes, a reward was promised to all merchants who could attract to Salente the commerce of some new nation.

Thus peoples soon hurried there in droves from all parts. The commerce of this city was similar to the ebbing and flowing of the sea. Treasures entered there like waves coming one after the other. Everything was carried there and everything left there freely. All that entered was useful. All that exited left other riches in its place. Strict justice presided in the port amid all these visiting nations. Frankness, good faith, and candor seemed, from the highest of these magnificent towers, to call merchants from the most distant lands. All of these merchants, whether they came from the east, where the sun emerges each day from the depths of the sea, or from this great sea where the sun, finishing its course, goes to extinguish its fires, lived as peacefully and securely in Salente as in their fatherland.

As for the interior of the city, Mentor visited all the storehouses, all the shops of artisans, and all the public spaces. He prohibited all foreign merchandise that could introduce luxury and softness. He regulated the dress, the diet, the furnishings, and the size and [160] ornament of houses, for all the different ranks. He banished all ornaments of gold and silver, and said to Idomeneus, "I know only one way to render your people modest in its expenses: it is for you to give them yourself as an example. It is necessary that you have a certain exterior majesty. But your authority will be sufficiently distinguished by your guards, and by the principal officers who surround you. Content yourself with clothes of very fine wool, dyed in purple. The heads of State, after you, should be clothed of the same wool, with the only differences being the color and a delicate embroidery of gold that you would have on the trim of your clothes. The different colors will serve to distinguish the different ranks, without requiring either gold or silver or precious stones. Regulate ranks by birth. Put in the first rank those who have a more ancient and more shining nobility. Those who would have the merit and the authority of the principal posts will be sufficiently content to come after these ancient and illustrious families, who have been so long in possession of the first honors. Those who have not the same nobility will give way to them without trouble, so long as you do not accustom them to forget themselves amid a too swift and too high rise to fortune, and take care to praise those who remain modest amid prosperity. The distinction least exposed to envy is that which comes from a long train of ancestors. As for virtue, it will be sufficiently excited and there will be enough enthusiasm to serve the state, as long as you reward fine actions with crowns and statues, and that these serve as a beginning of nobility for the children of those who will have done them. The people of the highest rank after you will have vestments of white, with a fringe of gold at the base of their habits. They will wear on their finger a ring of gold, and at the neck a medal of gold with your portrait on it. Those of the second rank will have clothes of blue: they will carry a fringe of silver, with the ring, and no medal; the third, of green, without ring or fringe, but with the medal; the fourth, of a yellow of the sun; the fifth, of a light red or pink; the sixth, of gridelin; and the seventh, who will be the lowest of the people, of a color mixed of yellow and white. Thus the clothing of the seven different ranks of free men. All the slaves [161] will be clothed in gray-brown. Thus, without any expense, each will be distinguished according to his condition, and all the arts that serve only to support sumptuousness will be banished from Salente. All the artisans who would have been employed in these pernicious arts will be useful to either the necessary arts, which are few in number, or in commerce, or in agriculture. No change in either the type of fabrics or in the form of the clothing will ever be permitted, as it is unworthy that men, destined to a serious and noble life, amuse themselves in inventing affected trimmings, or permit their women, to whom these amusements would be less shameful, ever to fall into this excess."

Mentor, like an able gardener pruning dead branches from his fruit trees, thus ensured the elimination of the useless sumptuousness that corrupted morals. He returned all things to a noble and frugal simplicity. He even regulated the diet of the citizens and the slaves.

"What shame," he said, "that the most elevated men make their greatness consist in sauces, by which they weaken their souls and insensibly ruin the health of their bodies! They ought to make their happiness consist in their moderation, in their ability to do good for other men, and in the reputation that their good actions must procure them. Sobriety renders the simplest diet very agreeable. It is that which provides, in addition to the most vigorous health, the purest and most constant pleasures. It is thus necessary to limit your meals to the best meats, but dressed without any sauce. This art poisons men by irritating their appetite beyond their real needs." Idomeneus understood well that he had done wrong in leaving the inhabitants of his new city to go soft and to corrupt their morals, in violating all the laws of Minos regarding sobriety. But wise Mentor made him take note that the laws alone, although renewed, would be useless, if the example of the king did not give them an authority that could not come from anywhere else. Idomeneus immediately regulated his table, where he allowed only excellent bread, the wine of the country, which is strong and agreeable, but in very small quantities, with simple meats, such as those that he had eaten with the other Greeks at the siege of Troy. No one dared to complain of a rule that the king imposed on himself, and all thus cured themselves of the profusion and delicacy into which they had begun to plunge themselves at meals. [162]

Mentor next prohibited soft and effeminate music, which corrupted all the youth. He was no less severe regarding the Bacchic music, which is hardly less intoxicating than wine and which produces morals full of anger and impudence. He limited all music to temple festivals, to sing there the praises of the gods and heroes who have set examples of the rarest virtues. He also permitted in the temples only the great ornaments of architecture, such as columns, pediments, and porticos; he provided models of a simple and gracious architecture in order to create, in a small space, a cheerful and comfortable home for a large family, and thus ensure that it might promote living healthily, that the living quarters be independent of each other, that order and tidiness be easy to maintain, and that the upkeep be inexpensive. He desired that any eminent house have a salon and a small peristyle, and small rooms for all free people. But he prohibited very severely the superfluous proliferation and the magnificence of accommodations. These different models of houses, fit for families of varying sizes, served to embellish at little cost a part of the city and render it regular, as opposed to the other part, already built in accord with the caprice and the sumptuousness of individuals, which had, despite its magnificence, a disposition less agreeable and less convenient. This new city was built in very little time, because the neighboring coast of Greece furnished good architects, and a very great number of masons from Epirus and from several other countries had been made to come, on the condition that after having finished their labors they would establish themselves around Salente, would take lands to clear there, and would serve to populate the countryside.

Painting and sculpture seemed to Mentor arts that it was not permissible to abandon. But he wanted to allow in Salente few men devoted to these arts. He established a school where masters of an exquisite taste presided, who examined the young students. "It is necessary," he said, "to allow nothing low and weak in these arts, which are not absolutely necessary. As a result, only young men of a genius that promises much, and that tends to perfection, ought to be admitted there. The others are born for less noble arts, and they will be employed more usefully in serving the ordinary needs of the republic. It is [163] necessary, he said, to employ sculptors and painters only to preserve memories of great men and great actions. It is in public buildings or in tombs that one must preserve representations of all that which has been done with an exceptional virtue for the service of the fatherland." Moreover, the moderation and frugality of Mentor did not prevent him from authorizing all the great buildings designed for racing teams of horses and chariots, for the combats of the wrestlers, for those of the cestus, and for all the other exercises that develop the body and render it more dexterous and more vigorous.

He eliminated a prodigious number of merchants who sold fabrics made in distant countries, embroideries of an excessive price, vases of gold and silver with figures of gods and men and animals, and finally liquors and perfumes. He even desired that the furnishings of each house be simple and made in such a manner as to last a long time, so that the Salentines, who loudly complained of their poverty, began to feel how much superfluous wealth they had. But it was a deceitful wealth that had impoverished them, and they became truly rich to the extent that they had the courage to cast it off. "It is to enrich oneself," they said themselves, "to despise such riches, which exhaust the State, and to diminish one's needs in reducing them to the true necessities of nature."

Mentor hastened to visit the arsenals and all the magazines, in order to know if the arms and all the other things necessary for war were in good condition; because it is necessary, he said, to be always ready to make war, in order never to be reduced to the misfortune of actually having to wage it. He found that several things were everywhere lacking. Immediately the workers were assembled in order to work in iron, steel, and bronze. Burning blazes and whirls of smoke and flames similar to those underground fires vomited by Mount Etna could soon be seen rising. The hammer resounded on the anvil, which groaned under redoubled blows that echoed in the neighboring mountains and seashores. One could be excused for thinking this to be the isle where Vulcan, bringing to life the Cyclops, forges thunderbolts for the father of the gods. Thanks to a wise foresight, one thus saw, in the midst of a deep peace, all the preparations of war.

Then Mentor exited from the city with Idomeneus, and [164] found a great stretch of fertile lands that remained uncultivated. Others were only half cultivated, by the negligence and poverty of the laborers, who, lacking men, also lacked the courage and bodily strength to bring agriculture to perfection. Mentor, seeing this desolate countryside, said to the king, "The earth here wants only to enrich its inhabitants. But inhabitants are lacking from the land. Let us take then all these superfluous artisans in the city, whose arts would serve only to disorder morals, and make them cultivate these plains and hills. It is truly a shame that all these men experienced in these arts that require a sedentary life are not used to work. But here is a means of remedying that. It is necessary to divide between them the vacant lands, and to call to their aid neighboring peoples who would do the toughest work under their supervision. These peoples would do it, as long as they were promised suitable rewards from the fruits of the lands that they would clear. They could even, in time, possess a part of them and be thus incorporated into your people, which is not numerous enough. As long as they were hard-working and obeyed the law, you would have the best subjects, and they would increase your power. Your urban artisans, transplanted into the countryside, will raise their children to work and acquire a taste for rural life. Moreover, all the foreign masons working to build your city ought to be employed in clearing a part of your lands and in making themselves laborers, and be incorporated into your people as soon as they have completed their work in the city. These artisans are delighted to commit themselves to passing their lives under a dominion that is now so mild. As they are robust and hard-working, their example will serve to excite to work the artisans transplanted from the city to the countryside, with whom they will be mixed. Soon all the country will be populated by vigorous families dedicated to agriculture. Besides, you will not find it hard for this people to multiply. They will soon become innumerable, provided you facilitate marriages. The manner of doing so is very simple. Almost all men are inclined to marry. Only poverty prevents them. If you do not burden them with taxes, they will support their wives and their children without difficulty, because the earth is never ungrateful; it always nourishes with its fruits those who cultivate it [165] with care. It refuses its goods only to those who fear giving it their labor. The more children the laborers have, the richer they are, if the prince does not impoverish them; because their children, from their earliest youth, begin to relieve them. The youngest tend the sheep in the pastures; the others, who are older, already lead great herds. The eldest work with their father. Meanwhile the mother of the family prepares a simple meal for her husband and her dear children, who must return fatigued from the day's work. She takes care to milk her cows and her ewes, from whom rivers of milk flow; she makes a great fire, around which the entire family, innocent and peaceful, takes pleasure in singing all evening in awaiting sweet sleep. She prepares cheeses, chestnuts, and fruits, preserved in the same freshness as if they had just been gathered. The shepherd returns with his flute and sings to his assembled family the new songs that he learned in the neighboring hamlets. The laborer returns with his plow and his tired herd walking, with heads bent, at a slow and belated pace, even as they are urged on. All the pains of work finish with the day. The poppies which sleep, by order of the gods, spreads over the earth, appease all dark cares by their charms and hold all nature in a sweet enchantment; each lies himself down, without thinking of tomorrow's pains. Happy these men without ambition, without distrust, without artifice, since the gods give them a good king, who does not trouble their innocent joy! But what horrible inhumanity it is to uproot, for schemes full of sumptuousness and ambition, the sweet fruits of their land, which they draw from nature's liberality and from the sweat of their brows! Nature alone could draw from its fecund breast all that would be necessary for an infinite number of temperate and hard-working men. But the pride and softness of some men reduces all the others to a horrific poverty.

"But what should I do," said Idomeneus, "if these people, who I spread across this fertile countryside, fail to cultivate it?"

"Do," Mentor responded to him, "exactly the opposite of what is commonly done. Greedy princes who lack foresight think only of imposing taxes on the most vigilant and the most industrious of their subjects [166] in order to derive a profit from their property. By so doing they hope to earn easy money. At the same time, they tax at a lower rate those whom laziness renders the most miserable. Reverse this bad order, which overwhelms the good, which rewards vice, and which introduces a carelessness as fatal to the king as to the entire State. Impose taxes, fines, and if it is necessary, even other rigorous penalties on those who neglect their fields, as you would punish soldiers who had abandoned their posts in wartime; by contrast, give favors and exemptions to the families who, multiplying themselves, augment in proportion the culture of their lands. Soon families will multiply themselves and everyone will be animated to labor. It will even become honorable. The profession of the plowman will no longer be despised, being no longer overwhelmed by so many sorrows. The plow will be held again in esteem, wielded by victorious hands that will have defended the fatherland. It will not be less fine to cultivate the estate inherited from one's ancestors, during a happy peace, than to have generously defended it during the troubles of war. All the countryside will flourish again. Golden fields will attest to the crowning glory of Ceres, and Bacchus, treading grapes underfoot, will make rivers of wine sweeter than nectar flow from the mountainsides; the cavernous valleys will resound with the concerts of shepherds who, along the clear rivers, will join their voices to their flutes, while their bounding flocks graze on the grass and among the flowers, without fearing the wolves. Will you not be too happy, O Idomeneus, to be the source of so many goods and of enabling all the peoples to live, in the shadow of your name, in such an amiable repose? This glory: is it not more moving than that of ravaging the earth and of spreading everywhere—from the lands of vanquished foreigners right up to one's homeland, amid victories—carnage, turmoil, horror, lassitude, consternation, cruel hunger, and hopelessness? O happy the king so loved by the gods, and so great-hearted, that he strives thus to be the delight of the

people and to display, in his reign, to all ages a spectacle so charming! The
entire earth, far from waging war in order to defend itself from his power,
would throw itself at his feet and beg him to reign over it."

Idomeneus replied to him: "But when the peoples will be thus in peace
and abundance, pleasure will corrupt them and they will turn the power that
I [167] will have given them against me."

"Do not fear," said Mentor, "this inconvenience. This is a pretext that is
always alleged in order to flatter prodigal princes, who want to overwhelm
their peoples with taxes. The remedy is simple. The laws that we come to establish for agriculture will render their lives laborious, and, in their abundance, they will have only that which is necessary, because we will remove
all the arts that furnish the superfluous. This abundance itself will be diminished by the ease of marriage and by the great multiplication of families.
Each family, being numerous and having little land, will need to cultivate it
through constant work. It is softness and laziness that renders peoples insolent and rebellious. The truth is that they will have bread, and easily; but
they will have only bread and the fruits of their own land won by the sweat of
their brow. In order to maintain your people in this state of moderation you
must regulate, right away, how much land each family can possess. You know
that we have divided all your people into seven classes, in accord with the
different ranks. It is necessary to allow each family, in each class, to possess
only that extent of land absolutely necessary in order to nourish the number
of people of which it will be composed. This regulation being inviolable, the
nobles will not be able to take from the poor. All will have land. But each,
having only a little, will have incentive to cultivate it well. If, many years from
now, land were to come to be in short supply here, one could create colonies
that would expand the State. I even believe that you must take care never to
allow wine to become too common in your kingdom. If too many vines are
planted, it is necessary to uproot them. Wine is the source of the greatest
evils of the people. It causes illnesses, quarrels, seditions, laziness, distaste
for work, and the disorder of families. Wine should then be reserved as a
species of remedy or as a very rare liquor, which is used only in sacrifices
or extraordinary celebrations. But do not hope to make so important a rule
observed, if you yourself do not set an example. Moreover it is necessary to
guard inviolably the laws of Minos for the education of children. It is necessary to establish public schools, where they can learn fear of the gods, love
of the fatherland, respect for the laws, and preference of honor to pleasures
and to [168] life itself. It is necessary to have magistrates who watch over

the families and the morals of individuals. Watch over yourself, you who are only king—that is to say, the pastor of the people—in order to watch night and day over your flock. By this you would prevent an infinite number of disorders and crimes. Those you cannot prevent, punish them severely from the start. It is an act of mercy to make examples up front in order to stop the course of iniquity. A little blood shed at the right moment can save having to spill much thereafter, and one puts oneself in a state of being feared, without having to use severity often. But what a detestable maxim to believe one finds security in oppressing one's people! To fail to instruct them, or lead them to virtue, or ever make yourself loved by them, and to push them to despair by your terror, to put them in the horrific necessity of either never being able to breathe freely or of shaking off the yoke of your tyrannical domination—are these the true means of reigning without disorder? Is this really the path that leads to glory? Remember that the countries in which the domination of the sovereign is the most absolute is where sovereigns are least strong. They take, they ruin everything, they alone possess the entirety of the State, yet all the State languishes. The countryside is left fallow and almost deserted. The cities diminish each day. Commerce dries up. The king, who could not be king all alone and who is only great by his people, destroys himself little by little through the insensible destruction of the people by whom he holds his riches and strength. His State exhausts itself of money and men, and this last loss is the greatest and most irreparable. His absolute power makes as many slaves as he has subjects. He is flattered, he seems to be adored, and men tremble at the least of his glances. But wait for the least revolution. This monstrous strength, pushed to too violent an excess, will not last as it has no foundation in the heart of the peoples. It exhausts and irritates the entire body of the State, it compels all the parts of the body to long for a change. At the first stroke that he is dealt, the idol is overturned, shatters, and is trampled underfoot. Hatred, horror, fear, resentment, mistrust—in a word all the passions unite themselves against so odious an authority. The king, who, in his vain prosperity, found not a single man sufficiently bold to speak the truth to him, [169] will find, in his misery, no man who deigns either to excuse him or defend him against his enemies."

After this discourse, Idomeneus, persuaded by Mentor, hurried to distribute the vacant lands, to fill them with all the useless artisans, and to execute all that had been resolved. He reserved only the lands that he had destined for the masons and which they could cultivate only after the completion of their work for the city. Already the reputation of the mild and moderate government of Idomeneus is drawing large numbers of peoples from all sides who are coming to incorporate themselves into his people and to seek their happiness under so amiable a domination. Already this countryside, so long covered in brambles and thorns, promises rich harvests and fruits until then unknown. The earth opens its breast by the cutting of the plow and prepares its riches for the reward of the laborer. Hope shines on all sides. One sees flocks of sheep in the valleys and on the hills, bounding on the grass, along with great herds of cattle that make the high mountains resound with their lowing. These herds serve to fertilize the countryside. It is Mentor who found the means of acquiring these herds. Mentor counseled Idomeneus to make with the Peucetes, a neighboring people, an exchange of all the superfluous things that the Salentines did not want to allow in Salente anymore for these herds that they lacked.

At the same time the city and the surrounding towns were full of beautiful youth who had long languished in misery and had not dared to marry, out of fear of adding to their miseries. When they saw Idomeneus take on sentiments of humanity and a desire to be their father, they no longer feared famine and the other plagues with which the heavens have afflicted the earth. Only cries of joy were heard, only the songs of the shepherds and the laborers celebrating their nuptial bonds. It almost seemed as if Pan had come with a crowd of satyrs and fauns mixed among the nymphs to dance to the sound of the flute in the shadows of the woods. All were tranquil and laughing. But the joy was moderate, and pleasures served only to refresh them from their long labors, and they were more lively and more pure for it. The old men, astonished to see that for which they had not dared to hope in the course of their many years, raised their trembling hands toward the heavens and cried out in an excess of joy mixed with tenderness: "Bless," they said, "O great Jupiter, the king who resembles you and who [170] is the greatest gift that you have given us. He was born for the good of men. Render him all the goods that we receive from him. Our grand-nephews, descended from these marriages that he favors, will owe everything to him, right up to their birth, and he will truly be the father of all his subjects." The young men and the young girls they married could only express their joy in singing the praises of the one to whom they owed this joy that was so sweet to them. His name was always on their lips, and still more in their hearts. They thought themselves happy to see him; they feared losing him. His loss would have been the desolation of each family.

Then Idomeneus admitted to Mentor that he had never felt any pleasure so moving as that of being loved and of rendering all men happy. "I would never have believed it," he said. "It seemed to me that the whole greatness of princes consisted only in making themselves feared, that the rest of men were made for them, and all that I had heard about kings who had been the love and the delight of their peoples seemed like mere fables to me. I recognize now that it's all true. But it is necessary that I recount to you how my heart had been poisoned, from my earliest infancy, with regard to the authority of kings. It is this that caused all the unhappiness of my life." Then Idomeneus began this narration . . .

7. Salente II [Pl. 2:289–296]

While Idomeneus questioned with curiosity the Cretans who had returned from the war, Telemachus listened to the wise counsels of Mentor. Then he looked on all sides with astonishment, and said to Mentor: "There is a change here, of which I do not wholly understand the reason. Did some calamity happen in Salente during my absence? How did it come about that one no longer sees here that magnificence that used to shine everywhere? I no longer see either gold or silver or precious stones. Dress is simple. The buildings that are being made now are less vast, and less ornate. The arts languish. The city seems deserted."

Mentor, smiling, responded to him: "Have you noted the state of the countryside around the city?"

"Yes," Telemachus replied, "I saw everywhere work honored and the fields cleared."

"Which is better," added Mentor, "a magnificent city of marble, gold, and silver with a neglected and sterile countryside, or a countryside fertile and cultivated, with a city of middling size and modest in its morals? A great city well populated with artisans busy weakening morals by the pleasures of life, when it is surrounded by a poor and poorly cultivated realm, resembles a monster with an enormous head and a body that is exhausted, deprived of nourishment, and out of proportion. It is number of people and abundance of nourishment that constitute the true power and the true wealth of a kingdom. Idomeneus now has a people innumerable and indefatigable in work, which fills the entire extent of his country. All his country is no longer only a single city. Salente is merely the center of it. We have transported from this city into the countryside the men who [290] were lacking in the countryside and who were superfluous in the city. Moreover we have attracted many foreign peoples to the country. The more these peoples multiply, the more they multiply the fruits of the earth by their labor; this multiplication so sweet and so peaceful adds more to a kingdom than a conquest. All that was cast out of this city were the superfluous arts that divert the poor from the culture of the earth for true needs, and corrupt the rich and throw them into sumptuousness and softness. But we have done no harm to the fine arts, or to the men who have a true genius for cultivating them. Thus Idomeneus is much stronger than he was when you so admired his magnificence. That dazzling glamour hid a weakness and a misery that would have soon overturned his empire. Now he has a great number of men, and he feeds them more easily. These men—accustomed to work, to pain, and to despise life out of love of good laws—are all ready to fight to defend these lands, cultivated by their own hands. Soon this state, that you believed diminished, will be the marvel of Hesperia. Remember, O Telemachus, that there are two things pernicious in the government of peoples for which there is almost never any remedy. The first is a royal authority that is unjust and excessively violent. The second is luxury, which corrupts morals. When kings accustom themselves to knowing no other laws than their absolute wills and put no brake on their passions, there is nothing to stop them. But by dint of total power, they undermine the foundations of their force. They no longer have any sure rule or maxims of government. All vie to flatter them. They no longer have a people; all that remains to them are slaves, of whom the number diminishes each day. Who will speak the truth to them? Who will stop this torrent? Everyone withdraws. The wise flee, hide themselves, and groan. Only a sudden and violent revolution can bring this unlimited power back into its natural course. Often even the stroke that could moderate it strikes without effect. Nothing portends a more awful collapse than an authority that has been pushed too far; it is like a bow that has been tightened too much, and which ultimately ruptures all at once, if it is not relaxed. But who will dare to relax it? Idomeneus was spoiled to the depths of his heart by this authority so flattering. He had been dethroned, [291] but he had not been disabused. It was necessary for the gods to send us here in order to disabuse him of this blind and excessive power that is inappropriate to men. Even so it took a sort of miracle for him to open his eyes."

"The other evil, almost incurable, is luxury. Just as excessive authority empoisons kings, luxury empoisons an entire nation. It is said that luxury serves to feed the poor at the expense of the rich, as if the poor could not earn their living more usefully by multiplying the fruits of the earth, without softening the rich by the refinements of voluptuousness. The entire nation accustoms itself to regard the most superfluous things as necessities of life; every day new necessities are invented, and one can no longer do without things that were unknown thirty years before. This luxury calls itself good taste, perfection of the arts, and politeness of the nation. This vice, which attracts countless others, is praised like a virtue; it spreads its contagion from the king down to the lowest of the dregs of the people. The close relatives of the king want to imitate his magnificence, the great that of the king's relatives, and the middling want to equal the great, because who judges themselves well? The low want to pass for middle-class. Everyone extends themselves beyond their means; some out of sumptuousness, and in order to boast of their riches; others out of a base shame, and in order to hide their poverty. Even those who are sufficiently wise to condemn so great a disorder are not wise enough to dare to be the first to raise their heads and set contrary examples. The whole nation ruins itself; all ranks become confused. The passion of acquiring property in order to support vain expenses corrupts the purest souls. It is no longer a question merely of being rich; poverty is a disgrace. Be wise, clever, virtuous; instruct men; win battles; save the fatherland; sacrifice all your interests: you are despised if your talents are not augmented by sumptuousness. Even those who lack property want to appear to have it; they dispense of it as if they had it; one borrows, one deceives, one contemplates a thousand unworthy artifices in order to get ahead. But who will cure these ills? It is necessary to change the taste and the habits of the entire nation. It is necessary to give it new laws. Who but a philosopher-king would wish to undertake this, who would know, by the example of his [292] own moderation, to shame all those who love sumptuous expense, and to encourage the wise, who will be relieved to be permitted to live in an honest frugality?"

Telemachus hearing this discourse was like a man awakening from a deep sleep. He felt the truth of these words and they engraved themselves in his heart, as a wise sculptor impresses the traits that he wants on the marble, such that he gives it sensitivity, life, and movement. Telemachus said nothing in response. But going back again over everything that he had come to understand, he let his eyes run over the things that had changed in the city. Finally he said to Mentor:

"You made Idomeneus the wisest of all kings. I no longer recognize him or his people. I admit that what you have done here is infinitely greater than the victories that we carried back. Chance and force play a great role in military success; it is necessary that we divide the glory of the battle with our soldiers. But all your work is the product of a single mind. You had to work all alone against a king and against all his people in order to correct them. The successes of war are always wicked and odious. Here, everything is the work of a divine wisdom. Everything is sweet, everything is pure, everything is amiable. Everything attests to an authority higher than man. When men desire glory, what will they not do in order to achieve it? How much do they fail to understand themselves in thinking that they can achieve solid glory in ravaging the earth and spilling human blood!"

Mentor's face attested to the joy he felt in seeing Telemachus thus disabused of victories and conquests, at an age when it would be natural to be intoxicated by the glory that he had acquired.

Finally Mentor added: "It is true that all that which you see here is good and praiseworthy. But know that still better things can be done. Idomeneus moderates his passions, and applies himself to governing his people with justice. But he does not correct his errors, which are unhappy testimonies to his ancient faults. When men want to quit the ways of evil, evil seems still to pursue them for a long time. They continue to exhibit bad habits, a weakened nature, inveterate errors, and almost incurable prejudices. Happy are those who have never lost their way! They can do good more perfectly. [293] The gods, O Telemachus, will ask more of you than of Idomeneus, because you have known truth since your youth, and you have never been given over to the seductions of an excessive prosperity."

"Idomeneus," Mentor continued, "is wise and enlightened, but he applies himself too much to details and fails to reflect on the big picture of affairs in order to form plans. The art of a king, who is above other men, does not consist in doing everything himself. It is a base vanity to hope to be able to carry out everything one's self, or to want to persuade everyone that you are capable of such. A king must govern by choosing and conducting those who govern under him. It is not necessary for him to attend to the details; to do so is to do the job of those who must work under him. He need only make them render accounts of their work to him, and know enough in order to judge these accounts discerningly. To choose and to apply men to govern according to their talents is to govern marvelously. The best and most perfect government consists in governing those who govern: it is necessary to observe them, to test them, to moderate them, to correct them, to animate them, to raise them, to humble them, to change their places, and always to keep them between your hands. To want to examine everything oneself is to be mistrustful, petty, and jealous for the trivial details that consume the time and freedom of mind necessary for great things. In order to form great plans, it is necessary to have a mind free and at ease. It is necessary to think at ease and in an entire disengagement from all dispatch of thorny affairs. A mind exhausted by details is like dregs of wine that have neither strength nor delicacy. Those who govern by details are always determined by the present, without expanding their views over an extended future. They are always carried along by present-day affairs, and, occupying themselves with these affairs alone, they are too much struck by them, they contract their minds; affairs can only be judged well when everything has been compared together, with everything placed in a certain order, such that the course and proportion of everything is evident. To fail to attend to this rule in government is to be like a musician who would content himself with finding melodious sounds but would not put himself to any trouble to unite them and harmonize them in order to compose a sweet and touching music. So too it resembles an architect who thinks his work is finished as soon as he [294] raises great columns, and many well cut stones, without thinking about the order and proportion of the ornaments of his edifice. While he builds a room, he fails to foresee that it might be necessary to build a staircase for it. When he works on the main part of the building, he takes no thought of either the court or the entrance. His work is only a confused assemblage of magnificent parts, which are not made for each other. This work, far from doing him honor, is an eternal monument to his shame; because the work attests to the fact that the worker does not know how to think in ways extensive enough to conceive all at once the general design of the whole of his work. This is a limited and subordinate cast of mind. One born with a genius limited to details is fit only to work under others. Do not doubt it, O my dear Telemachus, the government of a kingdom demands a certain harmony, like music, and just proportions, like architecture. Another analogy drawn from the arts will enable you to understand just how undistinguished men who govern by detail are. The one who in a concert sings only certain things, even though he sings them perfectly, is merely a singer. The one who conducts the concert, and who orders all parts at once, is alone the music master. So too the one who cuts the columns or raises a side of a building is only a mason. But the one who envisioned the entire edifice, and who has all the proportions of it in his head, is alone the architect. Thus those who work, who dispatch, who do the majority of business are those who govern the least. They are only subordinate workers. The true genius, who conducts the state, is the one who, doing nothing, makes everything happen; who thinks, who invents, who penetrates into the future, who returns back to the past, who arranges, who proportions, who prepares from afar, who braces himself always in order to fight against fortune, as a swimmer against the torrent of water, who is attentive night and day, in order to leave nothing to chance. Do you believe, Telemachus, that a great painter labors assiduously from dawn to dusk at his works? No: this difficult and servile work would extinguish all the fire of his imagination. He would no longer draw on his genius. It is necessary for him to work irregularly and by sallies, following where his taste leads him and his mind excites him. Do you believe that he spends his time grinding [295] colors and preparing brushes? No, this is the business of his students. He spares himself the cares of thinking of this; he dreams only of executing bold features, which give nobility, life, and passion to his figures. He has in his head the thoughts and the sentiments of the heroes that he wants to represent. He transports himself into their ages and into all the circumstances where they have been. To this species of enthusiasm he must join a wisdom that he retains, such that all parts might be true, correct, and proportioned to each other. Do you believe, Telemachus, that it takes less elevation of genius and effort of thought to make a great king than to make a good painter? Conclude then that the occupation of a king must be to think, to form great projects, and to choose men proper to execute them under him."

Telemachus responded to him: "It seems to me that I understand all that you say. But if things were to go thus, a king would often be deceived, not entering into all the details himself."

"It is you who are deceived," Mentor replied. "What prevents one from being duped is the general knowledge of government. Men who have no principles in affairs, and who have no true discernment of minds always feel their way along blindly. It is only by chance that they do not deceive themselves. They do not even know precisely what they are looking for, nor what they ought to strive for. They know only to distrust, and they distrust upright men, who speak out against them, rather than the deceivers who flatter them. On the contrary, those who have principles for government, and who understand men well, know what they ought to look for in them and how to manage them. At least they generally know well enough whether the men they avail themselves of are fit instruments for their plans, and whether they enter into their views sufficiently to stick to the goals that they propose. Moreover, as they never throw themselves into burdensome details, their minds are more free, enabling them to envisage in a single view the whole of the work, and to observe whether it advances toward its principal end. If they are deceived, at least they are hardly deceived in essentials. Moreover, they are above the petty jealousies that attest to a limited mind and a base soul. They understand that one cannot avoid being deceived in great affairs, since it is necessary that they there avail themselves of men, who are so [296] often deceivers. One loses more by irresolution, which leads to defiance, than one would lose in allowing oneself to be slightly deceived. To be deceived only in petty matters is a great happiness. Great men do not abandon themselves to being led, and it is the sole thing that a great man must trouble himself to ensure. It is necessary to reprove deception severely, when one discovers it. But it is necessary to expect some deception, if one does not want to be truly deceived. An artist in his studio sees everything with his own eyes, and does everything with his own hands. But a king, in a great state, cannot do everything, nor see everything. He must do only the things that no other can do under him. He must see only that which enters into the decision of important things."

Finally Mentor said to Telemachus: "The gods love you and prepare for you a reign full of wisdom. All that which you see here is done, less for the glory of Idomeneus, than for your instruction. All the wise establishments that you admire in Salente are only the shadow of what you will one day do in Ithaca, if you answer to your lofty destiny by your virtues. It is time that we think of leaving here. Idomeneus holds a boat ready for our return."

4

Correspondence

1. Letter to Louis XIV [Pl. 1:543–551]

The person, Sire, who takes the liberty of writing you this letter has no interest in this world.[1] She writes it neither out of bitterness, nor out of ambition, nor out of a desire to mix herself up in great affairs. She loves you without being known to you, and she sees God in your person. With all your power you cannot give her the goods she desires, and there are no evils that she would not willingly suffer in order to enable you to know the truths necessary for your salvation. If she speaks to you with vehemence, don't be shocked by it. Truth is free and powerful. You are hardly accustomed to hearing it. Men accustomed to being flattered readily take pure and simple truth for despair, for bitterness, and for excess. It is to betray you not to show it to you in its full extent. God is witness to the fact that the person who speaks to you does so with a heart full of zeal, respect, fidelity, and solicitude for all that concerns your true interest.

You were born, Sire, with an upright and fair heart, but those who raised you gave you for a science of governing only defiance, jealousy, an aversion to virtue, a fear of all spectacular merit, a taste for supple and fawning men, arrogance, and attention to your interests alone.

For nearly thirty years your leading ministers weakened and overturned all the time-honored maxims [544] of state so that your authority might rise to its heights—a project to which they were amenable since your authority was in their hands.[2] No longer were the state or the rules spoken of. One spoke only of the king and his good pleasure. Your revenues and your expenses have been pushed to the extreme. You have been raised to the heavens in order to have outshone, it was said, the greatness of all your predecessors together, that is to say, in order to have impoverished the whole of France so as to introduce a monstrous and incurable luxury to the court. They sought to raise you on the ruins of all the ranks in the state, as if you could be great by ruining all your subjects, on whom your greatness is founded. It is true that you have been jealous of authority, perhaps

Fénelon. Ryan Patrick Hanley, Oxford University Press (2020) © Oxford University Press.
DOI: 10.1093/oso/9780190079581.001.0001

even too much so in exterior things. But in essence each minister has been the master within the range of his administration. You believed yourself to be governing because you regulated the boundaries between those who governed. They have certainly displayed their power to the public, and one has felt it only too keenly. They have been hard, proud, unjust, violent, insincere. They have known no other rule either for the internal administration of the state or for foreign negotiations than that of threatening, crushing, and destroying everything that would resist them. They have spoken to you only in order to draw away from you all those of merit who could throw suspicion on them. They have accustomed you to receiving endless outrageous praises that border on idolatry, which for the sake of your honor you should have rejected with indignation. Your name has been rendered hateful, and the entire French nation has been rendered insufferable to all its neighbors. No traditional allies have been kept, because only slaves were wanted. For more than twenty years bloody wars have been waged. For example, Sire: in 1672 Your Majesty was made to launch the war in Holland for your glory, and to punish the Dutch who had made some raillery amid the misery into which they had been placed by disturbing the rules of commerce established by Cardinal Richelieu.[3] I cite this war in particular because it has been the source of all the others. Its sole foundation was motives of glory and vengeance, which can never render a war just. From this it follows that all the [545] frontiers that you have extended by this war are unjustly acquired in origin.[4] It is true, Sire, that the subsequent peace treaties seemed to cover up and atone for this injustice, since they gave you the conquered places. But an unjust war is not less unjust for having been successful. Peace treaties signed by the vanquished are not signed freely, but with a knife at their neck. They sign against their will in order to avoid even greater losses. They sign, as one gives over one's purse, when it is necessary to give it over or die. It is necessary then, Sire, to take up again the question of the origins of the war in Holland in order to examine all your conquests before God.

It is useless to say that they were necessary to your State: the property of others is never necessary to us. What is truly necessary for us is the observation of exact justice. It is not necessary even to pretend that you might be in the right to keep certain places because they serve to bolster the security of your borders. It is up to you to seek out this security by good alliances, by your moderation, or by places that you can fortify from behind. But in the end, the need to see to our security never gives us a title to take the lands of our neighbor. Ask learned and upright men about this: they will tell you that what I say is as clear as day.

This is enough, Sire, to recognize that you have spent your entire life outside the way of truth and justice, and consequently outside that of the Gospel. All the horrible troubles that have distressed the whole of Europe for more than twenty years—all the blood spilled, all the scandals committed, all the provinces ravaged, all the cities and towns burned to ashes—these are the disastrous consequences of this war of 1672, undertaken for your glory and for the confusion of the newspaper editors and medallion-makers of Holland.[5] Examine, without flattering yourself, and with good men, whether you can protect all that which you possess as a result of the treaties to which you reduced your enemies by so unjustified a war.

It is still the true source of all the ills France suffers. Since this war you have [546] always wanted to establish peace through mastery and to impose conditions, instead of settling them with equity and moderation. This is why the peace cannot last. Shamefully overwhelmed, your enemies have dreamed only of rising up again and reuniting against you. Are you really surprised by this? You have not even stayed within the terms of this peace that you imposed with so much arrogance. In peacetime you waged war and made enormous conquests. You established a Chamber of Reunion in order to be at once both judge and party.[6] This was to add insult and derision to usurpation and violence. You sought out equivocal terms in the Treaty of Westphalia in order to capture Strasbourg.[7] None of your ministers ever dared to allege these terms in any negotiation to show that you had had the least pretentions to this city. Such behavior united and animated all of Europe against you. Even those who have not dared openly to declare themselves eagerly desired your weakening and humiliation as the only hope for the freedom and peace of all Christian nations. You, Sire, who could have acquired so much solid and peaceful glory by being the father of your subjects and arbiter of your neighbors, you have been rendered the common enemy of your neighbors, and you have come to be regarded in your kingdom as a hard master.

The strangest effect of these bad counsels is the extent of the league formed against you. The allies would prefer to wage a losing war than to establish peace with you, because they are persuaded by their own experience that this peace would not be a true peace, that you would not abide by it any more than by the others, and that you would use it to overwhelm each of your neighbors individually and easily as soon as their alliances could be broken. Thus the more victorious you are, the more they fear you, and the more they unite in order to avoid the slavery by which they think themselves threatened. Unable to beat you, they hope at least to exhaust you in the long run. In the end their only remaining hope of security with you lies in putting you in a weakened condition in which you cannot harm them. Put yourself, [547] Sire, in their place for a moment, and see what it means to have preferred your own gain to justice and good faith.

Meanwhile your people, whom you ought to love as your children, and who have been up to now so devoted to you, are dying of hunger.[8] The cultivation of the land is almost abandoned. The towns and the countryside are being depopulated. All the arts languish and cannot feed the workers. All trade is wiped out. As a result you have destroyed half of the genuine domestic power of your state, in order to make and defend vain foreign conquests. Instead of drawing money out of these poor people, you ought to give them alms, and feed them. All of France is merely a vast hospital, desolate and without supplies. The magistrates are debased and exhausted. The nobility, of whom all property is held provisionally, live only by letters of state. You are pestered by a crowd of men who ask for favors and who murmur. It is you, Sire, who have brought on yourself all this confusion, because the entire kingdom having been ruined, you have everything in your hands, and it is possible to live only by your favor. Thus this great kingdom so flourishing under a king who is depicted to us every day as the delight of the people, and who would in fact now be so if flattering counselors had not poisoned him.

Even the people (it is necessary to say all) who have loved you so much, who had so much confidence in you, are beginning to lose their friendship, confidence, and even respect. Your victories and your conquests no longer bring them joy. They are full of bitterness and despair. Little by little rebellion is breaking out on all sides. They fear that you have no pity for their troubles, that you love only your authority and your glory. If the king, it is said, had a father's heart for his people, would he not rather put aside his glory to give his people bread, and enable them to catch their breath after so many troubles, than to hold on to some places on the frontier that only lead to wars? What response can you give to this, Sire? Public passions that were long unknown now become frequent. Even Paris, so near to you, is not exempt. The magistrates are compelled to tolerate the insolence of rebels and to pay them off under the table [548] in order to appease them; thus are paid those whom it is necessary to punish. You are reduced to the shameful and deplorable extreme of either allowing sedition to go unpunished, enabling it to grow, or of inhumanely slaughtering the people you have rendered so miserable, in stealing from them, by your taxes for this war, the bread they struggle to win by the sweat of their brows.

But while they lack bread, you yourself lack funds, and you do not want to see the extremes to which you have been reduced. Since you have always been fortunate, you cannot imagine yourself ever ceasing to be so. You are afraid to open your eyes. You are afraid of them not being opened. You are afraid of being compelled to sacrifice some part of your glory. This glory that swells your heart is dearer to you than justice, than your own tranquility, than the preservation of your people constantly dying from diseases caused by famine, than even your eternal salvation, which is incompatible with this idol of glory.

Thus, Sire, the state in which you are. You live as if you are blindfolded to fate. You flatter yourself on daily successes that determine nothing, and you cannot see from a more general viewpoint the broader scope of affairs which is falling into imperceptible decline without any remedy. While you take the field of battle and the cannon of your enemy in rough combat, while you take places by force, you do not imagine that you will fight on a terrain that gives away under your feet, and that you will fall despite your victories.

Everyone sees this and nobody dares to help you see it yourself. You will perhaps see it too late. True courage consists in not flattering one's self, and in taking a firm stance before necessity. You willingly lend an ear, Sire, only to those who flatter you with vain hopes. The men whom you deem the most solid are those who fear you and who avoid you the most. As you are king, you should seek out the truth, press your men to speak it without sugarcoating, and encourage those who are too timid. On the contrary, you seek only not to go deeper. But God will know well in the end to lift [549] the veil that covers your eyes and show you what escapes your sight. For ages He has held his arms raised above you. But He is slow to strike you, because He has pity on a prince who has been all his life haunted by flatterers, and because moreover your enemies are also His own. But He will surely know to separate His just cause from your unjust one, and to humiliate you in order to convert you, because you will only be a Christian through humiliation. You do not love God. You even fear Him only with the fear of a slave. It is Hell and not God that you fear. Your religion consists only in superstitions, in petty superficial practices. You are like the Jews of whom God said, "with their lips [they] glorify me, but their heart is far from me."[9] You are meticulously attentive to trifles, and hardened to terrible evils. You love only your glory and your ease. You refer everything to yourself as if you were the god of the world, and all the rest had been created only to be sacrificed for you. On the contrary, God has put you on the earth merely for your people. But, alas, you do not understand these truths. How would you know them? You do not know God, you do not love Him, you do not pray to Him from the heart, and you make no effort to know Him.

You have an archbishop who is corrupt, scandalous, incorrigible, false, crafty, insincere, hostile to all virtue, and who makes all good men groan.[10] You put up with him because he thinks only of pleasing you by his flatteries. Prostituting his honor for more than twenty years, he won your confidence. You hand good men over to him, you give him free rein to tyrannize the Church, and not a single virtuous prelate is treated as well as he.

As far as your confessor goes, he is not vicious.[11] But he fears solid virtue, and he only loves profane and loose men. He is jealous of his authority, which you have extended beyond all limits. Bishops had always been the king's confessors, and decided all affairs of conscience. You alone in France, Sire, fail to see that he knows nothing, that his mind is coarse and small, and that he combines [550] his artifice with this coarseness of spirit. Even the Jesuits despise him and are outraged at seeing him so vulnerable to the ridiculous ambition of his family. You have made a minister of state out of a religious man. He understands men no better than he understands anything else. He is the dupe of all those who flatter him and make him little presents. He neither doubts nor hesitates on any difficult question. Another man, very upright and very wise, would not dare to decide alone. As for him, he fears only having to deliberate with men who know the rules. He always goes boldly and fearlessly to mislead you. He will always lean toward laxity and to keeping you in ignorance. At least he will only lean toward parties conforming to the rules when he will fear scandalizing you. Thus one blind man leads another, and, as Jesus says, they both fall together into the pit.[12]

Your archbishop and your confessor have thrown you into the difficulties of the business of ecclesiastical appointments, in the bad business of Rome; they have left you to engage by M. de Louvois in those of St. Lazarus, and would have left you to perish in this injustice, if M. de Louvois had outlived you.[13]

It might have been hoped, Sire, that your council would have drawn you away from so wayward a path. But your council has neither power nor passion for the good. At least Mme de Maintenon and the Duke of Beauvillier ought to have put themselves in the service of your confidence in order to disabuse you.[14] But their weakness and their timidity dishonors them and scandalizes everyone. France is in peril. What are they waiting for in order to speak to you frankly? That everything be lost? Are they afraid of displeasing you? Then they do not love you, because it is necessary to be ready to upset those one loves rather than flatter them or betray them by one's silence. For what good are they if they do not show you that you must return the lands that are not yours, prefer the love of your people to a false glory, repair the harms that you have done to the Church, and dream of becoming a true Christian, before death overtakes you? I know well that when one speaks with this Christian liberty, one runs the risk of losing the favor of kings. But is your favor dearer to them than [551] your salvation? I also know well that one must pity you, console you, relieve you, speak to you with zeal, gentleness, and respect. But in the end it is necessary to speak the truth. Woe, woe to those who don't speak it, and woe to you if you are not ready to hear it! It is shameful that they had your confidence so fruitlessly for so long. It is up to them to withdraw themselves if you take too much offense, and if you only want to surround yourself with flatterers. You will perhaps ask, Sire, what they should say to you. Here it is: they should make clear to you that it is necessary to humble yourself under the all-powerful hand of God, if you do not wish Him to humble you, that it is necessary to beg for peace and by this shame to atone for all the glory that you have made your idol, that it is necessary to reject the unjust counsels of flattering politicians, and finally that, in order to save the state, it is necessary to return to your enemies as soon as possible the conquests that you in any case cannot hold without injustice. Are you not too happy amid your misfortunes, which God fashions in order to bring to an end the prosperities that have blinded you, and doesn't he compel you to make essential restitutions to your salvation, which you would have never been able to resolve yourself to make in a peaceful and triumphant state? The person who speaks these truths to you, Sire, so far from being opposed to your interests, would give her life in order for you to see what God wants you to see, and she does not stop praying for you.

2. Letter to the Marquis de Louville [CF 10:179–182]

. . . I will tell you—without knowing anything, by any channel—what can happen in your court were you to fail to limit yourself to your specific function, or fail to mistrust men. It is out of my deep friendship that I speak to you thusly.[15] Be patient; resist both your first and even your second thoughts;

suspend your judgment; go deeper into things little by little. Harm no one, but put your trust in very few. No joking about any ridiculous things; no impatience for any shortcoming; no excessive attachment to your prejudices against those of others. Take a broad view of things in order to see them in their totality, which is their only true point of view. Never speak anything but the truth; but suppress it any time you might speak it uselessly out of bad temper or excessive trust. Avoid, as much as you can, suspicions and jealousies. Even as modest as you are, you will never appease jealous minds. The nation in which you live is infinitely sensitive, and has an impenetrable profundity. Their natural spirit, owing to its culture, cannot attend to solid things, and turns itself entirely to sleight-of-hand: be on your guard. Take care also in everything you write. Write only sure and useful things. Give what is doubtful as doubtful. Write simply, and with a serious and modest precision; this does more honor than the most elegant and gracious letters. Accommodate yourself to the master you serve. He is good, he has a heart sensitive to the good; his mind is solid, and he will often close himself off, but he is still quite young. For all his solidity, he inevitably still has certain tastes typical of his age, and even a little dissipation. This has to be expected, but count on the fact that every year will give him some degree of application and some authority. Never speak to him too much at any one time; give him only what he asks of you. Stop yourself short as soon as you suspect he might be tired of it. Nothing is so dangerous as giving more nourishment than can be digested: the respect owed to the master and his well-being require a delicacy, finesse, and gentle insinuation that I pray that God will instill in you. If he seems not to want your opinion, keep yourself respectfully quiet, without lessening any marks of zeal and affection: it is necessary never to grow discouraged. Though the vivacity natural to his age will make him transgress some limits, his character is good, his religion is sincere, his courage is great, and he will always love those honest men who desire his true good without wearying him by an indiscreet zeal. What I fear for him is that poison of flattery, which the wisest kings almost never safeguard themselves against. This trap is what good hearts must fear. They love to be approved by men of merit, and deceitful men are always the most zealous to insinuate themselves by way of flattering praises. As soon as one is in power, no trust can be put in the sincerity of any praise. The worst princes are the most praised, because the wicked, who know their vanity, hope to take hold of them by this vulnerability. There is even more to be feared and hoped from those close to good princes as they can lavish honors and spur on violence.

No emperors were more praised than Caligula, Nero, Domitian. If the best kings were to consider this well, these examples would render them [180] fearful of the most merited praises. They would always fear being deceived by praise, and would make sure to take the safest route, which is to refuse all praise. True gentlemen admire little, and praise even the best things with simplicity and moderation. Praises grow tiresome to princes accustomed to cheers and applause and excessive and endless flattery. Dishonest men praise a prince only in order to extract some benefit from him: ambition toys with vanity, flattering it in order to lead it to its ends; the tailor calls M. Jordain "Monseigneur" in order to trick him out of an *ecu*.[16] A great king ought to be outraged at being supposed so vain and so weak. Nobody should be so bold as to praise him to his face; it is to lack respect for him. You know that Sixtus V severely prohibited praise.[17]

A king has no other honor nor any other interest than that of the nation he governs. He will be judged by the government of his kingdom, just as a watchmaker is judged by whether watches of his craftsmanship run well or poorly.

A kingdom is well governed, when one works ceaselessly, insofar as one can, to these ends: (1) to populate it; (2) to make it such that all men work in accord with their capacities to cultivate the earth well; (3) to make it such that all men might be well fed, as long as they work; (4) to allow neither idlers nor vagrants; (5) to reward merit; (6) to punish all disorders; (7) to hold all bodies and all individuals, however powerful they might be, in subordination; (8) to moderate the royal authority in the king's own person such that he might not do anything contrary to the laws out of arrogance, violence, caprice, or weakness; (9) not to deliver himself over to any minister or favorite. It is necessary to listen to diverse counsels, to compare them, and to examine them without bias. But one must never deliver one's self blindly, in any way, to any man: this ruins him, if he is good, and leads him to betray himself, if he is bad.

By this conduct, a king truly fulfills the duties of a king—that is to say, the father and pastor of the people. He works to render them just, wise, and happy. He must believe that he merely does his duty, when he takes the crook in hand to lead his flock to pasture, safe from wolves. He must believe his people to be well-governed only when everyone is employed, is fed, and is obedient to the laws. He must obey the laws himself because it is necessary to set an example, and he is only a simple man like the others, charged with dedicating himself to their tranquility and their happiness.

It is necessary for him to obey the laws and not himself. If he commands, he does so not for his sake, but for the good of those he governs. He must be only a man of the laws and a man of God. He carries the sword in order to make himself feared by the wicked. It was said of Solomon that *they feared the king, seeing that the wisdom of God was in him.*[18] Nothing makes a king more feared than to see him even-tempered, firm, self-possessed, never plunging himself into anything, attentive to everything, and never making a decision until after having made a dispassionate examination.

If a young prince is so happy as to have neither favorites nor a mistress, and if he trusts one of his ministers only so far as he acknowledges before God that his opinion is better than that of others, he will be soon feared, revered, and loved. He must carefully attend to the reasonable positions of each, but he must never allow his decisions to be made simply on the basis of the rank or the assertive manner of those who impose on him. He must accustom those of the first rank to propose their thoughts simply, and to await in silence his decision. This [181] ascendency over those who approach him is the most important point; but he cannot accomplish it all at once. A young king, though he might be no less a king and master than another who is older, cannot have the same authority over men. For example, the Catholic King will be extremely happy if he can, in forty years, make himself obeyed as the King our master is now obeyed in all his realm. A young king who arrives in a kingdom as a foreigner, and from a nation that Spain regarded as an enemy, must accustom himself to the nation, must submit himself to its traditions, must accommodate himself to its prejudices, and above all must instruct himself in the laws of the country, and preserve them religiously. To the degree that his diligence and his experience will grow, he will also see his authority grow. At first he must go easy, and only undertake those things that are absolutely necessary. What can't be corrected today will be corrected in ten years, little by little and almost by itself. He should listen readily, but believe only on the basis of clear evidence. He must not be won over simply by the first person to speak to him or the last person to speak to him. The first and last speakers should be regarded equally; it is the soundness of their reasons that should determine him. He must study men, never trust flatterers, examine the talents of each, ensure that a man's good qualities never cause him to lose sight of his faults, and fear becoming enamored. Every man has his faults; as soon as they are not seen in a man, he is poorly known, and he can no longer be trusted. The great duty of a king is to know how to choose men, place them, order them, correct them. He governs truly when he makes it such that his subordinates govern well.

If the King must take everything on himself, being so moderate, so diligent, what must not be done by those who have the honor of surrounding him! Every day I pray to God for His Majesty, and for you too, sir, whom I love and I honor from the depths of my heart.

I forgot to tell you that nobody is more persuaded than I am that the Catholic King is born with a perfect merit, and even with great sentiments of honor in all things. I have seen signs of it from his earliest childhood. I admit that being intrepid in war is a fine trait in a king. But courage in war is far less useful to so great a prince than courage in business. When will he find himself in the middle of a battle? Maybe never. On the contrary in his court he will every day be grappling with others and with himself. It is necessary for him to have unfailing courage against a deceitful minister, against an indiscrete favorite, against a woman who would wish to be his mistress. He needs courage against flatterers, against pleasures, and against diversions that might throw him into lassitude. He needs to be courageous in work, in disappointments, in failure. He needs courage against importunity, in order to know how to refuse without rudeness and without impatience. Courage in war, which is more dazzling, is infinitely inferior to such courage in all spheres of life and at all times. It is this that gives him true authority, that makes possible great success, that overcomes great obstacles, and that merits true glory. Francis I was heroic in battle; but weak among his mistresses and his favorites. In his court he shamefully squandered all the glory that he had won at Marignan.[19] And thus everything went awry, and nothing came off well. Charles the Wise could not go to war because of his disabilities, but his good and strong head yet directed the war; he was [182] superior to his ministers and to his generals.[20] The King our master won more esteem by his firmness in ordering the finances, in disciplining the troops, in correcting abuses, and by the orders that he gave for the war, than by his presence in several dangerous sieges. His patient courage at Namur there did more than even the valor of his troops.[21]

Tell him all these things, Sir, as you think it appropriate. I give them to you in the same form that I think them. You know how to adjust them as needed, and I do not doubt that you have entirely at heart the reputation and the happiness of the king to whom you are attached. As for me, I fervently wish that he might be a great king and a true saint, a worthy descendent of Saint Louis.

3. Letter to the Duke of Burgundy [CF 14:165–166]

I visited with the King of England several times in total freedom, and, My Lord, I believe I owe it to you to tell you the good opinion I have of him.[22] He seems sensible, gentle, and steady in everything. He seems to understand well the truths that are spoken to him. He shows a fondness for virtue, and for the principles of religion by which he seeks to order his conduct. He is his own master, and he acts calmly, like a man without a temper, without whims, without unsteadiness, without being dominated by imagination, one who constantly consults reason, and defers to it in all matters. He gives himself to others out of duty, and is full of respect for each individual. He seems neither to tire of submitting himself to others, nor impatient of ridding himself of them in order to be left alone all to himself; nor [166] does he seem distracted or withdrawn into himself when out in public: he gives himself entirely to what he is doing. He is full of dignity, without haughtiness; he proportions his attentions and his discourse according to rank and merit. He shows the gentle and moderate cheerfulness of a mature man. His recreations are governed by reason alone, and suited for relaxation, according to need, or to give pleasure to those who surround him. He seems to be everything to all men, without delivering himself to any one man. Moreover, this obligingness is free from both weakness and frivolity: he appears firm, decisive, exact. He easily takes on difficult tasks that must cost him. I saw him leave Cambrai after a bout of fever that had severely exhausted him in order to return to the army upon hearing about a battle that was very uncertain. None who were around him dared suggest to him that he should delay his departure and await other more positive news. If he had allowed even a few to see his irresolution, each would not have failed to tell him that he must yet wait a day; and he would have lost the opportunity of participating in a battle in which he showed great courage and which garnered him high repute, even in England. . . . In a word, the King of England gives himself and accommodates himself to others; he has uncommon reason and virtue; his firmness, his even-temperedness, his self-possession, his capacity to manage others, his gentle and kind solemnity, his cheerfulness free of baseness—all this predisposes the entire public in his favor.

5

Discourse Delivered at the Consecration of the Elector of Cologne

[Pl. 2:945–971]

Since I am destined to be your consecrator, prince whom the Church today sees with so much joy prostrate at the foot of the altar, I find no place in Scripture that does not make some impression on me in connection with your person. But these are the words that have touched me the most: "For whereas I was free as to all," says the Apostle, "I made myself the servant of all, that I might gain the more. *Cum liber essem ex omnibus, omnium me servum feci, ut plures lucrifacerem.*"[1] What greatness shows itself on all sides here! I see a house that has already filled the imperial throne for nearly four hundred years. It has given Germany two emperors, and two branches that enjoy the electoral dignity. It reigns in Sweden, where a prince, as his youth draws to a close, has become all at once the terror of the North.[2] I foresee only the highest alliances of the houses of France and Austria: on one side, you are the grandson of Henry the Great, the memory of whom will never cease being dear to France; on the other side, your blood flows in the veins of our princes, precious hope of the nation.[3] Alas! We can remember only with sadness the princess to whom we owe them, and who was too soon carried away from the world![4]

Will I dare add, in the presence of Emanuel, that the infidels have felt and that the Christians have admired his valor?[5] All the nations who see it up close are moved by the experience of his gentleness, his nobility, his goodness, his magnificence, his amiable sincerity, his constancy in all [948] tests of his commitments, his fidelity in his alliances that equals the probity and the delicacy of the most virtuous friends in their private society. With a heart similar to that of such a brother, prince, it is open to you to walk in his footsteps. You would be free to follow him; you could look forward to all that which is most flattering in our age. But you come to sacrifice to God this freedom and these worldly ambitions. It is of this sacrifice that I want to speak to you before the holy altar. I admit that respect demands that I commit myself to staying

Fénelon. Ryan Patrick Hanley, Oxford University Press (2020) © Oxford University Press.
DOI: 10.1093/oso/9780190079581.001.0001

quiet, but "love," as Saint Bernard said to Pope Eugene, "is not held back by respect . . . I will speak to you, not in order to instruct you, but to beseech you as a tender mother. I will appear indiscreet to those who do not love, and who do not feel all that a true love makes one feel."[6] As for you, I know that you have a taste for the truth and even for the hardest truth. I am not afraid of displeasing you in saying such: deign then to listen to that which I do not fear to say. On one hand, the Church has no need of the assistance of the princes of the world, because the promises of its almighty bridegroom suffice for it; on the other hand, princes who would become pastors can be very useful to the Church, as long as they humble themselves, as long as they dedicate themselves to work, and as long as all the pastoral virtues can be seen to shine in them.[7] Thus the two points that I propose to explicate in this discourse.

First Point

The children of this age, animated by the maxims of a profane politics, claim that the Church would not know how to manage without the assistance of princes and the protection of their arms, above all in countries where the heretics can attack them. Blind ones, who want to measure the work of God by that of men! It is to *maketh flesh his arm*;[8] it is to ensure *the cross of Christ should be made void.*[9] Does one believe that the bridegroom, all-powerful and faithful in his promises, suffices not for the bride? *Heaven and earth shall pass away, but my words shall not pass away.*[10] O feeble and weak men who we call the kings and the princes of the world, you have [949] only a power borrowed for a short time: the bridegroom, who lends it to you, entrusts it to you only as long as you will serve the bride. If you were to forsake the bride, you would also forsake the bridegroom; he would know to transfer his sword to other hands. Remember that it is he who is *the prince of the kings of the earth, the king of ages, immortal, invisible.*[11]

It is true that it is written that the Church *shalt suck the milk of the Gentiles,* that she will be *nursed with the breasts of kings,* that *they shall be thy nursing fathers,* that *the Gentiles shall walk in thy light, and kings in the brightness of thy rising;* but it is also said that *their kings may be brought, they shall worship thee with their face toward the earth* before the Church, that *they shall lick up the dust of thy feet,* that not daring to speak, *kings shall shut their mouth* before her bridegroom, that *the nation and the kingdom that will not serve* this new Jerusalem *shall perish.*[12] Too happy then the princes God deigns to employ in service! Too honored those he chooses for such a glorious trust!

And now, O ye kings, understand: receive instruction, you that judge the earth. Serve ye the Lord with fear: and rejoice unto him with trembling. Embrace discipline, lest at any time the Lord be angry, and you perish from the just way.[13] Jealous God *hath overturned the thrones of proud princes, and hath set up the meek* and moderate *in their stead,*[14] he makes *the roots of proud nations to wither, and hath planted the humble* in order to make them flourish;[15] he destroys all proud power all the way down to its foundations, *God hath abolished* even *the memory of the proud.*[16] *All flesh is grass, and all the glory thereof as the flower of the field,* as soon as *the spirit of the Lord hath blown upon it, the grass is withered, and the flower is fallen.*[17]

Thus princes must not boast of protecting the Church, nor flatter themselves so far as to believe that it would fall if they were not to carry it in their hands. If they were to cease supporting it, the Almighty would carry it Himself. As for them, *the nation and the kingdom that will not serve thee, shall perish,* according to the holy oracles.[18]

Let us cast eyes on the Church, that is to say on this visible society of children of God, which has lasted throughout all times: this is the kingdom of which *there shall be no end.*[19] All other powers rise and fall, and after having astonished the world, they disappear. The Church alone, against storms without and scandals within, remains [950] immortal. In order to triumph, it needs only to endure, and it has no other arms than the cross of its bridegroom.

Let us consider this society under Moses: Pharaoh wants to oppress him; the darkness grows palpable in Egypt; the land is covered in insects; the sea parts, its risen waters suspended like two walls; an entire people traverses the abyss with dry feet; a bread descended from the heavens nourishes them in the desert; the man speaks to the rock, and it sheds forth torrents: everything is miraculous for forty years, in order to deliver the captive Church.

Let us move on: we pass to the Maccabees. The kings of Syria persecute the Church, it cannot resolve itself to renew an alliance with Rome and with Sparta without declaring in a spirit of faith that it relies only on the promises of its bridegroom. *We needed,* said Jonathan, *none of these things, having for our comfort the holy books that are in our hands.*[20] And indeed, what does the Church need here below? All it needs is merely the grace of its bridegroom for it to give birth to the elect; their very blood is a seed that multiplies. Why would she beg for human aid, she who contents herself with obeying, suffering, dying—her reign, being of her bridegroom and thus not of this world, and all her goods being beyond this life?

But let us turn our attention toward the Church that pagan Rome, that Babylon drunk on the blood of the martyrs, endeavored to destroy. The Church remained free amid its chains, and invincible in the middle of its torments. God allowed the blood of his beloved children to drip for three hundred years. Why do you think he did this? It was in order to convince the entire world, by so long and so terrible an experience, that the Church, being suspended between heaven and earth, has need only of the invisible hand by which it is supported. Never was it so free, so strong, so flourishing, so fertile.

What became of these Romans who persecuted it? This people, which prided itself on being *the royal people*, was delivered to the barbarous nations; the eternal empire fell, Rome was buried in ruins with its false gods; the memory of it remains only because another Rome, rising from its ashes, which, being pure and holy, has become forever more the center of the kingdom of Jesus Christ.

But how is it that the Church conquered this Rome, victorious over the universe? Listen to the Apostle: *For the foolishness of God is wiser than men: and the weakness of* [951] *God is stronger than men. For see your vocation, brethren, that there are not many wise according to the flesh, not many mighty, not many noble. But the foolish things of the world God hath chosen, that he may confound the wise: and the weak things of the world hath God chosen, that he may confound the strong. And the base things of the world and the things that are contemptible, hath God chosen: and things that are not, that he might bring to nought things that are: That no flesh should glory in his sight.*[21] Thus we no longer boast of a wisdom convinced of folly, or a fragile and awkward power; we no longer speak of a simple and humble weakness, which can do all with God alone; we no longer speak of the folly of the cross. The jealousy of God went so far as to seem to exclude from the Church, during these centuries of trial, all that which might have seemed like human assistance: God, impenetrable in his counsels, wanted to overturn all natural order. From there comes what Tertullian seemed to doubt: *if the Caesars could have become Christians.*[22] How much blood and torment of the faithful did it cost to show that the Church holds nothing here below! "She possesses for herself," says Saint Ambrose, "only her faith alone."[23] It is this faith that vanquished the world.

After this spectacle of three hundred years, God remembered in the end his ancient promises; he deigned to do the masters of the world the favor of admitting them to the feet of his bride. In so doing they became *thy nurses,* and he gave them the honor of being able to *lick up the dust of thy feet.*[24] Was this an assistance that came in order to support the weakened Church? No, the one who had supported it for three centuries against men had no need of the weakness of men already vanquished by her in order to support her. But this was a triumph that the bridegroom wanted again to give to the bride, after so many victories; this was not a resource for the Church, but a favor and a forgiveness for the emperors. "What is there," said Saint Ambrose, "more glorious for the emperor, than to be named the son of the Church?"[25]

In vain someone will say that the Church is in the State. The Church, it is true, is in the State in order to obey the prince in all that which is temporal; but although it finds itself in the State, it never depends on it for any spiritual function. It is in this world, but only in order to convert it; it is in this world, but only in order to govern it in that which concerns salvation. She uses this world in passing, as if she used it not; she is there just as Israel was a stranger and [952] wayfarer in the middle of the desert: she is already of another world above this one. The world, in submitting itself to the Church, did not acquire the right of subjecting her: the princes, in becoming the children of the Church, did not become her masters; they must *serve* her, and not dominate her; *lick up the dust of thy feet,*[26] and not impose the yoke on her. The emperor, said Saint Ambrose, "is within the Church, but he is not above her. The good emperor seeks the assistance of the Church, and does not reject it."[27] The Church remained, under the converted emperors, as free as she had been under the idolatrous and persecuting emperors. She continued to say, amid the most profound peace, that which Tertullian would say for her during the persecutions: "*Non te terremus, qui nec timemus.* We do not frighten you, and we do not fear you. But take care," he adds, "not to fight against God."[28] In effect, what can be more disastrous to human power, which is only weakness, than to attack the Almighty? *And whosoever shall fall on this stone shall be broken: but on whomsoever it shall fall, it shall grind him to powder.*[29]

Is it a matter of civil and political order? The Church does not protect the kingdoms of the earth from weakening, she who holds in her hands the keys to the kingdom of Heaven. She desires nothing of all that which can be seen; she aspires only to the kingdom of her bridegroom, who is her own. She is poor, and jealous of the treasure of her poverty; she is peaceful, and it is she who gives, in the name of the bridegroom, a peace that the world can neither give nor take away; she is patient, and it is by her patience up to the death of the cross that she is invincible. She never forgets that her bridegroom ran away up to the mountain as soon as they wanted to make him king; she remembered that she must have in common with her bridegroom nakedness and the cross, since it is *a man of sorrows*, the man *bruise[d] in infirmity*, the man *filled with reproaches*.[30] She wants only to obey; she constantly gives the example of submission and zeal for legitimate authority; she would pour out all her blood in order to support it. This would be for her a second martyrdom after the one she endured for the faith. Princes, she loves you; she prays for you night and day; you have no resource more assured than her fidelity. Beyond the fact that she draws onto your persons and your peoples celestial benedictions, she inspires in your peoples an unquestioned affection for your persons, which are the images of God here below. [953]

If the Church accepts the pious and magnificent gifts that princes make her, this is not because she wants to renounce the cross of her bridegroom, and to enjoy deceptive riches; she wants only to procure to the princes the merit of casting them off; she wants to avail herself of them only in order to ornament the house of God, only in order to make the holy ministers subsist modestly, only in order to feed the poor who are the subjects of the princes. She seeks not the riches of men, but their salvation; not that which is theirs, but themselves. She accepts their perishable offerings, only to give them eternal goods.

Rather than submit to the yoke of the powers of the age, and to losing evangelical freedom, she returned all the temporal goods that she received from princes. "The lands of the Church," said Saint Ambrose, "pay the tribute; and if the emperor wants her lands, he has the power to take them; none of us resist him in this. The alms of the people will still suffice to feed the poor. Let us not be rendered hateful by our possession of these lands; let them take them, if the emperor wants them. I do not give them; but I do not refuse them."[31]

But is it a matter of the spiritual ministry given to the bride immediately by the one bridegroom? The Church exercises it with an entire independence of men. Jesus Christ says: *All power is given to me in heaven and in earth. Going therefore, teach ye all nations: baptizing them*, etc.[32] It is this omnipotence of the bridegroom that passes to the bride, and which has no limit; every created being without exemption is submissive there. As the pastors must give to the peoples the example of the most perfect submission and of the most inviolable fidelity to princes for the temporal, it is also necessary that princes, if they wish to be Christians, give in turn to the peoples the example of the most humble docility and of the most exact obedience to pastors in all things spiritual. All that which the Church binds, is bound; all that which it returns, is returned; all that which it decides here below, is confirmed in Heaven. Thus the power described by the prophet Daniel.

The ancient of days came, he says, *and gave judgment to the saints of the most High, and the time came, and the saints obtained the kingdom.*[33] Next the prophet depicts a powerful and impious king, who *shall speak words against the High One*, and *shall crush the saints of the most High: and he shall think himself able to change times and laws, and they* [954] *shall be delivered into his hand until a time, and times, and half a time. And judgment shall sit, that his power may be taken away, and be broken in pieces, and perish even to the end,* such that *the kingdom, and power, and the greatness of the kingdom, under the whole heaven, may be given to the people of the saints of the most High: whose kingdom is an everlasting kingdom, and all kings shall serve him, and shall obey him.*[34]

O men who are only men, although flattery tempts you to forget humanity and to raise yourselves above it, remember that God can do everything over you, and that you can do nothing against him. To disturb the Church in its functions is to attack the Most High in what he holds most dear, which is his bride; it is to blaspheme against the promises, it is to dare the impossible, it is to want to overturn *the everlasting kingdom.*[35] Kings of the earth, you band yourselves together in vain *against the Lord, and against his Christ;*[36] in vain you would renew the persecutions, in renewing them, you would merely purify the Church, and bring back for her the beauty of her ancient days. In vain you would say: *Let us break their bonds asunder: and let us cast away their yoke from us. He that dwelleth in heaven shall laugh* at your plans.[37] The Lord has given to his Son *the Gentiles for thy inheritance, and the utmost parts of the earth for thy possession.*[38] If you do not humble yourself under his strong hand, he *shalt break* you *in pieces like a potter's vessel.*[39] The power will be raised against whoever will dare to raise himself against the Church. It is not she who will raise him, because she knows only to suffer and to pray. But if the princes would want to enslave her, she would open her breast, she would say: Strike. She would add, like the apostles: *If it be just, in the sight of God, to hear you rather than God, judge ye.*[40] It is not me who speaks here; it is the Holy Spirit. If the kings failed *to serve it* and to obey it, their strength would be removed. The God of the armies, without whom one would protect the cities in vain, would not fight with them.

Not only can the princes do nothing against the Church, but still they can do nothing for it regarding the spiritual realm, in which they obey it. It is true that the pious and zealous prince is named the *bishop of the external*, and the *protector of the canons*: expressions that we will endlessly repeat with joy, in the moderate sense of the ancients who availed themselves of them.[41] But the bishop of the external must never undertake the function of the bishop of the internal. He holds himself, sword in hand, at the gate of the sanctuary; but he takes care not to enter there. [955] Even as he protects, he obeys; he protects the decisions but he makes none of them. Thus the two functions to which he limits himself: the first is of maintaining the Church in complete freedom against all its enemies without, so that it can within, without any hindrance, pronounce, decide, lead, approve, correct, and finally strike down all haughtiness that raises itself against the science of God; the second is of supporting these same decisions, as soon as they are made, without ever permitting himself, under any pretext, to interpret them. This protection of the canons turns itself then uniquely against the enemies of the Church, that is to say, against the innovators, against the indocile and pestilential minds, against all those who refuse correction. It is not pleasing to God either for the protector to govern, or for him to hinder anything that the Church will decree! He waits, he listens humbly, he believes without hesitating, he obeys himself, and encourages obedience as much by the authority of his example as by the power that he holds in his hands. But finally the protector of the freedom never diminishes it. Its protection would no longer be an aid, but a disguised yoke, if he were to want to determine the Church, instead of allowing himself to be determined by it. It is by this fatal excess that England broke the sacred bonds of unity, in wanting to give the authority of the head of the Church to the prince, who must always be only its protector.[42]

Whatever need the Church may have had of a prompt assistance against heresies and against abuses, it has still more need of preserving its freedom. Whatever support it receives from the best princes, it never ceases to say with the Apostle: *Wherein I labour even unto bands, as an evildoer. But the word of God* announces to us that it *is not bound* by any human power.[43] It is with this jealousy of independence in the spiritual, that Saint Augustine said to a proconsul, even as he saw himself exposed to the fury of the Donatists: "I would not wish that the Church of Africa was worn down to the point of having need of any earthly power."[44] Thus the same spirit that had made Saint Cyprian say: "The Bishop, holding fast to the Gospel, can be killed, but not conquered."[45] Thus precisely the same principle of freedom for the two states of the Church. Saint Cyprian defends this freedom against the violence of the persecutors, and Saint Augustine wants to preserve it with precaution, even with regard to the protector princes, in the midst of peace. What power, what evangelical nobility, [956] what fidelity to the promises of Jesus Christ! O God, give to your Church some Cyprians, Augustines, pastors who honor the ministry, and who would make men feel that they are the dispensers of your mysteries.

Moreover, while the promises may render the Church above all needs and all assistance, God does not yet disdain to make princes come to her aid. He prepares them from afar, He raises them, He instructs them, He trains them, He purifies them, He renders them worthy of being the instruments of His providence; in a word, He does nothing by them, until after having done in them all that pleases Him. Then the Church accepts this protection, as the offerings of the faithful, without requiring it; she sees only the hand of her own bridegroom in the benefits of princes. And indeed, it is He who gives them both power without and good will within in order to exercise this pious protection. The Church always goes back to her source; far from attending to worldly politics, she acts only in pure faith, and guards against believing that the Son of God, her bridegroom, is not sufficient for her.

Here let us depict the wise Maximilian, Elector of Bavaria.[46] Prince, it is with joy that I recall the memory of your ancestor. It is true that he did great things for religion: animated by a holy zeal, he armed himself against a prince of his house, in order to save the Catholic religion in Germany; superior to all worldly politics, he despised the highest and most flattering hopes in order to preserve the faith of his fathers. But God himself is self-sufficient, and the liberator of the bride of Jesus Christ owed to the bridegroom all the great deeds he did for the bride. No, no, it is necessary to see only God in this work: man disappears, every gift returns to its source, and the Church's only duty is to Jesus Christ.

Come then, O Clement, grandson of Maximilian; come aid the Church by your virtues, as your ancestor aided her by his arms. Come, not to support the unsteady ark by a reckless hand, but on the contrary to find in it your support. Come not to dominate, but to serve. If you believe that the Church has no need of your support, and if you give yourself humbly to her, you will be her ornament and consolation. This is the second truth of which I must speak. [957]

Second Point

Princes who become pastors can be very useful to the Church, as long as they dedicate themselves to the ministry in a spirit of humility, patience, and prayer.

I. Humility, which is so necessary to every minister of the altar, is still more necessary to those whose high birth tempts them to elevate themselves above all others. Listen to Jesus Christ: *The Son of man*, he says, *is not come to be ministered unto, but to minister, and to give his life a redemption* to others.[47] See thus: the Son of God, who you will represent amid his people, came not to enjoy riches, to receive honors, to taste pleasures, to exercise a worldly empire. On the contrary, he came to abase himself, to suffer, to support the weak, to heal the sick, to restrain rebellious and indocile men, to spread his benefits over those who would do him the greatest harms, to spread his arms always over a people who would speak against him. Do you believe that the disciple would be above the master? Would you wish that what was for Jesus Christ only a simple ministry might be for you an ambitious domination? As Son of God, he was *the brightness of* [the] *glory* of the Father and *the figure of his substance*; as man, he counted among his ancestors all the kings of Judah who reigned for a thousand years, all the great sacrificers, all the patriarchs.[48] Where the most august houses boast of not being able to discover their origin in the obscurity of ancient times, that of Jesus Christ showed clearly, by the sacred books, that his origin went up to the source of the human race. Thus a birth to which no other, under heaven, could be compared. Jesus Christ nevertheless came to serve even the least of men: he made himself the slave of all.

It was given to the apostles to do miracles even greater than those of the Savior. The shadow of Saint Peter suffices to cure the sick; the vestments of Saint Paul have the same power. But the apostles are only the emissaries of the Savior, sent in order to serve men; they are only the slaves of the peoples in Jesus Christ: *Nos autem* [958] *servos vestros per Jesum.*[49] Were you Peter, eternal foundation of the Church, you would be only the servant of those who serve God. Were you Paul, apostle of the nations, revered to the highest heaven, you would be only a slave destined to serve peoples in order to sanctify them.

And why is it that Jesus Christ confers on us His authority? Is it for us, or for the peoples over whom we exercise it? Is it so that we can satisfy our pride, in flattering that of other men? It is, on the contrary, so that we might suppress the pride and the passions of men, in humiliating ourselves, and in dying always to ourselves. How could we make the cross loved, if we reject it in order to embrace sumptuousness and pleasure? Who will believe the promises, if we do not seem to believe them in announcing them? Who will renounce himself in order to love God, if we appear empty of God, and idolatrous of ourselves? Who will attend to our words, if all our actions contradict them? The word of eternal life will be on our lips but a vain declamation, and the most holy ceremonies will be only a deceptive spectacle. What, these men so weighed down toward the world, so insensible to celestial gifts, so blind, so hardened—will they believe us, will they listen to us, when we will speak only of the cross and of death, if they discover in us no trace of the crucified Lord?

I grant that the pastor must not degrade the prince; but I ask also that the prince take care not to forget the humility of the pastor. Even if you will preserve a certain grandeur, which is inseparable from your temporal dignity, it is necessary for you to be able to say with Esther: Lord, *Thou knowest my necessity, that I abominate the sign of my pride and glory, which is upon my head in the days of my public appearance*; you know that it is with regret that I see myself surrounded by this splendor, and that I study myself to strip away all superfluity, in order to relieve the peoples and in order to assist the poor.[50]

Remember moreover that the temporal dignity is given to you only for the sake of the spiritual. It is in order to authorize the pastor of souls, that the electoral dignity has been joined in the Empire to that of the Archbishop of Cologne.[51] It is in order to facilitate for him the pastoral functions, and in order to affirm the Catholic Church, that one has attached this power so dazzling to his ministry of humility. Moreover, these two [959] functions reunite at a certain point. The pagans themselves have no more noble idea of a true prince, than that of *pastor of peoples*. Thus you are a pastor in two senses. If you are such as a sovereign prince, you are so to an even greater degree as a minister of Jesus Christ.

But how could you be the pastor of peoples, if your grandeur would separate you from them, and render you inaccessible to their conditions? How could you lead the flock, if you were not concerned for their needs? If the people were to see you always only from afar, always only in grandeur, always only surrounded by those who stifle confidence, how would they dare to pierce the crowd, throw themselves between your arms, tell you their pains, and find in you their consolation? How will you make them feel the heart of a father, if you show them only the haughtiness of a master? Thus what even the prince must not forget. Let us add what the apostolic man must feel.

If you were never to descend from your grandeur, how could you say with Jesus Christ: *Come to me, all you that labor, and are burdened, and I will refresh you*? How could you add: *Learn of me, because I am meek, and humble of heart*?[52] Do you want to be the father of the little ones? Be small yourself; shrink yourself to become proportionate to them. "If I know you well," said Saint Bernard to Pope Eugene, "you will not be less poor in spirit in becoming the father of the poor."[53] In effect, your riches are not your own; the founders have dispossessed their families only so that they could have been the patrimony of the poor; they are conferred to you, only so that you might relieve the poverty of your children.

But let us continue to listen to Saint Bernard, who speaks to the vicar of Jesus Christ: What did Saint Peter leave you by succession? "He could not give you that which he had not; he gave you that which he had, that is, care for all the Churches . . . . Such is the apostolic constitution: domination is forbidden; servitude is recommended."[54]

Come then, O prince, accomplish the prophecies in favor of the Church; come *lick up the dust of thy feet*.[55] Never disdain to regard any bishop as your brother, with whom you might possess *the episcopate in solidarity*.[56] Put your honor in supporting those of [960] common character. Recognize the holy priests as your coadjutors in Jesus Christ; receive their counsels; profit from their experience, cultivate, cherish even the poor clerics, who are the hope of the house of God; relieve all the workers who carry the weight and the heat of the day; console all those in whom you will find some spark of the spirit of grace. O you, who descend from so many princes and kings and emperors, *forget thy people and thy father's house*, say to all the ancestors: *I know you not*.[57] If someone thinks that pastoral humility and tenderness degrade your birth and your dignity, respond as David did when it was found indecent that he danced before the ark: *I will both play and make myself meaner than I have done: and I will be little in my own eyes*.[58] Descend as far as the last lamb of your flock: nothing can be low in a ministry that is above man. Descend, then, descend: fear nothing, as you could never descend too much in order to imitate *the prince of pastors*,[59] who *thought it not robbery to be equal* to his father, *emptied himself, taking the form of a servant*.[60] If the spirit of faith makes you descend thusly, your humility will constitute the joy of heaven and earth.

II. What patience is not necessary in this ministry? The minister of Jesus Christ is *debtor* to all, *to the wise and to the unwise*.[61] This is an immense debt, which renews itself each day, and which never abates. The more one does, the more one finds to do; and it is only, says St. Chrysostom, the one who, doing nothing, flatters himself of having done everything. Solomon cried to God, in view of the people of whom he was charged: *Thy servant is in the midst of the people which thou hast chosen, an immense people, which cannot be numbered nor counted for multitude. Give therefore to thy servant an understanding heart, to judge thy people*.[62] Scripture adds that in the mouth of Solomon this *discourse pleased God*; it will please him also in yours. Had you been Solomon, the wisest of all men, you would have care to ask of God *an understanding heart*. But docility—is it not the share of inferiors? Does it not seem that one must ask for wisdom from pastors, and docility from peoples? No, it is the pastor who needs to be even more docile than the flock. Without doubt it is necessary to be docile in order to obey well; but it is necessary to be still more docile in order to command well. The wisdom of man discovers itself only in docility. It [961] is necessary that he learn constantly in order to teach. Not only must he learn from God, and listen with an interior silence, according to these words: *I will hear what the Lord God will speak in me*;[63] but so too he must instruct himself in listening to men. "It is necessary," says Saint Cyprian, "not only that the bishop teaches, but also that he learns; because the one who grows every day, making progress in learning the most perfect things, teaches much better."[64]

Not only must the bishop constantly study the holy letters, the tradition, and the discipline of the canons, but he must also hear all those who want to speak to him. The truth is found only in going more thoroughly into things with patience. How unhappy the presumptuous who flatter themselves into believing that they penetrate it at the start! It is no less necessary to distrust his own prejudices than the disguises of the parties. It is necessary for him to fear deceiving himself, to believe easily that he deceives himself, and never to be ashamed to admit that he has been deceived. Elevation, far from protecting one against trumpery, is precisely that which exposes one to it the most; because the more one is raised up, the more one attracts the deceitful, by exciting their avidity, their ambition, and their flattery. To despise the counsel of others is to carry the most reckless of all counsels home to ourselves. To feel no need of it is to be without resource. The wise man, on the contrary, extends his wisdom by all that which he receives from others. He learns from all, in order to instruct all; he shows himself superior to everything and to himself by this simplicity. He would go to the ends of the earth to seek out a faithful and disinterested friend who would have the courage to show him his faults. He is not unaware that inferiors know details better than he, because they see the details closer up, and such details are less hidden from them. "I cannot," said Saint Cyprian to the priest and to the deacons of his Church, "respond alone to that which our FELLOW PRESBYTERS[65] . . . have written me; because I resolved, at the beginning of my episcopacy, to do nothing by my own private sentiment, without your counsel and without the consent of the people: but when I will arrive, by the grace of God, among you, we will then together, in accord with the demands of the honor we owe each other, deal with the things which have been done or which are to be done."[66] Thus never decide on any important point of discipline without ecclesiastical deliberation. The more important the business, the more [962] necessary it is to weigh them, and to trust in a counsel well chosen, and to distrust with sincerity one's own insight.

Behold, O prince, an innumerable people that you will lead. You must be amid them as Saint Augustine depicts Saint Ambrose to us: he passed all the days with the holy books in his hands, delivering himself to the crowd of men who would come to him as to a doctor in order to be cured of their spiritual sicknesses, *quorum infirmitatibus serviebat*.[67]

But this doctor, must he not vary the remedy according to the illness? Yes, undoubtedly: on these grounds it is said that we are *good stewards of the manifold grace of God*.[68] The true pastor limits himself to no particular conduct: he is gentle, he is rigorous; he threatens, he encourages; he hopes, he fears; he corrects, he consoles; he *became to the Jews a Jew* in legal matters, he is with those who are under the law as if he was there himself; *to the weak I became weak; I became all things to all men, that I might save all*.[69]

O happy weakness of the pastor, who grows weaker precisely by wholly lowering himself in order to proportion himself to the souls who lack power! *Who is weak*, says the Apostle, *and I am not weak? Who is scandalized, and I am not on fire* in order to raise him back up?[70] O pastors, no shrunken hearts for you! Enlarge, enlarge your depths. You know nothing, if you know only to command, only to reprimand, only to correct, only to observe the letter of the law. Be fathers. This is not all: be mothers, bear children in pain, suffer anew the pains of childbirth, at each effort that it would be necessary to make in order to finish shaping Jesus in a heart. *We became little ones in the midst of you*, said Saint Paul to the faithful of Thessalonica, *as if a nurse should cherish her children*.[71] Wait without end, O pastor of Israel; hope against hope; imitate the long-suffering patience of God for the sinners; support that which God supports, *rebuke in all patience and doctrine*: it will be given to you according to the measure of your faith.[72] Do not doubt that the rocks themselves might become children of Abraham in the end. You must do as God, to whom Saint Augustine said: "You have fashioned my heart, in order to remake it little by little by a hand so gentle and so merciful: *paulatim tu, Domine, manu mitissima et misericordissima pertractans et componens cor meum*.[73] [963]

But what about in the apostolic ministry? If you only want to intimidate men, and reduce them to doing certain exterior actions, raise the sword;

all tremble, you are obeyed. This is an exact administration, but not a sincere religion.[74] If men only tremble, the demons tremble as much as they and hate God. The more rigor and constraint you use, the more you run the risk of establishing only a disguised and deceitful self-love. Where then will be those the Father seeks, and who will adore Him in spirit and in truth? Let us remember that the worship of God consists in love: *Nec colitur ille, nisi amando.*[75] In order to love, it is necessary to enter into the depths of hearts; it is necessary to have a key to them; it is necessary to overturn all their motives, it is necessary to persuade, and to make them desire the good, in such a way that that one would desire it freely, and independently of servile fear. Can power persuade men? Can it make them desire what they do not desire? Does one not see that the least of the people neither believe nor always desire at the will of the strongest princes? Everyone keeps quiet, everyone suffers, everyone disguises themselves, everyone acts and appears to desire, everyone flatters, everyone applauds. But one neither believes nor loves; on the contrary, one hates all the more and bears more impatiently the constraint that reduces them to feign love. No human power can overpower the impenetrable fortress of a heart's freedom.

As for Jesus Christ, his reign is within man, because he desires love. Also he does nothing by violence, but everything by persuasion, as Saint Augustine says: *Nihil egit vi, sed omnia suadendo.*[76] Love does not enter into the heart by imposition; each loves only as much as it pleases him to love. It is easier to reprimand than to persuade; it is simpler to threaten than to instruct; it is more fitting to haughtiness and human impatience to beat those who resist than it is to edify them, to humiliate oneself, to pray, to die to oneself, in order to teach them to die to themselves. As soon as some disappointment is found in the heart, each is tempted to say to Jesus Christ: *Lord, wilt thou that we command fire to come down from heaven and consume* the indocile sinners?[77] But Jesus Christ responds: *You know not of what spirit you are*; he reprimands this indiscrete zeal.[78]

Correction resembles certain remedies composed of some poison: it is necessary to avail oneself of them only as [964] a last resort, and only by tempering them with a great deal of precaution. Correction secretly shocks all the way down to the last remnants of pride; it leaves in the heart a secret wound that easily becomes infected. The good pastor prefers as much as possible a gentle insinuation, adding there example, patience, prayer, paternal care. These remedies are less rapid, it is true, but they are more useful. The great art, in the conduct of souls, is to make them love you in order to make them love God, and to win confidence in order to achieve persuasion. The Apostle wants to move all hearts to tears, in such a way that one cannot resist him: *I Paul myself beseech you*, he says to the faithful, *by the mildness and modesty of Christ.*[79]

The pastor experienced in the ways of grace undertakes only the good works for which he sees that wills have already been prepared by the Lord. He sounds hearts: he would not dare to take two steps at a time; and if it is necessary, he has no shame in drawing back. He says like Jesus Christ: *I have yet many things to say to you: but you cannot bear them now.*[80] As for evil, he recalls to himself these beautiful words of Saint Augustine: "The Pastors conduct, not healed men, but men who have need of healing. It is necessary to suffer the faults of the multitude, in order to heal them, and it is necessary to tolerate the contagion, before making it stop. It is very difficult to find the proper middle in this work, in order to preserve there a peaceful and tranquil spirit."[81] Take care then not to try to uproot all the bad grain at once. *Suffer both to grow until the harvest,*[82] out of fear that you might uproot the good with the bad. All the times that you will feel your heart disturbed against some indocile sinner, recall these kind words of Jesus Christ: *They that are in health need not a physician, but they that are ill. Go then and learn what this meaneth, I will have mercy and not sacrifice. For I am not come to call the just, but sinners.*[83] All indignation, all impatience, all haughtiness contrary to this gentleness of the God of patience and consolation is the excessive rigor of the Pharisee. Fear not falling into dissipation in imitating God himself, in whom *mercy exalteth itself above judgment.*[84] Speak like Saint Cyprian, that intrepid defender of the purest discipline: "Let them come," he said of those who had sinned, "if they want to try our [965] judgment.... Here the Church is closed to nobody, and there is no man to whom the bishop refuses himself. We are always ready to extend to all those who would come our patience, our leniency, our humanity. I wish that all might return to the Church.... I pardon all things, I conceal many of them, out of the desire and zeal to reassemble our brothers. I do not examine even by the plain judgment of religion the offenses committed against God. I sin almost, in forgiving more than necessary the sins of others. I embrace with promptitude and tenderness those who would return in repenting and in confessing their sins with a humble and simple satisfaction."[85]

Alas! You could take some care to make yourself loved and to ease the yoke, yet what contradictions will you not find in your work! If you want to do evil, or at least leave off doing good by softness, flattering the passions of the multitude gets you applauded; friends are made at the expense of the rules. But if you want to do good and put down evil, it is necessary to refuse, to speak out against, to attack the passions of men; brace yourself against the torrent: everyone will unite against you. "Whoever," says Saint Cyprian, "does not imitate the wicked, offends them. Even the laws give way in order to flatter the sinner; and disorder, coming to be public, begins to seem permissible."[86] Abuses are accepted as customary; the people are jealous of them as of a right acquired by possession: one protests against reform as against indiscreet change. Even if the pastor employs the wisest and most temperate means, reform, which *edifies by a utility* that is real, *troubles* the minds *by an apparent novelty*.[87] The Church groans, feeling its hands tied, and seeing the disease resisting the remedy prepared for its cure.

The higher you are raised up, the more you will be exposed to this contradiction; the larger your flock will be, the more the pastor will have to suffer. It is said to you, as to Saint Paul: *For I will shew him how great things he must suffer for my name's sake*.[88] Work, and never see the fruit of your labors; work to persuade men, and feel their inconsistency; work, and see difficulties endlessly reborn; combat without, fear within; seeing everywhere sinners, and never knowing for sure where the truly just are. As Saint Augustine puts it: thus the lot of the ministers of Jesus Christ.

Germany, this blessed land that has given to the Church [966] so many holy pastors, so many pious princes, so many admirable monks, has been ravaged by heresy. The most happily preserved places have felt some trembling; discipline has suffered for it. How many times, in considering this sad spectacle, will you come to be reduced to say with the apostles: *we are unprofitable servants!*[89] Your feet will be almost unsteady, and your heart will be dry, when you will see the false peace of the blind and incorrigible sinners. O pastor of Israel, work in pure faith, without consolation if necessary: hold your soul in patience. Plant, water, wait for God to bring growth; if you were to procure only the salvation of a single soul, the labors of your entire life would be well spent.

But do you want me, O prince so dear to God, to leave you a summary of all your duties? Write not on tablets of stone, but on the living tablets of your heart, these great words of Saint Augustine: "May the one who conducts you believe himself happy, not by an imperious power, but by a charity devoted to servitude. For the sake of honor he must be above you in public; but he must be, by the fear of God, prostrate under your feet. It is necessary that he be the model of good works for all, that he corrects restless men, that he supports the weak, that he be patient with all, that he be ready to observe discipline, and reticent to impose it on others; and though both of these two points might be necessary, that he seeks nevertheless to be loved rather than to be feared."[90]

III. But how is it that a man appearing in mortal flesh, and surrounded with infirmity, can take on all of the celestial virtues in order to be the angel of God on earth? Know that God is *rich unto all that call upon him.*[91] He orders us to pray, from fear that we will lose, for want of prayer, the goods that he prepares for us. He promises, he invites; he prays, so to speak, that we might pray to him. It is true that a great love is necessary to feed a great flock; it is necessary to be almost no longer a man in order to merit leading men; it is necessary to stop failing to see the flaws of humanity in one's self. It is only after having said to you three times, as to Simon Peter, *Lovest thou me more than these?* and after having drawn three times from your heart this response, *Lord, thou knowest that I love thee* [967], that the great pastor says to you: *Feed my sheep.*[92] But in the end the one who demands so courageous and so patient a love is the same one who gives it to us. *You that have no money make haste, buy, and eat.*[93] He purchases it by desire alone, nothing of it is forbidden, except to the one who does not desire it. O infinite good, it is necessary only to desire you in order to possess you! This is the pure and burning gold, this is the treasure of the poor heart, which satisfies all desire, and which fills all void. Love gives everything, and love itself is given to whoever opens his heart to it. But see this order of the gifts of God, and take good care not to overturn it. Grace alone can give love, and grace gives itself only to prayer. *Pray without ceasing*, pray and never falter.[94] If all the faithful must pray thus, what will be the prayer of the pastor? You are the mediator between heaven and earth; pray, in order to help those who pray, in joining your prayers to theirs. Even more, pray for all those who do not pray; speak to God in favor of those to whom you would not dare to speak of God, when you see them hardened and hostile to virtue. Be, like Moses, the friend of God; go far from the people, on the mountain, to speak familiarly with Him face to face; return to the people, crowned with rays of glory that this inexpressible dialogue would have put around your head. May prayer be the source of your light in work. Not only must you convert the sinners, but still more you must direct the most perfect souls in the ways of God; you must *speak wisdom among the perfect*;[95] you must be their guide in prayer, in order to protect them from the illusions of self-love. Be then the salt of the earth, the light of the world, the eye that illuminates the body of your Church, and the mouth that pronounces the oracles of the tradition.

O! who will give me this spirit of prayer, which is absolute even to God, and who instills in the pastor all that he lacks for the sake of the flock? O spirit of prayer, it is you who will form the new apostles in order to change the face of the earth? O Spirit, O love, come to love; come teach us to pray, and pray in us; come to love yourself there. To pray always in order to love and to make God loved: this is the life of discipleship. Live this hidden life with Jesus Christ in God, prince become pastor of souls, and you will *taste, and see that the Lord is sweet.*[96] Then you will be a pillar of the house of God; then you will be the love and the delight of the Church. [968]

The great princes, who—so to speak—take from the Church without giving themselves to it, are great burdens and not supports. Alas! What do they not cost the Church! They do not feed the flock; it is on the flock that they themselves feed. The price of the sins of the people, the consecrated gifts, cannot satisfy their desire for splendor and ambition. What does the Church not suffer as a result of them! What wounds do they not inflict on its discipline! All the canons must fall before them; everything bends under their splendor. The dispensations they abuse teach others to undermine the holy laws: they are ashamed to be pastors and fathers; they want only to be princes and masters.

This will not be true of you, since you put your glory in your pastoral duties. How much more authority over men do the examples given by a bishop who is a great prince have than examples given by a bishop of a middling birth! How much better suited is his humility to humbling the proud! How much more touching is his modesty in suppressing luxury and sumptuousness! How much more amiable is his gentleness! How much more powerful is his patience in order to bring back the lost and indocile! Who would not be ashamed to be haughty and quick-tempered, when they see the prince, amid all his power, gentle and humble of heart? What will be the force of his word, when it will be supported by his virtues? For example, what was the glory of the Church of Cologne, when it had for its pastor the famous Bruno, brother of the Emperor Otto I![97] But why will we not hope to find in Clement a new Bruno? It is up to us, O prince, to dry the tears of the Church, and console it for all the evils that it suffers in these days of sin. You will make the deserts of the earth bloom again; you will bring back the beauty of the ancient days. What do I say? Raise your eyes, and see the countryside already white with sheep. *Be comforted, be comforted, my people, saith your God. . . . Every valley shall be exalted, and every mountain and hill shall be made low. . . . Get thee up upon a high mountain, thou that bringest good tidings to Sion: lift up thy voice with strength, thou that bringest good tidings to Jerusalem: lift it up, fear not. Say to the cities of Juda: Behold your God.*[98] O Church, which receives from the hand of the Lord such a bridegroom, *thus* children who *shall come from afar.* You will be more fruitful than ever in [969] your old age. *Behold these from the north and from the sea, and these from the south country. . . . Lift up thy eyes round about, and see all these are gathered together, they are come to thee: I live, saith the Lord, thou shalt be clothed with all these as with an ornament, and as a bride thou shalt put them about thee.* O mother who was believed sterile, *The children of thy barrenness shall still say in thy ears: The place is too strait for me, make me room to dwell in. And thou shalt say in thy heart: Who hath begotten these? I was barren and brought not forth, led away, and captive: and who hath brought up these? I was destitute and alone: and these, where were they?*[99]

Peoples, for the sake of the happiness of the one for whom this consecration is made, would that I could make you understand from afar my weak voice! Pray, peoples, pray; all the benedictions that you will draw on the head of Clement, will return on your own; the more grace he receives, the more he will spread it over all the flock.

And you assembled here who listen to me, never forget what you see today. Remember this modesty, this fervor for the holy religion, this indefatigable zeal for the house of God. Do not be surprised by it. From his childhood, this prince has been nourished on the words of the faith; the palace where he was born had, despite its magnificence, the regularity of a community of monks; the praises of God were sung in this court, as in the desert. The Lord will not forget all the marks of piety that came to be hereditary in this house; after the storm, he will in the end make happy days shine on it, and return to it its ancient radiance.

You see, my brothers, this prince prostrate at the foot of the altar. You come to hear all that which I have said to him. So! What have I not dared to say to him? So! What must I not say to him, since he fears only being ignorant of the truth? The greatest praise would praise him infinitely less than the episcopal freedom with which he desires that I speak to him. O, a prince shows himself great when he gives this freedom! This one will appear above vain praises, when all he wanted me to say to him is known!

And you, O prince on whom flows the unction of the Holy Spirit, resuscitate constantly the grace that you receive by the imposition of my hands. May this great day order all the other days of your life up to that of your death. Be always the good shepherd ready to give your life for your dear lambs, as you today desire to be, [970] and as you would wish to have been at the moment when, stripped of all earthly splendor, you will go to render account of your ministry to God. Pray, love, make God loved; render Him amiable in you; make it so that one feels Him in your person; spread afar the sweet perfume of Jesus Christ; be the power, the light, the consolation of your flock, such that your flock might be your joy and your crown on the day of Jesus Christ!

O God, You have loved him from eternity, You want him to love You and make You loved here below. Carry him in your breast through all dangers and temptations. Do not permit *the bewitching of vanity* of the age to *obscureth good things* that You have put in his heart.[100] Do not allow him to limit himself to his high birth, or to his natural courage, or to any worldly prudence. May faith alone do in him the work of faith, and at the moment when he comes to appear before You—the poor fed, the rich humiliated, the ignorant instructed, abuses reformed, discipline reestablished, the Church supported and consoled by his virtues—present him before the throne of grace, in order to receive from Your hands the crown that will never fade!

6

Examination of Conscience on the Duties of Kingship

[Pl. 2:973–1009]

Nobody wishes more than I, My Lord, that you might be many years away from the perils inseparable from kingship. I wish it out of zeal for the preservation of the holy person of the king, so necessary to his kingdom, and out of zeal for my lord the Dauphin. I wish it for the good of the state. I wish it for your good as well, because one of the gravest misfortunes that could happen to you would be to be the master of others at an age where you are still so far from being the master of yourself. But it is necessary to prepare you from afar for the dangers of a state from which I pray God will preserve you until the most advanced age of life. The best manner of making this state known to a prince who fears God and who loves religion is to prepare for him an examination of conscience on the duties of kingship. This is what I will try to do.

1.
[Instruction]

Do you know all the truths of Christianity?[1] Like the least of your subjects, you will be judged by the Gospels. Do you study your duties in this divine law? Could you endure a magistrate who always judged the people in your name without knowing your laws and your ordinances, which must be the standard of his judgments? Do you hope that God will allow you to be ignorant of His law, according to which He [974] wishes that you might live and govern His people? Do you read the Gospel without vain curiosity, with humble docility, in a practical spirit, and turning yourself against yourself in order to condemn all the things that this law will condemn in you?

Fénelon. Ryan Patrick Hanley, Oxford University Press (2020) © Oxford University Press.
DOI: 10.1093/oso/9780190079581.001.0001

2.

Have you persuaded yourself that the Gospel need not be the standard of kings as well as their subjects, that the art of governing exempts them from being humble, just, sincere, moderate, compassionate, and ready to pardon injuries? Has not some cowardly and corrupted flatterer told you, and have you not been quick to believe, that kings ought to govern themselves for the sake of their states by certain maxims of haughtiness, of severity, of dissimulation, in raising themselves above common rules of justice and humanity?

3.

Have you not sought out all kinds of counselors who are most disposed to flatter you in your maxims of ambition, of vanity, of sumptuousness, of softness, and of artifice? Have you not found it difficult to believe those firm and disinterested men who, desiring nothing from you, and not allowing themselves to be dazzled by your grandeur, would have respectfully spoken the truth to you, and would have spoken out against you in order to prevent you from making mistakes?

4.

Have you not been pleased, in the most hidden recesses of your heart, not to see the good that you have no desire to do, because it would have cost you too much to practice it, and have you not searched for reasons to excuse the evil to which you were carried by your inclinations? [975]

5.

Have you not neglected to pray to God in order to ask of Him awareness of His will for you? Have you sought in prayer the grace to profit from your reading? If you have neglected to pray, you have rendered yourself guilty of all the ignorance in which you have lived, and which the spirit of prayer would have stripped away. Reading the eternal truths counts for little if one does not pray to obtain the gift of understanding them well. Having not prayed well, you have merited the darkness in which God has left you for the correction of your faults and for the fulfillment of your duties. Thus the negligence, the lukewarmness, and the willful distraction in prayer that commonly pass for the least significant of all faults are nevertheless the true source of the ignorance and the fatal blindness in which the majority of princes live.

6.

Have you chosen for your spiritual counselors the most pious and most firm and most enlightened men, as one searches out the best military generals to command troops during war, and the best doctors when one is sick? Do your counselors include multiple people, such that one can protect you from the biases of others, since every man, however upright and skillful he may be, is always capable of bias? Have you feared the risks of rendering yourself dependent on a single man? Have you given to your counselors a total freedom of disclosing to you, without watering them down, the full extent of your obligations of conscience?

7.

Have you worked to instruct yourself in the laws, customs, and practices of the realm? The king is the highest judge in his state. It is he who makes the laws; it is he who interprets [976] them when the need arises. It is he who often judges in his council according to the laws that he has established or found already established prior to his reign. It is he who must set right all the other judges. In short, his job is to be at the head of all justice during peace, like being at the head of armies during war. And as war must only be waged with regret and in a manner that keeps it as short as possible, and with the goal of establishing a lasting peace, it follows that the office of commander of the armies is only a temporary office, compulsory and unpleasant for good kings, whereas that of judging the people, and overseeing all the judges, is their natural, essential, and ordinary function, inseparable from kingship itself. To judge according to the laws is to judge well. In order to judge according to the laws, it is necessary to know them. Do you know them, and are you in a position to set right judges who are ignorant of them? Do you know all the principles of jurisprudence, in order readily to understand what is at issue when a case is reported to you? Are you in a position to distinguish among your counselors those who flatter you from those who do not, and those who religiously follow the rules from those who would like to apply them in an arbitrary fashion according to their designs? Don't say that you follow the majority vote, because in the event that there is a division in your counsel in which your opinion must be decisive, you cannot be like a company president there; moreover you are there the sole true judge. Your counselors of state or ministers are only mere advisors. It is you alone who decide in the end. The voice of a single enlightened man must often be preferred to that of ten timid and weak or stubborn and corrupt judges. In such a case one must weigh rather than count votes.

8.

Have you studied the true form of the government of your kingdom? It is not sufficient to know the laws that govern landed property and other goods among individuals. This is without doubt the least part of justice. The justice that concerns us here is that which you must protect between your nation and yourself, between you and your neighbors. Have you carefully studied what is called the law of nations, law that it is even less permissible for a king to neglect, since it is this law [977] that governs his conduct in the most important functions, and since it is limited to the most evident principles of natural right for the entire human race?[2] Have you studied the fundamental laws and the customary practices that have the force of law for the general administration of your own particular nation? Have you sought to know, without flattering yourself, what the limits of your authority are? Do you know by what means others governed the kingdom in different ages? What the ancient parlements were,[3] and the Estates General that succeeded them? What the subordination of fiefs was? How things passed into their present state? On what this evolution is based? What anarchy is; what arbitrary power is; and, in between these two extremes, what the kingdom ruled by law is? Would you allow a judge to judge without knowing the ordinances, or a general to command the army without knowing the art of war? Do you believe that God would allow you to reign, if you reign without being taught what must limit and regulate your power? It is therefore necessary not to regard the study of history, morals, and all the details of the ancient constitution as a matter of idle curiosity, but as an essential duty of kingship.

9.

It is not enough to know the past. It is necessary to know the present. Do you know the number of people who compose your nation: how many men, how many women, how many laborers, how many artisans, how many lawyers, how many shopkeepers, how many priests and clergy, how many nobles, and how many soldiers? What would one say of a shepherd who didn't know the number of sheep in his flock? It is equally easy for a king to know the number of his people; he only has to want to know it. He must know if there are enough workers, if there are proportionally too many artisans, too many lawyers, too many soldiers for whom the state is responsible. It is necessary to know the nature of the inhabitants of the state's different provinces, their principal practices, their freedoms, their commerce, and the laws of their different transactions inside and outside of the kingdom. It is necessary to know the different tribunals established in each province, the rights of the [978] offices, the abuses of these offices, etc. Otherwise he will not know the value of the majority of things that will pass before his eyes. His ministers will impose on him without hesitation all the time. He will believe he sees everything, and will see only half. A king ignorant of all these things is only half a king. His ignorance renders him incapable of straightening out what is crooked. His ignorance does more evil than the corruption of the men who govern under him.

10.

[Of example]

It is typically said of kings that they have less to fear from their private vices than the failings to which they abandon themselves in kingship. As for me, I make bold to say the opposite, and I maintain that all their faults in their most private lives are of an immense consequence for the monarchy. Carefully examine then your morals. Subjects are the servile imitators of their prince, above all in the things that flatter their passions. Have you given them the pernicious example of a disgraceful and criminal love? If you have, your authority has served to honor vileness, you have broken the barrier between shame and righteousness, you have enabled vice and im-pudence to triumph. You have taught all your subjects no longer to blush at what is shameful—a disastrous lesson they will never forget. "It were better for him," says Jesus, "that a millstone were hanged about his neck, and he cast into the sea, than that he should scandalize one of these little ones."[4] Consider then the scandal of a king who allows himself to be seen sitting with vice on his throne, not only by his subjects, but still more by all the courts and all the nations of the known world! Vice is itself a contagious poison. The human race is always ready to catch this contagion. By inclination, it tends just to shake off the yoke of all decency. A spark causes a fire. A king's action is often multiplied and leads to a series of crimes that extend across several nations and several ages. Have you not given fatal examples of such? Perhaps you believe that your messes have been secret. No, the evil in princes is never secret. Good in them can be secret, because it takes great effort to [979] believe that they really have it in them. But as far as evil goes, it is expected and believed on the least suspicions. The public penetrates everything, and often, while the prince flatters himself that his weaknesses are overlooked, he is the only one who overlooks how much they are the object of the most malicious criticism. In him all equivocal commerce is subject to explication, all appearance of gallantry, all impassioned or amusing airs, cause a scandal and serve to alter for the worse the morals of an entire nation.

11.

Have you not permitted an immodest freedom in women? Do you admit them into your court only in cases of true necessity? In the court are they near the queen or the princesses of your house? Have you chosen for these places women of an advanced age, and of proven virtue? Have you excluded from these places young women of a beauty that would be a trap for you and your courtiers? It would be better for such women to remain in private life in the midst of their families, far from court. Have you excluded from your court all the women who are not needed for positions of service to princesses? Have you taken care to ensure that the princesses themselves be modest, reserved, and of a steady conduct in all things? In reducing the number of women of the court, and in choosing them for it as well as you can, have you taken care to dismiss those who introduce dangerous freedoms, and to prevent corrupted courtesans in particular from seeing them, outside the hours where all the court assembles together? Today all these precautions seem like scruples and excessive severities. But if one goes back to the times before the reign of Francis I, one will find that before the scandalous license introduced by this prince, the women of the highest rank, and above all those who were young and beautiful, did not go to court.[5] At most they appeared there very rarely in order to fulfill their duties to the queen; their honor lay in remaining with their families in the countryside. This large number of women who everywhere go freely to the court is a monstrous abuse, to which the nation has grown accustomed. Have you not permitted this [980] pernicious custom? Have you not attracted or retained by some distinction in your court some woman whose conduct is suspect, or at least who previously set a poor example to the world? It is not at court that these profane people must make their penance. They ought to make it in seclusion, if they are single, or in their families, if they are attached to the world by husbands still alive. But keep away from your court all those who have not been steady, as you have to choose between all the qualified women in your realm to fill the places.

12.

Have you taken care to suppress luxury and to forestall the ruinous inconstancy of fashions? This is what corrupts the majority of women. At court they throw themselves into expenses that they cannot keep up without resorting to crime. Luxury encourages in them the passion of pleasing; their passion for pleasing largely revolves around setting traps for the king. It would be necessary for him to be insensible and invulnerable in order to resist all these pernicious women that he surrounds himself with. It is a constantly precarious situation in which he puts himself. Have you not allowed the most vain and most wasteful people to find new ways of adding to your expenses? Have you not yourself contributed to so great an evil by an excessive magnificence? Even though you are the king, you must steer clear of everything costly that others would also like to have. It is useless to argue that none of your subjects can afford an appearance that is suited only to you. The princes closest to you would like to go a little further than what you will do. Great lords pride themselves in imitating princes. The gentlemen would like to be like the lords. The financiers would like to surpass the lords themselves. All the bourgeois would like to walk in the steps of the financiers, whom they have seen rise up out of the mud. No one does justice to themselves, sizing themselves up accurately. Little by little, luxury, by an imperceptible shift, passes from the highest condition to the lowest of the people. If you have embroidered trim, soon the valets will wear it. The only means of stopping [981] luxury in its tracks is to give yourself the example that Saint Louis gave of a great simplicity. Have you in fact given so necessary an example? It is not enough to give it in dress alone. It is necessary to give it in furniture, in equipage, in tables, in buildings. Look how the kings who preceded you were lodged and furnished. Look at what their meals and transport were like. You will be astonished at the immense luxury into which we have fallen. Today there are more coaches-and-six in Paris than there were mules a hundred years ago. Nobody had a private room. A single room sufficed, with several beds for several people. Now nobody can go without vast sets of rooms one after another. Each wants to have gardens that overturn all the earth, jets of water, statues, grounds without limits, houses of which the cost of upkeep surpasses the revenue of all the lands on which they lie. From where does all this come? From the example of a single person. Example alone can correct the morals of all the nation. We even see that the folly of our fashions is catching among all our neighbors. All Europe, so jealous of France, cannot refrain from entirely succumbing to our laws regarding our most frivolous and most pernicious things. Once again, such is the force of the example of the prince. He alone by his moderation can return his own people and his neighbors to common sense. Since he can, he must do so without fail. Have you done so?

13.

Have you not given a bad example either by speaking too freely, or by making barbed jests, or by speaking indecently about religious matters? Courtiers are servile imitators who take pride in having all the faults of the prince. Have you avoided all possible insinuations of irreligion even in your casual conversation? Have you made known your sincere indignation toward impiety? Have you left nothing in doubt on this front? Have you never been held back by an evil shame that would have made the Evangelist blush? Have you shown by your words and by your actions your sincere faith and your zeal for Christianity? Have you [982] put your authority in the service of silencing irreligion? Have you shrunk away with horror from evil pleasantries, equivocal discourses, and all other marks of libertinage?

14.

[Of justice]

Have you ever taken something from one of your subjects by simple authority and against the rules? Have you compensated him as a private individual would have done when you took his house, or enclosed his field in your grounds, or stripped him of his office, or raised his rent? Have you examined thoroughly the true needs of the state in order to weigh them against the inconveniences of taxes before burdening your people? Have you consulted on so important a question the most enlightened men, the ones most zealous for the public good, and the ones most capable of telling you the truth without either flattery or sugarcoating? Have you not called a necessity of state that which serves only to flatter your ambition, like war meant to allow you to make conquests and acquire glory? Have you not called your personal claims needs of state? If you had pretensions to hereditary rights in some neighboring state you needed to support this war out of your estate, your accounts, your personal loans—or, at least, only accept the assistance which the pure affection of your people would grant you, and not by overwhelming them with taxes in order to support pretensions of no concern to your subjects, since they will not be any happier if you were to gain another province. When Charles VIII went to Naples in order to claim the succession of the house of Anjou, he undertook this war out of his personal expenses.[6] The State did not think itself obligated to pay for this enterprise. At most, you could accept on such occasions those gifts the people make out of affection, and by virtue of the connection that exists between the interests of a zealous nation, and of a king who governs it like a father. But from this perspective you would be very far from overwhelming the people with taxes for your individual interests. [983]

15.

Have you not tolerated injustices even if you have abstained from doing injustice yourself? Have you chosen with all necessary care all the people that you must put in authority—the quartermasters, the governors, the ministers, etc.? Have you not chosen any of them out of weakness for those who proposed them to you, or by a secret desire that they might in due course extend your authority or your revenues beyond their proper limits?

Have you familiarized yourself with their administration? Have you let it be known you were ready to hear complaints against them and to dispense justice fairly in such cases? Have you done so when you have discovered their offenses?

16.

Have you not given to your ministers, or allowed them to garner, excessive profits that their services have not warranted? The rewards that the prince gives to those who serve the state under him must always have definite limits. It is not permissable to give them fortunes that surpass those of men of the highest rank, or that would be disproportioned to the current capacities of the state. No matter what services he has rendered, a minister must not be given immense goods all at once while the people suffer and while princes and lords of the first rank are in need. It is still less permissible to give such fortunes to favorites, who ordinarily have served the state even less than the ministers have.

17.

Have you given all the clerks of your ministers, and other persons who fulfill the subordinate positions, salaries sufficient for them to live decently, without taking anything extra from their services? At the same time, have you suppressed the luxury and the ambition of these people? If you have not done so, [984] you are responsible for all the secret acts of violence they have committed while in office. On the one hand they enter into these positions only in the expectation that they will live there in splendor and quickly acquire fortunes. On the other hand, their salary ordinarily is less than a third of the income necessary for the honorable accommodation of their families. Typically they have no wealth by birth. What do you want them to do? You put them in a position where they have a sort of necessity of secretly taking all they can glean from the dispatch of business. This is clear, and it is to shut one's eyes in bad faith not to see it. You should give them more and prevent them from putting themselves on too high a level.

18.

Have you searched out the means of relieving the people and of taking from them only when the true needs of the state compelled you to do so for their own advantage? The property of the people must only be employed for the sake of the genuine utility of the people themselves. You have your estate, which it is necessary to liquidate and draw from. It is intended for the subsistence of your house. You must limit this domestic expense, above all when the revenues of your estate are committed, and the people are exhausted. Subventions from the people must be employed for the true burdens of the state. In times of public poverty you must work to remove all burdens that are not absolutely necessary. Have you consulted the most skilled and well-intentioned people who can inform you of the state of the provinces, of the cultivation of the land, of the fertility of recent years, of the state of commerce, etc., in order to know what the state can afford to pay out without suffering? Have you settled up each year's taxes on this basis? Have you heard favorably the reproofs of good men? Far from reprimanding them, have you sought out and anticipated them, as a good prince must do? You know that in other times the king never took anything from his people by his own sole authority. It was the Parlement, that is to say the assembly of the nation, that accorded him the funds required for the special needs of the state.[7] Other than this he [985] lived off his estate. What changed this order, if not the absolute authority the kings have claimed? In our days one can yet see the parlements, which are bodies infinitely inferior to the ancient parlements or *états* of the nation, make remonstrances in order not to register financial edicts.[8] At least you must not issue any without having fully consulted people incapable of flattering you and who have a genuine zeal for the public good. Have you not imposed new taxes on the people in order to support your superfluous expenditures, the luxury of your tables and your equipages and your furnishings, the embellishment of your gardens and houses, the excessive gifts that you have lavished on your favorites?

19.

Have you not multiplied appointments and offices in order to draw new sums from their creation? Such creations are only disguised taxes. They all tend to oppress the people, and they have three inconveniences that simple taxes do not have. (1) They are perpetual, when one has not reimbursed them; and if one has paid them back, which is ruinous for your subjects, these creations begin anew. (2) Those who buy newly created offices want to get their money back as soon as possible, with interest. You give them the people to be skinned. For a hundred thousand francs you will be given upon creating an office, for example, you will hand over the people for five hundred thousand francs of humiliation that they will suffer without remedy. (3) You destroy, by this multiplication of offices, the good administration of the state, you render justice ever more venal, you render reform ever more impracticable, you plunge the entire nation into debt, because these creations become species of national debts, and finally you reduce all arts and all offices to monopolies that spoil and corrupt everything. Have you not reproached yourself for these creations, of which the successors will be pernicious for centuries to come? The wisest and best of all kings in a peaceful reign of fifty years could not repair the evils that a king can do through these sorts of creations in ten years of war. Have you not been too careless with [986] the courtiers who, under the pretext of sparing your finances from the rewards they have asked of you, have proposed various schemes to you? These schemes are always disguised taxes on the people; they disrupt the administration, weaken justice, degrade the arts, impede commerce, and burden the public—all in order to satisfy for a little time the avidity of a showy and wasteful courtier. Send your courtiers back to their lands for several years in order to put their affairs in order. Teach them to live frugally. Show them that you esteem only those who lead orderly lives and govern their affairs well. Show contempt for those who ruin themselves foolishly. By this, you will do them more good—without costing either you or your people a penny—than if you were to lavish on them all the wealth of the public.

20.

Have you never tolerated and willfully overlooked the fact that your ministers had appropriated private property for your use without paying fair compensation, or at least postponing payment of the price, in such a way that this postponement harmed those compelled to sell? It is thus that ministers take the houses of private individuals in order to enclose them in the palaces of the king or within their fortifications. It is thus that one dispossesses landlords of their domains or fiefdoms or inherited estates, in order to join them to palace grounds. It is thus that one establishes the captaincies of the hunt, in which the captains accredited by the prince forbid the lords to hunt in their own lands, even right next to the doors of their castles, and impose a thousand vexations on the countryside. The prince knows nothing of it, and perhaps wants to know nothing of it. It is up to you to know the evil that has been done by your authority. Inform yourself of the truth. Do not allow your authority to be extended too far. Listen favorably to those who would represent its limits to you. Choose ministers who dare to tell you when your authority has been pushed too far. Remove hard, haughty, and enterprising ministers. [987]

21.

In agreements that you have made with individuals, are you just, as if you were equal to the one with whom you are dealing? Is he as free with you as with one of his neighbors? Does he often not prefer to lose rather than claim his rights in order to redeem himself and to avoid potential vexations? Your lease holders, your customs officials, your administrators, etc.: do they not make decisions with an arrogance that you yourself would not have, and do they not stifle the voice of the weak seeking sympathy? Do you not often give to the man with whom you contract compensation in rents, access to your estate, newly created offices, which a stroke of the pen of your successor can revoke from him, because kings are always minors and their estate is inalienable? Thus one strips individuals of their guaranteed patrimonies in exchange for something that will be taken away from them in the future, with the inevitable ruin of their families.

22.

Have you not often granted to your financiers, in order to increase their estates, edicts or declarations or rulings with ambiguous terms, so as to extend your rights at the expense of commerce, and even set traps for merchants and confiscate their merchandise, or at least harass and inconvenience them in their commerce until they pay some sum in ransom? This does harm to both the merchants and to the public who sees its entire trade destroyed little by little by this.

23.

Have you not allowed enlistments that were not truly voluntary? It is true that people must contribute to the defense of the state. But only in wars that are just and absolutely necessary, and only when one selects in each village free young men [988] whose absence would harm neither fieldwork, nor commerce, nor the other necessary arts, and who have no family to support. In addition, the pledge to give them their leave after a small number of years of service, such that others would come and relieve them and serve in their place, should be inviolable. But to allow the taking of men without choice and against their will, to make a family abandoned by its head languish and often perish, to tear the farmer away from his plow, to hold him ten or fifteen years in service, where he often dies in misery in hospitals lacking essential resources, to bash in his head or cut off his nose if he deserts—nothing can excuse this before either God or man.

24.

Have you taken care to release each convict immediately after the term decreed by the judge for his punishment? The condition of these men is horrific. Nothing is more inhumane than further prolonging their terms. Don't respond that one would weaken the chain gang by observing this point of justice. Justice is more important than the chain gang. Only the justice that you have done without injury, and without taking what is not yours, counts for true and real power.

25.

Have you given your troops pay sufficient to live without plundering? If you have not done so, you put your troops under the evident necessity of having to commit the plunders and assaults that you make a pretense of forbidding them. Will you punish them for having done what you well know they cannot avoid doing, and without which your service would necessarily be neglected from the start? On the other hand, will you not punish them when they publicly steal from your defenses? Will you render the laws despicable, and allow your authority to be so disgracefully toyed with? Will you be in manifest contradiction with yourself, and will your authority be only a deceitful game, in order to appear [989] to suppress disorder and to use it to serve your own interests all the while? What discipline and order can one hope for from troops when officers can only survive by plundering the subjects of the king, violating his decrees at every moment, taking men by force and deceit in order to impress them, and when soldiers would die of hunger, if they did not always deserve to be hanged?

26.

Have you not done injustices to foreign nations? A poor wretch is hung for having stolen a pistole on the highway in his extreme need, but a man who conquers—that is, one who unjustly subjugates the country of a neighboring state—is treated like a hero. The usurping of a meadow or a vineyard is regarded as an unpardonable sin in the judgment of God, at least if one does not make restitution, and yet one counts for nothing the usurping of cities and provinces. To take a field from an individual is a great sin. To take the land of a nation is an innocent and glorious deed. Where then are the ideas of justice? Will God judge similarly? *"Existimasti inique quod ero tui similis."*[9] Must one be less just in great things than in small? Is justice no longer justice when it concerns great interests? The millions of men who make up a nation—are they less our brothers than a single man? Will one have no scruple about doing injustice to millions of men across an entire country, though one would not dare to do an injustice to a single man for the sake of a meadow? Everything that is taken by simple conquest is then taken very unjustly, and must be returned. So too everything taken in a war waged on evil grounds. Peace treaties are meaningless when you, from a position of superior strength, force your neighbors to sign the treaty in order to avoid even greater evils. In such a case he signs like someone who hands over his wallet when a thief holds a gun to his head. The war that you began inappropriately and then waged successfully, far from providing you with a secure conscience, commits you not only to the restitution of usurped lands, but moreover to the reparation of all unnecessary injuries to your neighbors. [990]

As for peace treaties, it is necessary to consider them null and void not only in cases of injustices brought about by violence, but also in those cases where you may have mixed some artifice, or some ambiguous term, in order to appeal to them when it suits you. Your enemy is your brother. You cannot forget him without forgetting humanity. It is never permissible for you to injure him when you can avoid doing so without injuring yourself, and you can never seek out any advantage against him by arms except in cases of extreme necessity. Treaties are not matters of arms or war, but matters of peace, justice, humanity, and good faith. It is still more despicable and criminal to deceive a neighboring people in a peace treaty than to deceive a private individual in a contract. To put ambiguous and deceitful terms in a treaty is to sow the seeds of future war, and to put powder kegs under the houses in which we live.

27.

When there have been questions of war, did you begin by first examining your rights, and by having those who are the most intelligent and the least flattering toward you do so as well? Did you defy the counsels of certain ministers who had some interest in drawing you into war, or who at least sought to flatter your passions in order to draw from you that which might gratify theirs? Have you sought out all the reasons that could be given against you? Have you listened favorably to those who detailed them? Have you taken the time to know the sentiments of all your wisest counselors without forestalling them? Have you not regarded your personal glory as a reason to undertake something, out of fear of spending your life without distinguishing yourself from other princes? As if princes could find some solid glory in disturbing the happiness of peoples of whom they ought to be the fathers, as if the father of a family could be estimable by actions that harm his children, and as if a king could find glory in putting his hope in something other than his virtue—that is to say, in something other than his justice and the good government of his people! Have you not believed that war was necessary [991] in order to acquire places that suited you and were at your disposal, and that would guarantee the security of your borders? Bizarre rule! By these standards one will little by little go as far as China. The security of a border can be established without taking the property of others. Fortify your own positions, and do not usurp those of your neighbors. Would you like it if a neighbor took from you anything he deemed useful for his security? Your security is not a title of ownership over the property of others. Your true security lies in being just, in keeping good allies by upright and moderate conduct, in having a large population, well fed, well disposed, and well disciplined. But what is more contrary to your security than making your neighbors feel that they can never find any security with you, and that you are always ready to take from them whatever suits you?

28.

Have you carefully examined whether the war in question was necessary for your people? Maybe it was only a matter of some claim to a succession that concerns you personally but in which your people have no real interest? What does it matter to them whether you have one more province? They can, out of affection for you, if they treat you like a father, make some efforts to help you claim successions in states that are legitimately owed to you. But can you overwhelm them with taxes against their will in order to raise funds needed for a war that is useless to them? Moreover, even supposing that this war concerned the state directly, you must examine whether it is more useful than damaging. It is necessary to compare the fruits that can be drawn from it—or at least the harms that can be feared if one does not engage in it—with the inconveniences it will bring in its wake. All things considered, there is almost no war, even one that ends happily, that does not do more harm than good to a state. One has only to consider how much it ruins families, how much death it spreads, how much it ravages and depopulates all the countryside, how much it destabilizes a state, how much it overturns its laws, how much it authorizes licentiousness, how much it would be necessary for years afterward [992] to struggle to repair the harms that two years of war do to the good governance of a state. Would any sensible and rational man bring a suit, even one firmly grounded in law, if he was convinced that such a suit (even if he were to win it) would do more harm than good to the large family for which he is responsible?

This accurate balancing of the harms and benefits of war would convince a good king always to avoid war given its disastrous consequences, because where are the benefits that can counterbalance all the inevitable harms—to say nothing of the perils of a defeat? There is only one case where war would be necessary despite its evils. It is when by avoiding it one would merely give too much control and advantage to an enemy who is unjust, deceitful, and too powerful. In that case, in seeking to avoid the war out of weakness, one would fall still more perilously; one would make a peace that would not be a peace, but would only appear to be one. In that case, it is necessary to make war vigorously albeit reluctantly, out of a sincere desire for a good and lasting peace. But this unique case is rarer than one imagines, and often one believes it real, though it is highly chimerical.

When a king is just, sincere, inviolably faithful to all his allies, and powerful in his country owing to wise government, he does well to put down the restless and unjust neighbors who want to attack him. He has the love of his people and the trust of his neighbors. Everyone is concerned to support him. If his cause is just, he has only to take all the gentlest routes before launching the war. He can, being already strongly armed, offer to believe some neutral and disinterested neighbors, to take something upon himself for the sake of peace, avoiding everything that would embitter minds, and hold open all the paths of possible accommodation. If all this comes to nothing, he can wage war with more confidence in the protection of God, with more zealous subjects, and with more assistance from his allies. But it will very rarely come about that he would be reduced to wage war under such circumstances. Three-quarters of wars are waged merely out of haughtiness, duplicity, avidity, and rashness. [993]

29.

Have you been faithful in keeping your word to your enemies in matters of surrender, ransom of prisoners, etc.? There are laws of war that must be adhered to no less religiously than the laws that govern peacetime. Even during war there is yet a certain law of peoples that is the foundation of humanity itself. This forms a sacred and inviolable bond between all men, which no war can break. Otherwise war would be merely an inhuman crime, merely a perpetual train of betrayals, assassinations, abominations, and barbarous acts. You must do to your enemies only that which you believe they have the right to do to you. There are brutalities and tricks of war that are reciprocal and that everyone expects. As for everything else, good faith and complete humanity are necessary. It is not permissible to return fraud for fraud. It is not permissible, for example, to make promises that you have no intention of keeping, just because you have been given such promises. Moreover, during a war between two nations independent of each other, the stronger or nobler king must not dispense himself from being equally subject to the common laws of war. A prince dealing with a private citizen must observe the rules of engagement just as much as his subject, and as soon as the prince engages him, he becomes his equal in this transaction alone. The most noble and powerful prince must pride himself in being the most faithful in following all the rules of restitution regarding prisoners and ransoms that protect his people from captures, massacres, arsons, etc.

30.

It is not enough to respect the capitulation treaties with regard to enemies; it is also necessary to respect them religiously with regard to conquered peoples. Just as you must keep your word to the enemy garrison as it withdraws from a taken city and not justify some sort of trickery on the basis of some ambiguous terminology, so too you must keep your word to the people of this city and the territories under its control. What does it matter to whom you have promised [994] conditions for this people? Whether the promise was made to the people or the garrison, it is all the same. What is certain is that you have promised these conditions for this people. It is up to you to respect them inviolably. Who will trust you if you fail in this? What is sacred if so solemn a promise is not? This is a contract made with these people to make them your subjects. Will you begin by violating your foundational title? They are obligated to obey you only in accord with the terms of this contract, and if you violate it, you do not deserve for them to observe it.

31.

During war have you not done unnecessary harms to your enemies? These enemies are always men, always your brothers, if you are truly human yourself. You must harm them only when you cannot avoid doing so and in order to safeguard against those harms they are preparing to do to you, and thereby bring about a just peace. Have you not invented and introduced, unnecessarily, and by passion or by pride, new kinds of hostilities? Have you not authorized ravages, arsons, sacrileges, and massacres that have settled nothing, and without which you could have still defended your cause, and despite which your enemies have equally continued their efforts against you? You must give account to God, and repair, to the entire extent of your power, all the ills that you have authorized, and that have been done needlessly.

32.

Have you executed peace treaties promptly? Have you never violated them under specious pretexts? With regard to ambiguous preexisting peace treaties, instead of drawing from them justifications for war, it is necessary to interpret them by the practice that immediately followed their establishment. This immediate practice is the infallible interpretation of their words. The parties, immediately after the treaty, were in perfect agreement; they knew better what they meant than can be known [995] fifty years later. Thus possession is decisive in this regard, and to want to disturb it is to want to elude what is most assured and most inviolable in the human race. As for treaties that one is tempted to go back on for idiosyncratic legal reasons, it is necessary to observe three things. (1) As soon as one accepts the rule of succession for States, it is necessary to subordinate the customs and laws of individual countries to the law of peoples, which is infinitely superior to them, and to the inviolable faith in the peace treaties that are the sole foundation of the security of human nature.[10] Would it be proper for the custom of a single country to stand in the way of a peace necessary for the salvation of all Europe? Just as the administration of a city must give way to the essential needs of the state as a whole, of which it is only a member, so too the jurisprudences of provinces must fade before this law of nations and the guarantee of their alliances. (2) Sovereign princes, who make these solemn treaties, make them in the name of their nations as a whole, and with the forms in use in their age, in order to give them all the supreme authority of the laws. Thus, in this regard, they depart from the particular laws of the provinces. (3) If weakening the peace treaties under an extremely specious pretext is allowed even once, even on the grounds of specific laws, legal tricks will always be found to annul all the exchanges, transfers, donations, compensations, and other pacts, on which the security and the peace of all are founded. War will become an evil without remedy. Treaties will remain valid only until an advantageous opportunity to begin the war again comes about. Peace will be only an interlude and moreover an interlude of uncertain length. All the boundaries of states will vanish into thin air. In order to give some stability to the world, and some security to nations, it is necessary to privilege above all else two points that are like the two poles of the earth. First, that every peace treaty sworn between two princes is inviolable for them, and must always be taken simply in its most natural sense, and interpreted in light of its immediate execution. Second, every peaceful and uninterrupted possession for as long a time as jurisprudence requires for the least favorable claim based on prescription, must confer a secure and legitimate ownership to the one who has that possession, whatever defect there may have been in [996] its origin. Without these two fundamental laws the human race can never enjoy any security or rest. Have you always followed them?

33.

Have you done justice to the merit of all the leading subjects whom you could employ? In not doing justice to individuals with respect to their property, such as their lands and their rents, etc., you have injured only these individuals and their families. But in disregarding virtue and talents in choosing men, you have done an irreparable injustice to your state. Those whom you have not chosen for the posts have effectively lost nothing, because these posts would have been for them merely opportunities dangerous to both their worldly repose and their salvation. But you have in fact unjustly deprived your entire realm of assistance that God had prepared for it. Men of elevated mind and upright heart are rarer than one might believe them to be. To find them it would be necessary to go to the ends of the earth: *Procul et de ultimus finibus pretium ejus*, as the wise man said of the courageous woman.[11] Why have you deprived the state of the assistance of these men who are so superior to others? Is it not your responsibility to choose the best men for the best places? Wasn't this your principal duty on this front? A king no longer does the job of a king when he attends to details to which others who govern under him might attend. His essential job is to do what nobody other than him can do, namely to choose well those who are to exercise his authority under him. This is to put each in the place suited to him, and to do everything in the state not by himself (which is impossible), but by men that he chooses, that he prompts, that he instructs, that he corrects: this is the real work of a king. Have you let go of all the rest, which others under you can do, in order to apply yourself to this essential responsibility which you alone can fulfill? Have you taken care to examine a certain number of sensible and well-intentioned men, by whom you could be informed of all the subjects of each profession who are on the rise and distinguish themselves? Have you questioned everyone separately, in order to see whether [997] their testimonies on each subject might be the same? Have you had the patience to examine by these different methods the sentiments, the inclinations, the habits, the conduct of each man you can install? Have you seen these men yourself? To dispatch details in a chamber in which one is constantly shut up is to steal one's most precious time from the state. A king must see, speak, and listen to many men, he must learn by experience how to study men, and must get to know them via frequent interactions and free access. There are two manners of knowing them. One is conversation. If you study men well, without appearing to study them, conversation will be more useful to you than many of the works that one might think important. You will note the inconstancy, the indiscretion, the vanity, the artifice of men, their flatteries, their false maxims. Princes have an infinite power over those who approach them, and those who approach them have an infinite weakness in approaching them. The sight of princes awakens all the passions, and reopens all the heart's wounds. If a prince knows how to profit from this influence, he will soon feel out the principal weaknesses of each man. The other manner of testing men is to put them in subordinate employments, in order to see if they will be suited to superior employments. Follow men in the employments that you entrust them with, never lose sight of them, search out what they do, make them give an account of what they have promised to do. This is what to speak to them about when you see them; you will never lack a subject of conversation. You will see their character by the decisions they have taken. Sometimes it is appropriate to hide your true sentiments from them in order to discover theirs. Ask them for counsel. You will take of it only what pleases you. Such is the true function of the king. Have you fulfilled it? Have you not neglected to know men by a laziness of mind, by a humor that renders you withdrawn, by a haughtiness that distances you from society, by details that are only trifles in comparison to this study of men, and finally by amusements in your chambers under pretext of secret business? Have you not feared and separated out the strong and distinguished subjects from the others? Have you not feared that they would see you up close, and would discover your weaknesses, if you were to approach them personally? Have you not feared that they would not flatter you [998], that they would speak out against your unjust passions, your bad tastes, your base and indecent motives? Have you not preferred to make use of self-interested and false men, who flatter you, who pretend never to see your faults, and who applaud all your fantasies? Or even certain mediocre and flexible men, whom you easily control, whom you hope to dazzle, who never have the courage to resist you, and who govern you all the more, as you do not defy their authority, and you do not fear that they appear of a genius superior to your own? Is it not by such corrupt motives that you have filled the principal posts with weak or depraved men, and kept far from you all the good men who could assist you in great affairs? Taking the lands and the offices and the money of others is not an injustice comparable to that which I am describing.

34.

Have you not accustomed your domestics to a lifestyle beyond their means, and to rewards that burden the state? Your *valets de chambre*, your *valets de garde-robe*, etc.,—do they not live like lords, while real lords languish in your antechamber to no avail, and others, from the most illustrious houses, are reduced to hiding their misery in the depths of the provinces?[12] Have you not authorized, under the pretext of adorning your court, a luxury in dress, furniture, equipage, and architecture in all these subordinate officers who enjoy neither high birth nor solid merit, and who believe themselves to be above men of quality because they speak with you familiarly and easily obtain favors? Are you sufficiently afraid of their importunity? Are you not more afraid of annoying them than of bringing them to justice? Have you not been too sensible to petty marks of zealousness and tender attachment to your person from those who hover around you in order to testify to their desire to please you, and to advance their fortune? Have you not rendered them unhappy by leaving them to imagine hopes disproportionate to their condition and to your affection for them? Have you not ruined their families, [999] in letting them die without sufficient recompense to their remaining children, after having let them live in a ridiculous sumptuousness that consumed the great favors they drew from you during their lives? Has this not also been the case with other courtiers each according to his degree? While they live they suck the entire kingdom dry. Whenever they die they leave their families ruined. You give them too much, and you make them spend even more. Thus those who ruin the state also ruin themselves. It is you who are the cause of this, in assembling around you so many useless, gaudy, lazy men, who claim a title from you on the basis of their most foolish dissipations in order to ask of you new gifts that they can again waste.

35.

Have you not been biased against someone without having examined the facts? To do so is to open the door to calumny and false reports, or at least to recklessly take on the prejudices of men who approach you and in whom you confide. It is not permissible for you to listen to and to believe only a certain number of men. They are merely men, and even if they might be incorruptible they are not infallible. Whatever trust you have in their wisdom and in their virtue, you are obliged to examine if they are not being deceived by others, and if they do not persist in it. Every time that you deliver yourself to a single person, or to a certain number of people bound together by common interests or common sentiments, you willingly expose yourself to being duped and to doing injustice. Have you not sometimes shut your eyes to certain powerful reasons, or at least have you not taken certain definitive courses of action when in doubt, in order to please those who surround you and whom you fear annoying? Have you not taken a course of action on uncertain advice, stripping men who have talents and distinguished merit of positions? One says to oneself: it is impossible to verify these accusations; the surest route is to strip this man of his position. But this supposed precaution is the most dangerous of all traps. [1000] Nothing is improved by it, and one gives in to everything the accusers maintain. One judges the depths without examining, as one excludes merit and one lets oneself fear everyone that the accusers want to render suspect. Men known as reporters offer themselves for this service, insinuate themselves by this awful art, and are therefore manifestly unworthy of all belief.[13] To believe one is to leave oneself willingly exposed to slitting the throats of the innocent. A prince who lends an ear to those who make their living by spreading such lies is unworthy of knowing either truth or virtue. It is necessary to drive out and unmask these vermin of the court. But as it is also necessary to be well informed, the prince must have good and honest men whom he obliges, against their nature, to watch over things, to observe, to know what happens, and to warn him in private of them. He must choose for this function men to whom such tasks are the most repugnant, and who have the greatest horror of the infamous art of reporting. These would inform him only of true and important facts; they would not tell him all the trifling details that he need take no notice of, and on which he must be answerable to the public. At least they would not give him questionable information, which insofar as it is questionable it will be up to him to examine it more deeply, or suspend his judgment if it cannot be clarified.

36.

Have you not lavished excessive benefits on your ministers, on your favorites, and on their minions, while you have allowed men of merit who have long served you and who lack protection to languish in need? Typically the great fault of princes is to be weak, feeble, and unfocused. They are almost never swayed by either the merit or the genuine faults of men. The depths of things are not what touch them. Their decisions ordinarily come from what they do not dare refuse to those whom they are in the habit of seeing and believing. Often they suffer them with impatience, and do not fail to remain subjugated. They see the faults of such men, and are content with seeing them. They are satisfied not to be their dupes, after which they follow them blindly. To them they sacrifice merit, innocence, distinguished talents, and the longest service. Sometimes they will listen favorably to a man who will dare to speak against these [1001] ministers or these favorites, and they will see the facts clearly verified; then they will grumble, and will let it be known to those who dared speak that they will have the prince's support against the minister or favorite. But soon the prince grows weary of protecting those who are attached to him alone. This protection requires him to go into too much detail, and out of fear of seeing a minister with an unhappy face, the upright man who enables him to know the truth will be abandoned to the minister's fury. After all this do you deserve to be informed? Can you hope to be? Who is the wise man who will dare to go directly to you and bypass the minister, whose jealousy is implacable? Do you not deserve to see only through his eyes? Are you not delivered to his most unjust passions, and to his most unreasonable prejudices? Do you leave yourself some remedy against so great an evil?

37.

Do you not allow yourself to be dazzled by certain vain and bold men who possess the art of making themselves valued, while you neglect and keep far from you merit that is simple, modest, timid, and hidden? A prince shows the vulgarity of his taste and the weakness of his judgment when he does not know how to discern just how superficial and full of despicable vices are these bold and artfully imposing minds. A wise and penetrating prince esteems neither scatterbrained minds nor great talkers, nor those who make their choices with a confident tone, nor the disdainful critics, nor the mockers who turn everything into a joke. He scorns those who find everything easy, who applaud all that he desires, who consult only his eyes or the tone of his voice in order to guess his thoughts and to agree with him. He shrinks well away from depending on the confidence of these men who have only exteriors without depth. On the contrary, he seeks out, he anticipates, he attracts judicious and solid persons who are free from eagerness, who distrust themselves, who fear high offices, who promise little and who try to do much, who hardly speak but always think, who speak in a skeptical manner, and who know how to disagree with others respectfully. Such subjects often languish in obscurity, while the first places are occupied by vulgar and bold men who have fooled [1002] the prince and who serve only to show how much discernment he lacks. As long as you fail to seek out unknown merit, and to hold back men who are overzealous and lack solid qualities, you will be answerable before God for all the errors that will be made by those who act under you. The art of the skillful courtier costs the state everything. The smallest and most corrupt minds are often those that best learn this disgraceful art. This art spoils all the others: the doctor neglects medicine, the prelate forgets the duties of his ministry, the military general thinks more about currying favor than defending the state; the ambassador applies himself more to negotiating for the sake of advancing his own interests in the court of his master than to negotiating for the sake of advancing his master's interests at the court to which he is sent. The art of currying favor spoils men of all professions, and suffocates genuine merit. Humble then these men, whose talent consists only of pleasing, flattering, dazzling, and insinuating themselves in order to make their fortune. If you fail here, you will fill places unworthily, and true merit will always be left behind. Your duty is to push back those who advance themselves too much, and to advance those who remain pushed back in doing their duty.

38.

Have you not piled up too many offices on the head of a single man, either to satisfy his ambition, or to spare yourself the pain of having many men to whom you would be obliged to speak? Once a man is a man of fashion he is given everything and it is hoped that he will do everything on his own. This is not because he is loved, since nothing is loved. It is not because he is trusted, since everyone's probity is distrusted. It is not because he is thought perfect, since everyone delights in criticizing everything. It's because one is lazy and undisciplined. One doesn't want to have to deal with so many people. In order to see them less, and in order not to be observed up close by so many people, a single man is made to do that which four men would struggle to do well. As a result the public suffers; projects requiring dispatch languish, and surprises and injustices are more frequent and more irremediable. This man is overwhelmed, and would be [1003] offended were he not to be. He has the time neither to think nor to dig more deeply into things, neither to make plans nor to study the men who serve him. He is swept along day by day, always attending to a flood of details. Moreover, this host of responsibilities falling on a single head, and often a very weak one at that, excludes all the better subjects who could have developed themselves and done great things. All talents stay stifled. The laziness of the prince is the true cause of this. The smallest reasons determine the greatest affairs. From this are born innumerable injustices. *Pauca de te*, said Saint Augustine to Count Boniface, *sed multa propter te*.[14] Perhaps you will do little evil yourself, but your authority put in bad hands will do infinite evils.

Supplement

States that neighbor each other are not only obligated to treat each other according to the rules of justice and good faith. They must go even further, and, for the sake of their individual security as much as for the common interest, form a sort of society and general republic.

It is necessary to count on the fact that in the long run the greatest power always prevails and overcomes the others if the others do not unite to form a counterweight. It is not permissible in human affairs to hope that a superior power will remain within the limits of an exact moderation, and that in its power it will want only what it could have obtained in a state of great weakness. Even if a prince were to be so perfect as to make so marvelous a use of his prosperity, this marvel would end with his reign. The natural ambition of sovereigns, the flatteries of their counselors, and the prejudices of whole nations, prevent us from believing that a nation that is capable of subjugating others will abstain from doing so for centuries on end. A reign that exhibited a justice so extraordinary would be the ornament of history, and a prodigy that would never be seen again. It is thus necessary to count on what is real and what is familiar from everyday life, namely that every nation seeks to prevail over all those that surround it. Every nation is thus obligated for the sake of its own security to keep incessant watch in order to prevent the excessive aggrandizement of [1004] all its neighbors. Preventing a neighbor from becoming too strong is not an evil; it is to safeguard oneself and one's other neighbors from servitude—in a word, it is to work for liberty, for tranquility, for the public salvation, insofar as the aggrandizement of one nation beyond a certain limit changes the general system of all the nations that have relations with it. For example, all the changes in succession that occurred in the house of Burgundy, then those which raised the house of Austria, changed the face of all Europe. All Europe came to fear universal monarchy under Charles V, above all after Francis I had been defeated and taken at Pavia.[15] It is certain that a nation which had never been mixed up directly with Spain, would yet be left the right, for the sake of public liberty, of preventing this rapid growth in power that seemed ready to swallow up everything.

Individuals have no right to oppose the growth of their neighbors' wealth simply because they suppose that this growth of another could be their ruin. There are written laws and magistrates to punish injustices and assaults between families unequal in property; but the case is not the same with states. Too great a growth of a single state can be the ruin and the servitude of all those that neighbor it: there are neither written laws, nor established judges, that can serve as a barrier against the invasions of the strongest. One is always right to suppose that the strongest, in the long run, will take advantage of its strength when there is no other near equal that could stop it. Therefore, every prince has both the right and the duty to prevent in his neighbor an increase of power that would cast his people, and all other neighboring peoples, into imminent danger of servitude without recourse.

For example, after he had conquered Portugal, Phillip II, King of Spain, wanted to make himself the master of England.[16] I know well that his right was unfounded, because he had it only by Queen Mary, his wife, who died childless. Elizabeth, illegitimate, could not reign. The crown belonged to Mary Stuart and her son. But in the end, supposing that the right of Philip II had been incontestable, all Europe nevertheless would have had reason to oppose his establishment in England, because this so powerful realm, annexed to Spain, Italy, Flanders, the [1005] east and west Indies, would put him in a state of making the law, above all by his naval forces, for all the other powers of Christendom. So: *Summum jus, summa injuria.*[17] A particular right of succession or donation should have given way to the natural law of the security of all nations. In a word, everything that reverses the balance and gives the decisive blow for universal monarchy cannot be just, even when it might be founded on written laws in a particular country. The reason for this is that these written laws of a people cannot prevail over the natural laws of liberty and common security that are etched in the hearts of all peoples of the world. When a power rises to a point that all the other neighboring powers together can resist it no longer, all the others have the right to join forces to prevent this growth, after which there would be no time left to defend the common liberty. But, in order legitimately to make these sorts of leagues designed to prevent the too great growth of a state, it is necessary that the case be true and pressing: it is necessary to limit it to a defensive league, or at least not make it offensive, in such a way that the just and necessary defense will find itself trapped in the designs of an aggression; even still it is always necessary, in the treaties of offensive leagues, to establish precise limits, in order never to destroy a power under the pretext of restraining it.

This attention to maintaining a sort of equality and balance between neighboring nations is what assures them a common tranquility. In this regard, all neighboring nations connected by commerce form a great body and a sort of community. For example, Christendom forms a sort of general republic, which has its interests, its fears, and its precautions to observe. All the members composing this great body are duty-bound to each other for the common good, and are duty-bound to themselves as well for the security of the fatherland, to prevent all progress of any member who would overturn the balance and who would turn themselves to the inevitable ruin of all the other members of the same body. Everything that changes or alters this general system of Europe is too dangerous, and brings countless evils in its wake.

All neighboring nations are so bound by their interests to each other and to the greater part of Europe that the [1006] least progress of individual nations could alter this general system of equilibrium that can alone establish public security. Take away a stone from an arch and the entire building falls, because all the stones support themselves in pushing back against each other.

Humanity thus imposes a mutual duty of defense of common preservation, between neighboring nations, against a neighboring state that becomes too powerful, just as there are mutual duties between fellow citizens for the liberty of the fatherland. If the citizen owes much to his fatherland, of which he is a member, it is all the more true that each nation owes even more to the tranquility and to the preservation of the universal republic of which it is a member, and in which are contained all the fatherlands of individuals.

Defensive leagues are thus just and necessary when it is truly a matter of preventing too great a power that would be in a position to invade everyone. This superior strength does not therefore have the right to break the peace with other inferior states, precisely owing to their defensive league; because they have both the right and obligation to make such a league.

As for an offensive league, it depends on the circumstances. It is necessary that it be founded on infractions of the peace, or on the occupation of some land of the allies, or on the certainty of some other similar foundation. Even still it is always necessary, as I have already said, to limit such treaties to conditions that prevent what one often sees: namely a nation making use of the necessity of engaging another that aspires to universal tyranny in order to aspire to such itself in its own right. Skill in making treaties of alliance, as well as justice and good faith, consists in making them very specific, very far from all equivocation, and precisely limited to the particular benefit that you want to draw directly from them. If you do not take care in this respect, the commitments you take on will turn against you, lowering your enemies too much and elevating your allies too much. It would be necessary for you either to suffer what will destroy you or to fail to keep your word—things almost equally catastrophic.

Let us continue to examine these principles, taking the particular example of Christendom, which is the most proximate to us.

There are only four kinds of systems. The first is to be absolutely superior to all other powers, [1007] even united together: this is the state of the Romans and of Charlemagne. The second is to be the power superior to others within Christendom, which nevertheless serve more or less as a counterweight in uniting together. The third is to be a power inferior to another, but which supports itself, by its union with all its neighbors, against this predominant power. Finally, the fourth is a power more or less equal to another, which preserves peace by this species of balance that it safeguards without ambition and in good faith.

The state of the Romans and of Charlemagne is not a state that it would be permissible for you to desire: (1) because, in order to achieve it, you have to commit all sorts of injustice and assaults and take what does not belong to you, and to do so via wars abominable in their length and scope. (2) This goal is very dangerous: often states fall by this mad ambition. (3) These immense empires, which have done so many harms in forming themselves, create new ones, still more appalling, soon after collapsing to earth. The first minority, or the first weak reign, makes the overgrown masses shudder, and separates peoples accustomed neither to the yoke nor to mutual union. What divisions, what confusions, what irremediable anarchies follow! One need only remember the evils that the rapid fall of Charlemagne's empire caused in the West, and, in the East, the reversal of Alexander's, whose captains caused even more harms in dividing his spoils than he had himself made in ravaging Asia.[18] This is then the most dazzling, the most flattering, and the most disastrous system for those who manage to execute it.

The second system is that of a superior strength to all the others, which, against it, form something like a balance. This superior strength has the advantage over the others of being wholly unified, wholly simple, wholly absolute in its ordering, wholly certain in its measures. But, in the long run, if it never stops uniting all the others against it in exciting jealousy, it necessarily succumbs. It exhausts itself and is exposed to many internal and unforeseen accidents, or attacks from outside can suddenly topple it. Moreover, it wears itself out for nothing, and makes ruinous efforts for the sake of a superiority that gives it nothing useful, and exposes it to all sorts of dishonor and dangers. Of [1008] all states it is certainly the worst; all the more because it cannot avoid, in all its astonishing prosperity, turning into the first system, which we have already seen to be unjust and pernicious.

The third system is that of a power inferior to another, but in such a way that the inferior, united to the rest of Europe, forms a balance against the superior power and ensures the safety of all the other lesser states. This system has its impracticalities and inconveniences; but it risks less than the previous one, because one is on the defensive, one exhausts oneself less, one has allies, and one is not ordinarily, in this state of inferiority, in the condition of blindness and senseless presumption that threatens with ruin those who prevail. One almost always sees that with a little time, those who had prevailed begin to wear down and degenerate. As long as this inferior state is wise, moderate, strong in its alliances, careful not to give them any offense, and does nothing that in their opinion is not in the common interest, it holds this superior power until it drops.

The fourth system is of a power more or less equal to another, with which it forms a balance for the sake of public security. To be in this state, and not to want to leave it out of ambition, is to be most wise and happy. You are the common arbiter, all your neighbors are your friends—or at least those who do not render themselves suspect to others by their actions. You do nothing that does not seem to be done for your neighbors as much as for your people. You fortify yourself always, and if, as is almost guaranteed in the long run, you succeed by dint of wise government to have more domestic forces and more foreign alliances than the power that is jealous of you, then it is necessary to assert yourself more and more in this wise moderation that limits you to preserving the balance and the common security. It is always necessary to remember the evils that great conquests cost the state both within and without; that they are fruitless; that they are risky to undertake; finally, the vanity, futility, the short duration of grand empires, and the ravages they cause in falling.

But, as it is not permitted to hope that a power superior to all others will long persist without abusing this superiority, a genuinely wise and [1009] just prince must never wish to leave to his successors—who will be, in all likelihood, less moderate than he—this continual and violent temptation to an open superiority. For the good of his successors and his people as well, he must limit himself to a sort of equality. It is true that there are two sorts of superiorities: one outer, which consists in extent of lands, fortified places, passages for entry into the lands of his neighbors, etc. This serves only to cause temptations as fateful to oneself as to one's neighbors, and to excite hatred, jealousy, and leagues. The other is inner and solid; it consists in a people more numerous, better disciplined, more applied to the cultivation of the earth and the necessary arts. This superiority is typically easy to acquire, reliable, a shelter from envy and leagues, and more likely than even conquests and fortresses to make a people invincible. One could not go too far in seeking this second superiority, or in avoiding the first, which has only a false luster.

7

Political Memoranda

1. Memorandum on the Deplorable Situation in France [Pl. 2:1034–1044]

I do not know well enough the full extent of general affairs to meddle in judging the dangers and resources of France, nor, as a result, do I know how far one should go in order to establish peace.

Perhaps the change in the ministry will relieve our troubles.[1] Perhaps the renewal of coinage will eliminate cash notes, and will reestablish credit.[2] Perhaps an abundant harvest will come, after this barrenness, making it easier for us to feed our troops. Perhaps a general of the army will reestablish military discipline, and by some victory will humble the pride of our enemies.

In order to determine the proper course of action, it would be necessary to make a general examination encompassing all the different parts of the government; all the wealth of the realm; all the debts of the King; the causes of the plunge in credit; the sources of commerce; the state of the crown's revenues; the number of unnecessary people working in the field and at trades that cannot be allowed to go on; the approach to military recruiting; the condition of the officers who have not been paid; that of the shopkeepers whom they have impressed as their troops; the degree of exhaustion of each province and the state of mind of those who live there; the state of all points on our borders, as much for fortifications as for the munitions necessary in case of attack; the state of our navy and our coasts exposed to invasion; the interests, the resources, and the dispositions of every foreign court; and finally the true power of the armies [1035] of our enemies, the actual state of mind of their generals, and the plans formed in their councils.

As each of our ministers deals directly with the King on matters concerning his office, I fear that none of them may be in a position to collect, in an accurate and comprehensive view, all these different parts of government in order to compare them, to judge their proportionality, and to fit them together.

Fénelon. Ryan Patrick Hanley, Oxford University Press (2020) © Oxford University Press.
DOI: 10.1093/oso/9780190079581.001.0001

When one builds a house, even if the masons and carpenters and plumbers and joiners and locksmiths, etc., all do excellent work in their respective arts, the work as a whole will go poorly if there is not a leading man who directs everything to the same end, and who has in his head all the works of all these different workers in order to render them proportionate to each other, and in order to make of them an orderly whole. So too we need a man well instructed in the whole of our affairs, who makes an exact comparison of our troubles and our resources, both those of our enemies and our own. Without this knowledge of the whole, each gropes along blindly.

As for me, were I to take the liberty of judging the state of France by the little bits of the government that I can glimpse on this frontier, I would conclude that we are still alive only by a miracle, that this is a crumbling old machine that is still moving forward only because of the impetus given it in the past, and that will end up falling apart at the first shock. I would be tempted to believe that our greatest evil is that nobody sees the depths of our condition; that a sort of resolution of not wanting to see it has been taken; that no one dares to acknowledge that we are at the limits of our strength; that all are reduced to closing their eyes and to opening their hands, always grasping without knowing whether they will find anything to grasp; that only a miracle today will supply that which will be necessary tomorrow; and that nobody will want to see the full extent of our ills in order to undertake a sufficient remedy for them, until it will be too late.

This is what I see, and what I intend to speak of every day to the wisest and best-instructed people.

Soldiers are unable to get emergency loans. They are often unable even to get bread for days on end, and when they do it is almost nothing but oats, poorly cooked, and full of filth. These poorly fed soldiers fight poorly, it seems. They can be heard grumbling, and saying things that are alarming for combat. [1036]

The subordinate officers suffer proportionally even more than the soldiers. The majority, after having exhausted their family's credit, eat and drink the bad bread and water of ordinary rations. Many of them lack the means to return to their provinces. Many others languish in Paris, where they ask in vain for assistance from the minister of war. Still others are in the army in a state of discouragement and despair that frightens everyone.

The general of our army does not know how to prevent the disorder of the troops. Can soldiers be punished who have been made to die of hunger, and who pillage only to avoid collapsing altogether? Would it be desirable for them to be unable to fight at all? On the other hand, by not punishing them, what evils must we not expect? They will ravage the entire countryside. The people fear the troops who must defend them as much as those of the enemies who want to attack them. The army can only move with difficulty, because it ordinarily has bread only for a day. It is even compelled to incline toward the side by which it alone can receive subsistence, namely that of Hainaut.[3] It lives only on grain that comes to it from the Dutch.

Our fortresses, which we thought were the strongest, are far from finished. The examples of Menen and Tournai have shown that the King has been betrayed there by the masonry, which was worthless.[4] Each fortress even lacks munitions. If we were to lose another battle, these fortresses would fall like a house of cards.

The people no longer live like men, and it is no longer possible to count on their patience, given how excessively it has been tested. Those who have lost their wheat crops have no other resource. Others slightly behind them are on the verge of losing them. As they have nothing left to hope, they have nothing left to fear.

The funds of all the towns are exhausted. Ten years of advance revenues have been taken from them for the King, and new advances are shamelessly and threateningly demanded that would double those already made. All the hospitals are overwhelmed. The townspeople for whom these institutions were founded are driven out, and instead they are filled with soldiers. These hospitals are owed very great sums, and instead of being paid, their debts are piled up higher and higher every day. [1037]

The French who are prisoners in Holland die of hunger there for want of any payment on the part of the King. Those who have returned to France on leave dare not return to Holland even though honor obliges them to do so, as they neither have enough to make the trip, nor enough to pay what they owe in the enemy's lands.

Our injured lack food, clothing, and medicine. They do not even find refuge because they are sent to hospitals that are overwhelmed by advances for the King, and all full of sick soldiers. Who would want to expose themselves to injury in combat, unsure whether they will be either healed or helped? The soldiers are heard to say in their despair that if the enemies come, they will lay down their arms. By this you can judge what is likely to come of a battle that would decide the fate of France.

The entire countryside is overwhelmed by the demand for wagons for military transport. All the horses of the peasants are being killed. This serves only to spoil the plowing for the coming years, and to leave no hopes of survival to either the people or the troops. By this you can judge how much French domination grows hateful to the entire country.

The intendants, despite themselves, do almost as much damage as the marauders. They seize even the public storehouses. In public they deplore the shameful necessity that reduces them to this. They admit that they would not know how to keep the promises they are compelled to make. It is no longer possible to serve without swindling all sides. It is a life for Bohemians, not men who govern. The nation seems to be universally bankrupt. Notwithstanding the violence and fraud, one is often constrained to abandon certain very necessary works, as soon as it is necessary to make an advance of two hundred pistoles in order to use them for a more pressing need.

The nation is falling into disgrace. It is becoming the object of public derision. Our enemies openly proclaim that the government of Spain, which we so derided, never fell as low as ours. Our people, our soldiers, and our officers no longer have either affection, or esteem, or confidence, or hope of rising again, or respect for authority. Each seeks only to elude the rules, and to await the end of the war, whatever it might cost.

If a battle in Dauphiné were lost, the Duke of [1038] Savoy would come into the country with masses of Huguenots. He would be able to stir up several of the kingdom's provinces. If a battle in Flanders were lost, the enemy would penetrate right up to the gates of Paris. What recourse would remain to you? I have no idea, but God wills that someone might know!

If one can make cash flow, feed the troops, relieve the officers, reestablish the discipline and reputation that have been lost, suppress the audacity of the enemies by a vigorous war, it cannot be done too soon. In this case, it would be shameful and horrible to seek peace eagerly. In this case, nothing would be more inappropriate than to have sent a minister to Holland to obtain it. In this case, you need only to discipline well and to pay well the troops and to beat the enemies. Would that so necessary a change might be made as soon as possible, and that those who say that too much has been conceded for the sake of peace come as soon as possible to relieve the war and the finances. Yet they stay quiet, and persist in wanting to risk losing France for Spain.

In response it will surely be said that it is easy to note the inconveniences of war, and that I should limit myself to proposing expedients for its support, in order to achieve a peace that would be respectable and fitting for the King.

I respond that it is no longer a matter of comparing the propositions of peace to the inconveniences of war. If it is found through this careful comparison that no sure success in war can be promised, and that engaging in such puts France at risk, there is nothing left to deliberate. The sole glory that all good French can wish for the King is that in this extremity he turns his courage against himself, and that he generously sacrifices everything in order to save the realm that God has conferred on him. Since he has received it from God, he does not even have the right to risk it, or expose it to the invasion of the enemies, like a thing with which he can do whatever he wants, but is to govern it as a father, and transmit it as a precious gift to his posterity.

Beyond the invasion of our enemies, which is much to be feared were we to lose a battle, it must be foreseen that the enemies may next winter ask us for some new bases for the expenses of this campaign. I would not at all be astonished to see them ask, beyond [1039] their preliminaries, for Valenciennes, Bouchain, Douai, and even Cambrai.[5] They would have several pretexts for so doing. (1) In taking Tournai, they took only that which was already offered to them.[6] The costs of this siege are infinite. (2) They will say that in thus increasing their demands, they would compel you to conclude the war, whereas if you were assured of making peace on a clear fixed condition, you would slow it down as much as possible, and you would risk battles, reckoning that in losing them you would risk nothing. (3) They will say that this is to fortify their Barrier against your enterprises. (4) They will claim that these places will serve as hostages in order to assure your good faith with regard to the giving up of Spain, because you will break your promises less brazenly when your country will be open as far as the Somme.[7]

From this I conclude that if you cannot reasonably hope either to exhaust our enemies before being exhausted yourself, or to divide them against themselves, or to conquer them, you cannot possibly today refuse conditions, however harsh and shameful, to which you will be compelled to submit in six months or a year, after having, so to speak, worn France out altogether, and after you are exposed to total ruin—to say nothing of the even harsher conditions that our enemies might add when you will come back to them in the last resort. It seems that wisdom and courage lie in foreseeing a prospect so near, and in complying as soon as possible.

The Dutch negotiation does not seem to have been carried out very well. (1) Things should have been prepared before sending M. de Torcy. A man more agreeable than M. Rouillé should have first been sent into this country.[8] A man who inspires confidence was needed there. We needed from him precise knowledge of the specific difficulty that prevented bringing matters to a conclusion, we needed to choose sure means to alleviate this difficulty, and we needed to let the minister leave only with powers and instructions that would guarantee that he would return only with a signed peace. (2) When the enemies seemed to M. de Torcy to insinuate to him that they wished the King might take up arms in order to dethrone his grandson, he should have asked for a clear and decisive explanation on this point, he should have declared that he would not dare to propose such a thing to the King, he should have been summoned in secret and should have awaited in Holland the return of the courier by whom he would have informed [1040] the King what this proposition amounted to. In waiting he should have availed himself of all well-meaning republicans in order to make all the deputies of the provinces and the people themselves understand how unjust and hateful it was to demand this condition, and to disturb the peace on such an article. Finally it was necessary for him to make use of the expectation that a response from France would be sent a little slowly, in order to find expedients that could have assured the abandonment of Spain without this odious condition. It seems to me that the negotiation was abruptly concluded at the very point where it was yet to begin, and where it was crucial to capitalize.

The enemies complain bitterly that M. de Torcy failed to explain to them his difficulties on this article, that he did not in good faith seek out with them sufficient assurances for this abandonment, without resorting to so harsh a means, that the difficulties of this minister have turned on Savoy and on Alsace, and not on this article 37.[9] The enemies even go so far as to maintain that they have never insisted on this article, and that they only wish that the minister of France might seek out assurances with them, in order to prevent us from indirectly assisting the King of Spain at the expense of the peace treaty, as we assisted Portugal against the promise made in the treaty of the Pyrenees. They say the French have not even dared to say that this harsh condition had been required by the allies, and that we say only that it is "insinuated" in the preliminaries. One does not break off, they add, on an alleged insinuation of a harsh article. It was necessary to explain it, to seek out expedients, and to see the extent to which the allies would be reduced. But making the King take up arms against his grandson was never spoken of.

Our enemies say, the clear intention of France has been to play with us just as she always does. She wanted to appear to abandon Spain to us, without really abandoning anything. She wanted only to move the war in Flanders, where she is in desperate straits, and where the center of her realm is at the brink of being exposed, to another far-distant country, reachable for us only by sea, with infinite expense and disadvantages. It is on this point that we have taken care not to be deceived. What marks the bad faith of France is that she broke off the negotiation entirely as soon as she saw that we would not wish to let ourselves [1041] be fooled on this essential point, which is the sole aim of the entire war. Instead of sincerely seeking means of establishing security, M. de Torcy, who came to us to request peace with so much eagerness, dreamt only of hastily breaking it off.

The enemies also speak thusly: France, which would like to withdraw its troops from Spain, has not dared to do it, seeing well that the Spanish, as soon as they were left to themselves, would not fail to prefer the preservation of their monarchy intact under Charles to the inevitable dismemberment of this monarchy under Philip, for which they would even be obliged to support a long and ruinous war. Since one does not dare leave the Spanish to themselves, it is apparent that a genuine abandonment of Philip, made in good faith by France, would soon compel the entire Spanish nation to recognize Charles. It is thus apparent that France does not sincerely want to recall Philip, and that she wants to withdraw entirely from the present difficulty by an imaginary consent to his return without wanting to take any effective means of procuring it.

It seems that neutral parties always suspect some finesse in this process by France, which is already only too much accused of artifice throughout all of Europe.

The King of Spain could be made to understand that our own sovereign King would ultimately be obliged to remove him, sooner than leave him in a miserable state exposed to being made prisoner of his enemies. The King could say to him: "I will never wage war against you. But also I will never assist you against my word. If you find yourself in imminent danger of succumbing, the only effort I could make for you will be to bring you down, in order to save you from a captivity shameful for you and for me." This discourse would strip the young King of all hope of relief, and would make him feel the absolute necessity of sacrificing himself for the sake of peace. Thus the use to which I would like to limit this expedient.

The most effective expedient, unless I am mistaken, would be to send to Spain a man who is wise, beloved, of known virtue, of an intimate confidence, who was a talented speaker, and who would speak not only to the King and to the Queen, but also to all the Councils and to all the nobility of Spain. He could say to them: "The King my master [1042] thanks you, and praises to the skies the generosity with which you have so constantly supported his grandson on the throne, against your own manifest interests. He entrusted this prince to you only because you have asked it of him in order to preserve in his hands your monarchy whole and intact. One can no longer hope for this advantage, for which alone you have asked this prince. The more the King my master is touched by everything that you have done him, the less he wants to allow his grandson to be the cause of the degradation and of the dismemberment of your monarchy. No longer able to support it, he believes you should hand it over entire. It is to him that you conferred this deposit. It is he who returns it to you. He only does so as a last resort, after having exhausted his realm, and risked France itself for Spain. In giving you back your monarchy, he asks you once again for his grandson, who must not any longer be the cause of your suffering, of trouble for all of Europe, and of extreme risk for an exhausted France."

In the event that the King of Spain could not reconcile himself to descend from the throne in order to save France, this discourse would serve to open the eyes of the entire Spanish nation, and put it in complete freedom to follow its true interests. This declaration by France would relieve the Spanish of all fear of a change. Then they would do only that which the King would counsel them to do out of a sincere affection. Then the King of Spain could no longer make this nation hope for any secret and indirect assistance from France. This course would be the noblest one that the King could take amid the present difficulties.

It will be said to me in response that in this case the King would dethrone his grandson with his own hands. But I respond that it would be less sad and less disgraceful for him to dethrone him himself, than to see him dethroned by his enemies before his eyes. If the King of Spain can be supported without ruining France, it is undoubtedly necessary to do so with vigor. But if he cannot be, true courage lies in facing up to doing nobly and without compunction the only thing that remains for him to do in order to save France.

As far as peace negotiations go, I would like to see us be prepared for them, to know with certainty to what precise ends they might work, and to settle on the necessary means to relieve this difficulty. I would like to see that the good republicans of Holland who might desire it be addressed. I [1043] would like to see them negotiated publicly. Secrecy is impossible. It is necessary to count on the fact that Spain will always know all the offers that we have made to abandon it. We can only hope to succeed in a negotiation in spite of the party who crosses it by making our offers and our true interest known to the entire body of the Dutch nation, which is weary of so a long war and which must not desire our ruin. I would like to see all suspicions of finesse removed, and above all that this negotiation might be trusted to a man of a high reputation for uprightness and probity, the choice of whom would signal that we wish to proceed in good faith. As long as the return of the King of Spain could be assured, peace negotiations would proceed quickly. You will become strong in the course of what follows, in spite of the most disadvantageous peace, provided that you break up the league, that you win the confidence of a part of your neighbors, that you work to reestablish it inside the realm, and that you facilitate in peacetime the multiplication of families, the cultivation of the earth, and commerce. The most solid glory of the King lies in paying certain especially pressing debts, remedying innumerable harms that war has introduced, and showing kindness to his people. He can still become the common arbiter and mediator of Europe, as long as our neighbors are carefully handled in peacetime.

As far as the expedients related to the conditions of peace go, some are so dangerous that they need to be decisively rejected.

That of giving the enemies a passage through the middle of France suits neither them nor us. If in order to go to Spain their troops were to pass through France—which is exhausted, and has several provinces full of Huguenots—we would have to fear an invasion. Moreover our enemies, traversing France in an armed body, would ravage everything. It would be better to die than to accept this condition. If on the contrary they were to divide themselves into multiple small bodies and cross France by different routes, they would need to fear that their troops might be overcome in the course of so long a march by peoples reduced to desperation, and that the King might slaughter their troops were he as untrustworthy as they imagine him to be.

It was rumored that the enemies wanted to [1044] request places of safety. But what places could they desire beyond the frontier places that open onto the realm, and which have been offered to them? Moreover the coastal places, which, like La Rochelle, could only be used as storehouses in their sea voyages to Spain, would serve only to multiply the difficulties and the expense of loading and unloading for the sake of a subpar route. They could only desire this storehouse, which is useless to them against Spain, for the sake of an end that is secret and pernicious to France. The places that they would demand beyond Spain, such as Bayonne or Collioure, would not be any more useful to them, since they would have more difficulty unloading in these places, than of unloading immediately at Barcelona, or in the other ports of the two seas, which they control.

We could give them hostages. But as it would be necessary not to expose the persons who would serve this function to any danger, it would be of chief import to express in formal terms that the King would not surrender respon-sibility for all the soldiers or French officers who, being discharged from the service after the peace, would pass furtively into Spain in order there to seek work and bread. The King could only commit himself to withdrawing all his troops from this realm, to not sending money there, to recommending his grandson to the Spanish nation with the most effective entreaties, and to punishing very rigorously all the French who, under some sort of specious pretext, would try to pass into Spain in spite of His Majesty's defenses.

As a last resort, one could also, after having exhausted all other possibili-ties, agree to put the cities of Valenciennes, Douai, Bouchain, and Cambrai in receivership for five or six years, in the hands of the Swiss Catholic Cantons, so that these cantons could open this gate of France to our enemies, if we were to fail to keep our word, and on the condition that they would faith-fully return them to us at the end of the time period if we were to observe our treaty in good faith.

2. Plans of Government (*Tables de Chaulnes*) [Pl. 2:1085–1105]

Project for the Present [1085]

Peace to be made
{
must be purchased at whatever cost. Arras and Cambrai very dear to France

If by very great misfortune peace was impossible at any other price it would be necessary to sacrifice these places

If it is not achieved, diligence in order to have ready by the end of March
{
fodder

grain

transport

river position against the enemies

+ Castille[10]
}
}

War to be supported

- **choice of a general**
  - who has esteem and confidence
  - who knows how to make an excellent defense
- **none of the new Marshals of France. They would be**
  - neither more cunning
  - nor more authorized
    - humiliation for the good lieutenants general

choice of a modest number of good lieutenants general joined to the general [1086]

- **presence of the person of M. le D.[11] pernicious without**
  - an able and zealous general
  - closely united second general
  - well-chosen lieutenants general
  - authority to make immediate decisions
  - firmness of a man of 50 years
- **avoid battle**
  - in covering our places
  - even allowing to take small ones
- **in the last resort fighting at risk of being**
  - beaten
  - taken
  - killed with glory
- **generals**
  - Villeroi   hard-working with command and dignity
  - Villars   fierce and little loved, because he scorns, etc.
  - Harcourt   sickly, little experience, good mind
  - Berwick   organized, vigilant, timid in counsel, curt, firm, and a good man

War to be supported (*cont.*)

- **generals (*cont.*)**
  - Bezons — irresolute and limited, but a sensible and upright man
  - Montesquiou[12]

- **general officers**
  - not to engage all the courtiers to continue in service
    - revulsion
    - lack of application
    - bad example
  - good treatment of well-reputed older officers
  - regular council of war. General officers, many very mediocre
    - good to listen to
    - not always to believe

- **council of war at court** — composed
  - of marshals of France and other experienced men [1087]
  - who might know what a secretary of state cannot know
  - who speak freely on inconveniences and abuses
  - who form battle plans in concert with the general charged with executing them
  - who give their opinions during the campaign

War to be supported (*cont.*) { council of war at court (*cont.*) { composed (*cont.*) { who yet do not prevent the general from deciding without awaiting their opinion, because it is crucial to profit from moments.

Plan of Reform after the Peace

Military corps {

reduced to 150,000 men {
- never general war against Europe
- no entanglements with the English
- easiness of peace with the Dutch
- one could easily have one against the other
- easy alliance with half of the Empire

few bases {
- no general war
- works and garrisons go to ruin
- many places fall { as soon as money is lacking / as soon as a civil war comes
- military superiority, which is easy, does everything

modest number of regiments {
- but large and well disciplined
- without any corruption on any account
- never given to young men lacking experience
- with many mature officers

Military corps (*cont.*)
- limited number of regiments (*cont.*)
  - good treatment of soldiers
    - regarding pay
    - regarding supplies (elite group)
    - regarding hospitals [1088]
  - good appointments
    - to colonels
    - to captains
  - seniority of an officer counts for nothing, if it is unsupported
  - care not to allow those evidently without talent to stay in the service
  - to advance men of distinguished talent
  - enlistment very open, with guarantee of leave after five years
  - never any amnesty
  - instead of the *Hôtel des Invalides*,[13] small pensions to each disabled veteran in his village
- project of reform. Listen to
  - MM. the marshals
    - de Harcourt
    - de Tallard
  - M. de Puységur[14]
- fortifications
  - by the soldiers
  - by the neighboring peasants
  - limited to medium-sized garrisons[15]

Regulation of expenditures at court
- Elimination of all nonessential court pensions
- moderation in
  - furnishings
  - equipage
  - dress
  - tables
  - Exclusion of all unnecessary women

Regulation of expenditures at court (*cont.*) {
- Sumptuary laws like the Romans
- cessation of buildings and gardens
- Diminution of almost all appointments
- end of all redundancies { make each stay in his post
- Exact calculation of the funds for the house of the king
- no augmentation under any pretext.

Reduction of all work for the king. Let the arts flourish {
- by means of wealthy individuals
- by means of foreigners

Exact calculation of all the appointments {
- of governors, lieutenants general, etc.
- of chief military staff, etc.
- of unavoidable pensions
- of wages of offices { of the parlements, etc [1089] and other courts, etc.

Exact calculation of all the debts of the King {
- Distinguishing those which carry interest from those which must not
- reckoning with each *rentier*[16] {
  - with reduction for wear and tear { significant and evident
  - with remission of many others
  - with general reduction to 30 *denier*
  - with exception of certain privileged cases.
- clearing each account, if possible
- finishing by a rough assessment, if one cannot see clearly

Calculation of the total {
- of the funds necessary for the household of the King and court
- of all appointments, wages, and necessary pensions
- of the interest coming in on all debts
- of the subsistence of the entire military corps

Comparison {
precise of this total expense

with the total of the revenues that can be drawn in allowing to be reestablished {
Agriculture

useful arts

commerce
}
}

Establishment of *assiette*[17] {
which is a small meeting of each diocese, as in Languedoc

which includes the bishop with the lords of the country and the third estate

which regulates the raising of taxes in accordance with the land register, etc.

which is subordinate to the *états de la province*[18]
}

Establishment of local *états* {
in all the provinces as in Languedoc {
not less submissive than elsewhere

less feeble
}

composed of deputies from the three estates of each diocese

with power of {
administering, correcting, distributing funds, etc.

hearing the reports of the deputies of the tax boards

calculating the taxes on {
the natural riches of the country

of the commerce that flourishes there
}
}
}

Cessation {
of salt tax[19]

great farms[20]

capitation[21]

and royal tithe[22] {
sufficiency of the sums that the *états* would raise in order to pay their part of the sum total of the expenses of the state. [1090]

order of the *états* always easier to bear than that {
of the *fermiers* of the king[23]

or *traitants*[24]
}
}
}

Cessation (*cont.*) — without the inconvenience
- of perpetuating ruinous taxes
- of rendering them arbitrary

→ no more financiers

For example taxes by the *états du pays* on salt, without *gabelle*

Establishment of Estates General[25]

utility

- *Etats* of the whole realm will be peaceful and connected like those of
  - Languedoc
  - Britanny
  - Burgundy
  - Provence
  - Artois, etc.

  ordered and uniform conduct, as long as the king does not alter it

- Deputies interested
  - by their property
  - by their hopes

  → to please the king

- Deputies
  - interested to spare their own country, where their property resides
  - instead of the financiers having an interest in destroying in order to enrich themselves

- Deputies seeing up close
  - the condition of the land
  - the commerce

  → of their province

composition

- of the Bishop of each diocese
- of a Lord of ancient and high nobility → elected by the nobles

Establishment of Estates General (*cont.*)
- **composition (*cont.*)**
  - of a considerable man of the third estate
    - elected by the third estate
  - Free election
    - no recommendation of the King, who would call it to order
    - no perpetual deputy, but capable of being continued
  - no deputy will receive promotion from the king, until 3 years after his post ends

Superiority of the Estates General over the *états de provinces*
- correction of things done by the *états de province*, on complaints and evidence [1091]
- general revision of the accounts of the local *états* for funds and ordinary expenses
- deliberation over the funds to raise with regard to extraordinary charges
- Undertakings
  - of war against neighbors
  - of navigation for commerce
  - of correction of emerging abuses

Authority of the *états*
- to gather together every 3 years at some fixed town, unless the king proposes some other
- to continue deliberations for as long as they might judge necessary
- to extend their deliberation over all matters[26]
  - of justice
  - of police
  - of finance
  - of war

Authority of the *états* (*cont.*)

to extend their deliberation over all matters (*cont.*)
- of alliances and peace negotiations
- of agriculture
- of commerce

in order to examine the population count
- made in each *assiette*
- reviewed by the local *états*
- and reported to the Estates General
- with the inventory of each family
  - which ruins itself by its own fault
  - which grows by its work
  - which has so much, and which owes so much

in order to punish abusive lords

in order to leave no land uncultivated
- large parks[27]
- large hunting grounds[28]
- abuse of the *capitaineries*[29]

in order to abolish
- all privileges
- all letters of state[30]
- all trading of currency without merchandise, necessary bankers excepted [1092]

Church

Temporal power

Definition. Coercive authority in order to enable men to live in society with
- subordination
- justice
- and uprightness of morals

Examples. thus lived the Greeks, the Romans

temporal authority complete in these examples, without any authority over religion

Spiritual power {

Definition. Noncoercive authority in order to {
- teach the faith
- administer the sacraments
- enable practice of the evangelical virtues
} { by persuasion / for eternal salvation }

Example of the ancient Church up to Constantine

Example of the Protestant Church in France[31] {
- It made pastors
- It assembled the faithful[32]
- It administered, preached, judged, corrected, excommunicated
- It did all this without temporal authority
}

example of the Catholic Church { in Holland / in Turkey }

church permitted and authorized in a country must be even more free in its functions there

our Kings left the Protestants in France free { to elect / to depose } { their pastors / commissioners to the Synods }

The Sultan left the Christians free { to elect / to depose } { their pastors }

putting the Church in France in the same state, one would have the freedom [1093] that one does not have {
- to elect
- to depose
- to assemble
}

protection of the prince must { support, facilitate, etc / not interfere, and subjugate }

The temporal comes from the community of men, which is called the nation

The spiritual comes from God, by the mission of his Son and the apostles

The temporal is in one sense older. It freely received the spiritual

The spiritual is in another sense older. The worship of the Creator before the institution of human laws

Reciprocal independence of the 2 powers

princes can do nothing with regard to the pastoral duties
- of judging faith
- of teaching
- administering sacraments
- making pastors
- excommunicating

pastors cannot coerce for the sake of the temporal administration.

mutual assistance
- prince can punish innovators against the Church
- pastors can bolster the prince
  - in exhorting subjects
  - in excommunicating rebels

The 2 powers separated during 300 years of persecution
- united and in concert
- not merged

since peace

They must remain distinct and free from each other in this alliance

prince is layman subordinate to the pastors for the spiritual, like the least layman, if he wants to be Christian

pastors are subordinate to the prince for the temporal, like the least subjects. They must give examples.

Reciprocal independence of the 2 powers (*cont.*) {

Thus the Church can excommunicate the prince, and the prince can condemn the pastor to death

each must utilize this right only in the last extreme. but it is a genuine right [1094]

Church mother of Kings {

She bolsters their authority in binding men by conscience

She directs peoples in order to elect kings according to God

She works to unite kings to each other

But she has no right {

of establishing

of deposing { the Kings {

Scripture does not maintain it

it indicates only voluntary submission with regard to the spiritual

Kings protectors of the canons {

protection means neither decision nor authority over the Church. It means supporting her {

against her enemies

against rebellious children

protection is ready assistance {

in order to follow her decisions

never in order to prevent them absolutely { no judgment. no authority as the prince is master with regard to the temporal, just as if there were no Church, the Church is mistress of the spiritual, as if there were no prince. The prince is obedient only in protecting the decisions

Prince is only *évêque du dehors*[33] in what he puts into execution separate from the administration regulated by the Church

Kings protectors of the canons (*cont.*)

a simple protector of the canons means a man

- who never makes any canon or rule
- but who puts them into execution when the Church has made them

From this it follows that the prince must never say in this vein

- we want
- we enjoin
- we order[34]

Blending of the 2 powers

mixed assemblies

- councils where the princes and ambassadors were with bishops
- individual councils of Charlemagne. regular capitularies[35]
  - of ecclesiastical discipline
  - of secular administration

Christianity became like a Christian republic, of which the pope was the head [1095] examples

- amphictyons[36]
- Dutch Republic

Pope became sovereign, crowns fiefs of the Holy See

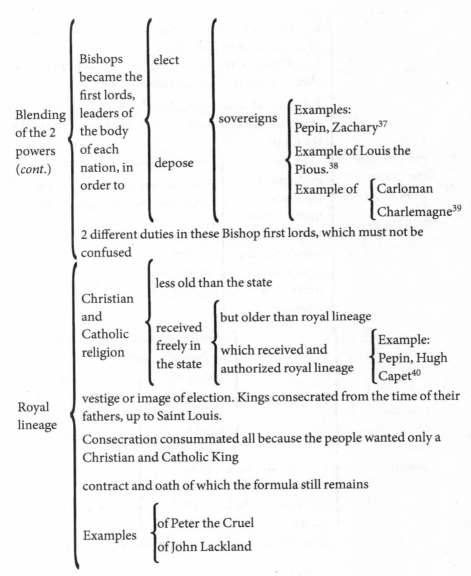

Blending of the 2 powers (*cont.*) { Bishops became the first lords, leaders of the body of each nation, in order to { elect / depose } { sovereigns { Examples: Pepin, Zachary[37]

Example of Louis the Pious.[38]

Example of { Carloman / Charlemagne[39] } } }

2 different duties in these Bishop first lords, which must not be confused

Royal lineage {

Christian and Catholic religion { received freely in the state { less old than the state

but older than royal lineage { which received and authorized royal lineage { Example: Pepin, Hugh Capet[40] } } }

vestige or image of election. Kings consecrated from the time of their fathers, up to Saint Louis.

Consecration consummated all because the people wanted only a Christian and Catholic King

contract and oath of which the formula still remains

Examples { of Peter the Cruel / of John Lackland }

Royal lineage (*cont.*) {

Examples (*cont.*) {

of the Emperor Henry IV

of Fredrick II

of the count of Toulouse Albigensian

of Henry IV king of France

of the Greeks in Italy of the time of Gregory II[41]

Examples of heretics {

King of Sweden James, king of England his grandfather James I

Rome {

center of unity, leader of the divine institution in order to confirm brother Bishops always up to consummation

It is necessary to be always in the communion of this seat, principally for the faith

person of the pope, according to the ultramontanes, can become heretic { then he is not pope[42]

Ossius, Bishop of Cordova, president at the Council of Nicaea, in the name of the pope[43] [1096] { Legates to the other councils

necessity of a center of unity, independent of { individual princes / national churches

power over the temporal { direct absurd and pernicious / indirect evident[44] when it is reduced to deciding on the oath[45]

Secular power[46] could with regard to the temporal

- strip church of all fiefs, revenues, rights, authority, honors, as before Constantine

- prince could not do it in violation of the constitution of the state against the nation.

- then the Church would again find itself, as before the donation, free with regard to the spiritual alone

- Interest of the individual churches in having a leader independent of their temporal prince.

- Independence of the spiritual greater if there were no temporal to deal with.

- this would be a reversal of the constitution, akin to degrading the lords, and leaving everything to the third estate[47]

- this would be to violate the first clause of the contract and the oath of the King

- large debts of the clergy are
  - destruction of a part of the foundations
  - alienations of the seigneuries by usufruction[48]

  against their oath

Spiritual power could with regard to the spiritual

- revoke the concordats in order to reestablish the canonical elections
- withdraw all patronage from spiritual title
- grant no exemption from canons

Liberties of the Gallicans[49] on the spiritual

- Rome exercised an arbitrary power that disturbed the order of the individual Churches
  - expectations [1097]
  - frivolous appellations
  - odious taxes
  - abusive exemptions

It is necessary to admit that these initiatives are sharply diminished

now the initiatives come
- from the secular power
- not from that of Rome
  - King in practice more authoritative than the pope in France

Liberties with regard to the pope, servitude toward the King

authority of the King over the Church devolved to the lay judges
- the laity dominate the Bishops
- third estate dominates first lords
  - Examples
    - *arrêt d'Agen*[50]
    - Primate of Lyon[51]

Liberties of the Gallicans[49] on the spiritual (cont.)

enormous abuses
- of the *appel comme d'abus*[52]
- of the royal cases — to be reformed

abuse of not permitting the provincial councils — national ones dangerous

abuse of not allowing bishops to confer together with their leader

abuse of wanting the laity to request and examine bulls on the faith

schismatic maxims of the parlement
- Kings and judges cannot be excommunicated
- King names man who confers, etc.
- *collatio est in fructu*

possessoire real, *pétitoire* imaginary[53]

otherwise Church, under pretext of the oath of the contracting parties, would judge everything. Today the laity, under pretext of *possessoire*, judges everything.

The rule would be
- that the Bishops of France would continue their canonical practices
- that the King would protect them in order to stay in power canonically according to their desire
- that Rome would maintain them against the usurpations of the lay power

Liberties of the Gallicans[49] on the spiritual (cont.)

The rule would be (cont.) { that they would remain subordinate to their leader { in order to consult him continually — for pronouncements — in order to correct them, depose them, etc.

abuse of the assemblies of the clergy[54] [1098]

clear and present danger of schism by the archbishops of Paris

Liberties of the Gallicans on the temporal

Entire liberty for the purely temporal with regard to the pope { for the King and people — even for the clergy

utility of the Church of not being able to alienate without him

right of the King to reject bulls that would usurp the temporal

no right of examining those which are limited to the spiritual, send them back to the Bishops[55]

Ways of bringing reform.

Reestablish free commerce of the Bishops with their leader in order { to consult — to be authorized

Reach agreement with Rome on the procedure for deposing Bishops. Example: the former bishop of Gap.[56]

do nothing in general { without consulting with the papal nuncio — and without communicating with Rome via a French Cardinal

Allow to elect popes the most enlightened and most pious subjects

defy outrageous maxims of the parliamentarians

Ways of bringing reform (*cont.*)

- place some pious, wise, moderate bishops in the Council
  - not pro forma
  - but for every mixed affair
- remember that they are all naturally
  - the first lords
  - and councilors of state
- accept the Council of Trent
  - of which the main points were accepted in the ordinances [1099]
  - with modifications for the purely temporal points
- make an office of
  - pious lay magistrates
  - good Bishops with the nuncio
    - in order to establish the *appel comme d'abus*

put an end to all exemptions of chapters and of noncongregating monasteries

- pursue the reform or suppression of recalcitrant orders
  - Examples
    - Cluny
    - Cordeliers[57]
- Leave to the Bishops, the *appel simple*[58] exempted, freedom over their proceedings with regard to
  - visiting
  - correcting
  - prohibiting
  - deposing all ecclesiastics, *curés*

Ways of bringing reform (cont.)

- leave to the Bishops freedom of judging themselves in their official domains
- nominate to the pope for the Cardinalship only men
  - learned, pious, etc,
  - who reside often in Rome
- Leave them in the conclaves entire freedom of following their oath for the most worthy
- Request wise and zealous Nuncios, not political and uninitiated
- have a council of conscience
  - in order to choose pious and capable bishops
  - forming it not by ranks, but by merit
  - not making it right now
- plan for uprooting Jansenism[59]
  - requesting of Rome decision on relative and alternating necessity
  - making all the bishops accept the Bull[60]
  - deposing those who will refuse it
  - taking away the doctorates of abbes, tutors, grand vicars, professors, superiors of seminaries
  - giving doctrinal rules
    - to the Oratory
    - to the Benedictines
    - to the canons regular [1100]

Nobility

Peerage list

- made in each province on basis of careful research
- state of the honors and the demonstrable evidence of each family
- state of all the branches
  - of which the rootedness is clear
  - of which it is doubtful
  - which seem illegitimate
    - each child registered
- General Registry at Paris
- no branch recognized without registration.
- Inventory in alphabetical order
  - of the *Chambre des comptes* of Paris[61]
  - of the *Trésor des chartes*[62]
  - of *chambres des comptes* elsewhere
    - with distribution to each family of that which belongs to it

Education

- one hundred children of high birth pages of the King
  - Studies
  - exercises
    - chosen on basis of good nature.
- lesser nobility or from poor branches, cadets in the regiments
  - parents
  - friends
    - of colonels
    - of captains
- household of the King filled only by chosen nobles
  - guards
  - heavy cavalry
  - light cavalry[63]
- no military posts that can be bought. nobles preferred
- butlers, ordinary gentlemen, etc., all verified nobles.[64]

Every house will have a property never to be substituted. Majorasgo of Spain[65] [1101]

Freedom of wholesale trade, without infringement

Freedom of entering into public office.

marriages of mismatched station forbidden to both sexes

prohibition against purchases of lands, of noble names,[66] of taking these names

Ennoblements prohibited except in the case of outstanding services rendered to the State

Support of nobility

Order of the Holy Spirit for only those houses
- distinguished by their brilliance
- by their antiquity beyond known origin

Order of the Saint-Michel in order to honor the services of the good inferior nobility

neither the one nor the other for the soldiers without proportionate birth

no Dukedoms beyond a certain number
- Dukes of high birth. Insufficient favor[67]
- ceremonial regulated
- would need to await vacant place to obtain them
- would be admitted only in the Estates General

letters for Marquis, Counts,[68] Barons, as for Dukes

Soldiers

separate honors for the soldiers

Various orders of knighthood with distinctions for
- Lieutenants general
- battle sergeants
- colonels, etc.

privileges purely honorific.

Bastardy
- Dishonor it in order to suppress vice and scandal
- strip illegitimate children of the King of the rank of princes — They would not have it
- strip all others of the rank of gentlemen, the name and the arms, etc.

Foreign princes
- Leave the long-established ranks
- cut out all those which seem doubtful and contested.
- arrange that each child after the first-born would only have the honors[69] when the King will judge him worthy of them [1102]
- do not easily give to these houses, responsibilities, governments, advantages
- They will never accept another sovereign than the first-born of their house
- Bouillon and Rohan, first-born Dukes, younger children cousins, etc.[70]
- No other family with any distinction than those of the Dukes.

Justice

Chancellor
- must keep watch over all the tribunals, and regulate the boundaries between them
- must know the talents and the reputation of each principal provincial magistrate
- to procure to each advancement according to his talents, his virtue, his services
- to relieve of responsibilities those who exercise them poorly.
- The chief chancellor of the third estate must have a lesser rank than before

Council {
- composed not of *maîtres des requêtes*[71] without merit admitted for sake of money but of men freely chosen in all the tribunals of the realm
- established in order to redress with the chancellor all the inferior judges
- counselors of state sent from time to time into the provinces to reform abuse

Parlements {

remove little by little the *paulette*, etc.[72] {
- responsibilities sharply diminished
- responsibilities to diminish still further by reform
- Keep for the term of their life all judges of integrity and sufficiently instructed
- have their worthy children succeed them freely
- allotment of fair wages from public funds
- examples of advancement for those who perform better
}

few judges [1103]

few laws

Laws that avoid difficulties {
- over wills
- marriage contracts { few of free arrangement[73]
- sales and exchanges
- imprisonments and decrees[74]
}

Parlements (*cont.*) { **wide choice** {
- of *premiers présidents*[75]
- *procureurs généraux*[76]
- preference of nobles to commoners of equal merit for the places of { president counselor[77]

Bailliages[78] {

no *presidiaux.*[79] { their rights given to the *bailliages.*[80]

reestablish the right of *the bailli d'épée* to exercise his function there

Lieutenant general and criminal lieutenant nobles, if possible[81]

number of counselors determined {
- not on the basis of the money that one hopes to derive
- but according to the real needs of the public

no justice to local Lords, nor to the King in the villages of his lands. All immediately at the neighboring *bailliage.*[82]

reservation to the Lord of certain rights[83] {
- over their vassals for their fiefs
- of security and military service over their peasants

Office of jurisprudence {

assemble legal experts chosen {
- in order to correct and harmonize all the customs
- in order to simplify procedure
- in order to cut back the prosecutors, etc.

account rendered to the chancellor by this office in the council of state

Comprehensive examination in order to make a good code. [1104]

Suppression of tribunals[84]
- no more *grand Conseil*[85]
- no more *Cour des Aides*[86]
- no more Treasurers of France
- no more elected

Commerce

Freedom
- wide commerce
  - of good and abundant commodities in France
  - or of the works made by good workers
- commerce of money by usury, beyond necessary banking, strictly forbidden
- Type of censor in order to authorize
  - gain from true commerce[87]
  - not gain from usury
  - to know the means by which each grows rich
- Deliberate in the *états*
  - General
  - local
  - if it is necessary to discontinue
    - all entrance all exit
    - from the kingdom
- France sufficiently wealthy, if it sells well its grains, oils, wines, textiles, etc.
- that which it will buy from the
  - English
  - Dutch
  - are delicacies and curiosities not at all comparable
  - leave free
- rule constant and uniform
  - in order never to either annoy or quibble with foreigners.
  - in order to make it easy for them to buy at reasonable price.

Freedom (*cont.*)

Leave to the Dutch profit
- from their austere frugality and work
- from the danger of having few sailors in their ships
- from their good administration in order to join together in commerce
- from the abundance of their ships for freight

bureau of trade that the Estates General and [1105] local *états*, as well as the council of the King, consult on all general arrangements

Type of Mount of Piety[88] for those who will want to trade, and who lack the means to move forward

manufactures to be established, in order to make better than foreigners, without exclusion of their works

arts to be made to flourish, in order to sell
- not to the King until he has paid his debts
- but to foreigners and wealthy French

Sumptuary laws[89]
- nobles are ruined to enrich the merchants by luxury
- the morals of all the nation are corrupted by this luxury
- this luxury is more pernicious, as profit from fashion is not useful

Study of the financiers
- there would be no more need of them
- Type of censor would examine in detail their profits
- The financiers could turn their industry toward commerce[90]

The entire regulation by the Council of the commerce and administration of the kingdom, of which the report of the results always delivered to the Council of State where the King is present, etc.

Modest navy, not excessive, proportionate to the needs of the state,
which agrees not to undertake alone wars by sea against powers which place
all their forces there.

    To regulate:
        prices
        commerce from port to port, etc.

Permit every foreigner to come live in France and to enjoy there all the
privileges of natural-born and naturalized citizens, in declaring their intention to the clerk of the royal *bailliage*, on the certificate of citizenship and
good character that he would carry, and the oath that he would take, etc. All
of this without cost etc.

Augment the number of governments of the provinces in fixing them at a
lesser extent at which a man can carefully supervise them with care with the
lieutenant general and lieutenant of the king. Twenty at least in France, would
be the measure of the number of the local estates. Residence of the governors
and officers. No intendants *Missi dominici*[91] only from time to time.

3. Measures to Take after the Death of the Duke of Burgundy [Pl. 2:1106–1123]

Study of . . . [92]

I

It would be a great injustice and a great misfortune to suspect N.[93] on the
basis of popular imaginings[94]

II

I would like to study more thoroughly and in deep secrecy
    The evidence of what he did in Spain
    The specific facts now being alleged

III

If he is not guilty, holding him suspect and excluding him may lead to a needless civil war.

IV

If he is guilty, it is crucial to safeguard the lives of the king and the young prince,[95] who is at every moment in danger.

V

If he is not guilty, and if he is well intentioned, it [1107] would be crucial to treat him with trust, and to engage him through honor, etc.

VI

What strikes me is that his daughter, who is said to be brazenly irreligious, would not know how to live there without him, and knowing all the monstrous things that are said about their relations, he still spends his life all alone with her.[96] This irreligion, this indifference to all libel, this abandonment to so strange a person, seems to render credible everything that seems so difficult to believe.[97]

VII

There are crimes that one can never be sure of proving judicially until after complete inquiry into the case. It is terrible to begin this one in uncertainty.

VIII

Proof is often much more difficult against a person of such high rank. Who will not be afraid of coming out on the losing end of so odious an accusation? Each will fear a sudden death of the king, or an indulgence of his part, in order to preserve the honor of the royal household. Each will fear an eternal resentment of this house. Hopes of reward or protection are not at all proportionate to such fears. As soon as detailed testimonies are sought, each will backpedal.

IX

If unfortunately the crime were proved, would a grandson of France,[98] who could soon come by right to the succession of the crown, be sentenced to an infamous death? Could he be safely held in prison indefinitely? Would he not be freed when his son-in-law and his daughter should have authority? [1108]

X

Supposing even that one had the power to declare him excluded him from the succession, what wars would we not have to fear, if all this came about? Moreover, his son, who is innocent, could not be excluded. What wouldn't he have to fear from the father of the King[99] excluded shamefully from the crown?

XI

All investigations either feeble and superficial, or rigorous and not entirely successful at finishing him off, would produce countless needless evils. On the one hand he would be implacable with regard to a defamatory investigation. On the other he would be triumphant with regard to that on which he could not be convicted. He would be excluded from the regency, and he would nevertheless have all its actual authority under the name of his son-in-law, whom he would govern through his daughter.

XII

Public indignation must not be counted on. The horror of the recent spectacle excites this indignation. It will lessen over time. A grandson of France calumniated so horribly and without clear proof would soon arouse further indignation. Moreover, the present morals of the nation throw everyone into the most violent temptation of attaching themselves to the strongest by all sorts of base acts, dirty tricks, black deeds, and treasons.

XIII

This prince, were he pushed to the limit, would discover great resources, in the present weakness, in the decline of a reign about to end, in his genuinely brutal though seemingly mild spirit, in his great revenues, in the support of his son-in-law, in his and his daughter's irreligion, and in the frightful counsels that he would never lack. [1109]

XIV

Were he excluded from the council of the regency, it would seem that the king holds him suspect. This exclusion will be seen as very damning. In this case his interest would be that investigation is made, to which all submit. Then he would respond after the death of the king to this[100] calumnious exclusion. No more is needed, when one is the strongest, in order to reverse what seems hateful and irregular.

XV

In the investigation, one could hardly expose the crime of N., without finding that his daughter was complicit in his action. In this case what would one do with her? She can become queen! Her condemnation could put the Duke of Berry, having become king, in a position of never having children![101]

XVI

[102] If the young prince were to fall, after so horrible a scandal, the King of Spain would want to come into France in order to claim the throne, and the Spanish could well refuse to receive in his place the Duke of Berry, governed by this daughter and father-in-law whom they find so despicable.

XVII

In this case there could easily be a war between the 2 brothers. The King of Spain, following the counsels of his wife the Queen and of the Spanish nation, would maintain that the renunciation of the late Monsignor and of the late Dauphin, was as null and void as that of Queen Theresa of Spain.[103] They would want to reunite the two monarchies, in order not to fall into hands so odious and so defamed. [1110]

XVIII

Despite all these reasons for not making a showy investigation, I would like to see one made in great secrecy, in order to protect the lives of the King and of the young prince, assuming that one finds evidence that merits this extension. But secrecy is at once difficult and absolutely necessary.

XIX

Would it be possible to examine in great secrecy this prince's chemist, and see the inventory of the drugs that he mixed? It would be necessary to take them, and make experiments of them on criminals condemned to death.[104]

XX

If unfortunately the prince is guilty, and if he were to see that no one wants to go any further, what will he not dare to undertake?

Plan for the Council of Regency[105]

I

If you form a large council, you will introduce there disorder, division, absence of secrecy, and corruption. If you make it smaller, it will be more envied, more spoken against, easier to discredit, especially if the best subjects are in short supply. [1111]

II

You can succeed in establishing this council only by admitting to it men presently in favor.[106] Make it very large if you want to give them a necessary counterweight of upright and firm men.

III

If you install N. there, you will deliver the state and the young prince to the one who is suspected of the blackest wickedness. Exclude N. for this suspicion, you will prepare the overthrow of this council, which will seem founded on a horrible slander against a grandson of France.

IV

All things considered, I would not dare say that it is convenient to admit to this council a prince suspected of wickedness, who would find himself the master of everything he should find lying between him and the supreme authority.

V

Moreover, independently of this suspicion, one can hardly hope that being under his daughter's sway, he might contribute
> to the good education of the young prince
> to good order in order to reestablish the state

VI

In order to take the edge off this exclusion, I would like to see the Duke of Berry given only the simple precedency with his vote counted, like those of the others, and in order to bring an end to the plurality of suffrages. It would be necessary to elect a subject by the plurality of votes, if one of the council members were to die.[107] [1112]

VII

I would exclude, as well as N.
> all the princes of the blood
> all the natural princes
> all the foreign princes who do not regard the King as their sovereign

VIII

I would also exclude the Lords who have been given a rank of prince. This is a predicament for the rank to avoid. The only one that it is tempting to admit is the Prince of Rohan.[108]

IX

The ambitious lords, adaptable and unmethodical, would eagerly seek to enter into this council. But all upright men would fear it, and would flee this job as a frightful predicament. Little to hope. Everything to fear. The day after the death of the king, each of the upright and firm counselors would have to fear the authority of the Duke of Berry and that of the Duke of Orleans, and inside the council, division and outbreaks of cabals. It would be endlessly difficult to compose this council of men fit to justify hope.

X

I do not dare speak my thoughts on the choice of prelates worthy of entering into this council.

XI

As for the lords, have a look at [1113]

The Dukes
   of Chevreuse
   of Villeroi
   of Beauvillier
   of Saint-Simon
   of Charost
   of Harcourt
   of Chaulnes[109]
The Marshals
   of Huxelles
   of Tallard[110]

XII

It is natural that favor puts there
   The Duke of Guiche
   The Duke of Noailles
   The Duke of Antin
   The Maréchal d'Estrées[111]
     It is necessary to think of counterweights

XIII

One could not exclude any of the ministers from this council. As for the secretaries of state, one could call on them only for expedient actions.

XIV

It would be necessary for the King to authorize as soon as possible this council of Regency, in an assembly of notables, which conforms to the government of the nation.

XV

Moreover it would be necessary for the King in his *lit de justice* to register it in the Parlement of Paris.[112] Similar registration in all the other parlements, sovereign courts, *bailliages*, etc. [1114]

XVI

The King, in the assembly of notables, could make all the notables take an oath to maintain this council, and the councillors of this council to govern with zeal, etc., The Duke of Berry could even take the oath.

XVII

It would be infinitely desirable for the King to put this council into operation right away. He would not be any less the master of everything. He would accustom the whole nation to submit to this council. He would test each councilor. He would unite them, redress them, and bolster his work. If it is necessary the day after his death to begin a thing that has become so extraordinary, it will be immediately reversed. For a long time the nation was more accustomed only to the absolute will of a single master. Everyone will run to the Duke of Berry alone.

XVIII

If the King cannot be persuaded of so necessary a thing, it would at least be necessary[113] for His Majesty to assemble this council five or six times a year, that he moreover consult individually each of the councillors, and that he let them in on classified affairs, so that they were not all at once new at the day of need.

XIX

Not a moment should be lost in establishing this council. The surprising nature of the spectacle, the public outcry, the fear of a final misfortune can unsettle. But if under pretext of not aggrieving the King, one waits for him to come around in the ordinary course of things, nothing will be gained. [1115]

XX

Moreover, there is not a day where we would not be threatened either by a sudden natural death, or a catastrophic accident, followed by the blow that the public supposes to come from N.

XXI

Every day one must fear a weakening of the head, more dangerous than even the death of His Majesty. Then everyone will find themselves all at once in the most horrible confusion, and without remedy.

XXII

His Majesty cannot, either as a matter of honor or in good conscience, put himself in danger of leaving the realm, and the young prince his heir, without any resource
> for the government of France
> for the education and the safety of the child

XXIII

I admit that the establishment of this council makes us fear terrible inconveniences. But, in the present state, only very imperfect things are possible, and it would be still worse to do nothing at all. One cannot be content with ordinary and moderate precautions.

Education of the young prince.

I

If the Duke of Beauvillier can be named governor, he must sacrifice himself, and abandon himself blindly, [1116] without listening to his reservations. The case is unique. Were he even to exclude only one bad candidate, he would do an inestimable good. He must sacrifice himself to the State, to the Church, to the King and to the prince that he so loved.

II

If he were named, he could obtain a sort of coadjutor such as
> the Duke of Chaulnes
> the Duke of Charost[114]

He would be much relieved by a friendly confidant, and the succession would be safely guaranteed.

III

Not only is a governor proper to form the young prince needed, but also one sufficiently authorized and resolute as to maintain, in case of minority, so precious an education against the cabals.

IV

It is necessary for the preceptor to be an ecclesiastic. He will better teach religion. He will better lay foundations against the ambitious enterprises of the laymen. He will be more respected. But as I know almost no person in the clergy, I cannot propose any candidate. He would have to be entirely united to the governor.

V

It seems to me that, in this specific case, it would be necessary to choose a Bishop. This status will give him more authority over the prince, and over the public. He will be less exposed to the revolutions of the cabals. The pope's approval could be secured for a Bishop to charge himself with this task in a case so extraordinary for the faith.

VI

The subjects of the episcopal order that I consider from afar, and without being able to attend to any, much less know them to their depths, are the gentlemen

of Meaux
of Soissons
of Nîmes
of Autun
of Toul[115]

VII

The Abbé of Polignac is a courtier who would be in favor.[116] Moreover he has intellect and acquired knowledge. But I do not want him.

VIII

An undergovernor is necessary who has sense, probity, and religious sincerity, with an intimate attachment to the governor.

IX

An underpreceptor and a reader are necessary who would be intimately united to the preceptor.

X

An excellent choice for the *gentilshommes de la manche*, and for the first *valet de chambre*, etc., is necessary.[117] None unfit for good company.[118] None doubtful on Jansenism. The gentlemen

Du Chesne

de Charmon.[119] [1118]

XI

One can confer with Monsieur Bourdon on the choice of the ecclesiastical subjects. It is important to act together with him in secret.[120]

XII

It is not a question of waiting until the customary age. This is an exceptional case. The King can fail all at once; it is necessary to put this machine into motion while he is alive, and to have it firmed it up before he fails. A prince can be left in the hands of women, and given men who will see him every day, who will accustom him to them, and who will begin his education imperceptibly.

XIII

The King could include the form of the education in the act of regency. Thus the education would be registered and authorized with the same solemnity that would authorize the council of regency for the future minority.

XIV

His Majesty could even extract from the prince, who must naturally be the head of the regency, a promise that he will not disturb, for any reason, this project of education thus authorized. [1119]

The King[121]

I

I believe that it is very important to increase, without lots of noise and without affectation, every precaution over his food, etc., as well as that of the young prince who remains

II

It is to be desired that all the ministers unite themselves in order to render His Majesty very easily able to purchase the peace that is so dear. This is the only way of clearing it up for the rest of his life, and of prolonging it.

III

They can make him understand that this is necessary for his glory and his conscience. He must not expose himself to leave a small child with the entire realm in so near a danger.

IV

He can have represented to him the dire extremes that would come about if he were to fall into a state of languor, in which he could never decide anything, and no minister would dare to take anything on himself.

V

He can be made to foresee the possibility of a lost battle, and of enemies entering into the heart of the realm. [1120]

VI

He can be made to see the possibility where France would have the misfortune of losing him. Thus one would have everything to fear

    from the Huguenot party

    from the Jansenist party

    from the malcontents of various states

    from the princes excluded from the regency

    from debts

      paid

      or not paid

    from very numerous troops lacking discipline

The remedy is to establish without any delay a council of regency, that everyone becomes accustomed to respecting.

VII

He can have shown to him the consolation, the glory, and the trust in his salvation, that he will draw from a prompt peace, if it gives him the means of beginning to make his people feel some relief, after the evils of all the long wars.

VIII

He can be made to consider that he immediately would have to reform his troops, which he could do only with very great danger in the disorder of a minority.

IX

He must be shown how important it is that he reestablishes as soon as possible some order in the finances, without which there can be no hope for any breathing room for the people, before the disorders of a minority. During a regency, a prince intent on troubling the state would have an easy means of succeeding there. If the Council of Regency pays the debts, it would not be able to relieve the people, and peoples overwhelmed will [1121] not continue to carry this oppressive yoke, when they see a prince offering them his protection against this council. If on the contrary the council removes or suspends the payment of debts in order to relieve the people, the *rentiers* who are in such great number and so insistent, will make a formidable party against the council that will have mistreated them.[122]

X

The same can be said of the courtiers and military men who have large pensions. If the Council of Regency pays them, it overwhelms the people. If it refuses them, or delays them their payment, it would become hateful. One way or another a strong party will be formed for a prince who will want to satisfy his resentment and his ambition.

XI

If the Duke of Berry, under the sway of his spouse and his father-in-law, on the death of the King were to find himself ready to govern—without which there would be a Council of Regency again in actual possession, and again affirmed in the exercise of authority—the people and troops, accustomed to obey only the order of a single master, would not accustom themselves easily to prefer the decisions of a council without experience, and perhaps sharply divided, to the wills of a son and of a grandson of France, united together with a great party.

XII

If the minor prince were hypothetically to die, the Duke of Orleans could prevent the return of the King of Spain, above all if the Spanish were to refuse to receive the Duke of Berry.

XIII

There would be no one who was ready to arrange [1122] things in order to bring this civil war to an end. At least a council already established could work toward peace and good order with some provisional authority.

XIV

It seems to me entirely appropriate that the Good Duke might go to see Madame de Maintenon, that he speak to her with an open heart[123] and that he represent to her all these things, so that she concurs effectively in this work.

XV

This is precisely what can attract the blessing of God and the good wishes of all France. This is to work toward peace, to the glory and to the salvation of the King. What would she not have to deplore, if the King were missing in this confusion?

XVI

It is not by every day sparing the King the sight of some thorny and distressing details that one will work effectively to relieve him and maintain him. The thorns will be reborn under his feet at every moment. He can find comfort only in complying from the start in total rigor. A prompt peace, the destruction of the Jansenist party, order brought to finances, methodical reform of the troops, the establishment of a good council authorized and put in charge as soon as possible—these are what can put the King in a position to long endure, and put the kingdom in a position to support itself against all dangers. One will owe everything to Madame de Maintenon, if she inclines the King toward this.

XVII

The Good Duke can speak with all the knowledge owed to the good offices that Madame de Maintenon has rendered him in the past. He can declare to her that he speaks without interest, neither for himself, nor for his friends, and without bias and without conspiracy. [1123] He can add that, as far as his sentiments on religion go, he has never had ones other than those of the Holy See, that he is attached to nothing extraordinary, and that he would even be horrified by his friends if he were to find in them some obstinacy, or artifice, or penchant for novelty.

XVIII

I do not believe that Madame de Maintenon would act gracefully, nor even with a certain force of elevated prudence. But what does one know of what God wills? He sometimes uses the weakest instruments, at least to stop certain misfortunes. It is necessary to try to appease Madame de Maintenon and to speak the truth to her. God will do His will in everything.

8

"On Pure Love"

[Pl. 1:656–671]

The Lord hath made all things for Himself, as Scripture says.[1] He dedicates to Himself all that He makes; and His rights hold over everything, forever. The free and intelligent being that He created is as much His as those of His creations that lack freedom and intelligence. All that is in the created being without intelligence He relates essentially and totally to Himself, and so too He desires that the intelligent being joins himself entirely and without reserve to Him alone. It is true that He desires our happiness; but our happiness is neither the primary end of His work, nor an end equal to that of His glory. It is in fact for the sake of His glory that He wishes even our happiness; our happiness is only a secondary end, which He relates to the final and essential end of His glory. He is Himself His sole and essential end in all things.

In order to enter into this essential purpose of our creation, it is necessary to put God ahead of ourselves and to ensure that we desire our beatitude only for His glory; otherwise we would reverse the order that He established. It is thus not merely our self-interested desire for our beatitude that must lead us to desire His glory. It is on the contrary the desire for His glory that must lead us to desire our beatitude as a thing that He is pleased to relate to His glory. It is true that not all just souls are capable of such an explicit preference of God to themselves, but an implicit preference is necessary at a minimum, and an explicit preference, which is more perfect, is suited only to those souls to whom God gives the insight and the strength to prefer Him to themselves, such that they desire their own beatitude solely for the sake of His glory.

What makes it so difficult for men to understand this truth and what makes this speech so [657] hard for them to hear is that they love themselves and indeed want to love themselves out of self-interest. In some basic and superficial sense they understand that it is necessary to love God above all things. Yet they do not understand what it means to love God above one's self, and to love one's self only as one loves Him. They utter these profound words without trouble because they fail to understand all their power. But

Fénelon. Ryan Patrick Hanley, Oxford University Press (2020) © Oxford University Press.
DOI: 10.1093/oso/9780190079581.001.0001

they would be reduced to trembling as soon as they were told that it is necessary to prefer God and His glory to ourselves and to our beatitude such that we would love His glory even more than our beatitude, and such that we would genuinely join one to the other, regarding His glory as a primary end to which other ends are subordinate.

It would have been remarkable had men done all they must in order to understand a rule so clear, so just, and so essential to the created being. But, since man *is fixed in himself,* as St. Augustine says,[2] he sees nothing beyond the narrow limits of the self-love in which he is enclosed; he forgets at every moment that he is a created being, that he has no duty to himself insofar as he is not his own, and that he owes himself without reserve to the good pleasure of the one to whom he owes his existence. Tell him this oppressive truth and he does not dare deny it. But its real meaning escapes him, and imperceptibly he always wants to revert back to calculating his advantage with God.

It is argued that God has given us a natural inclination for beatitude, which is God Himself.[3] In so doing He could have wanted to facilitate our union with Him, and to have instilled in us an inclination for our happiness similar to the inclination He instilled in us for the nourishment we need in order to live. But it is necessary to distinguish carefully the pleasure that God has made us to feel at the sight of Him, which is our beatitude, from the violent inclination that the disobedience of the first man instilled in our hearts and that renders us self-centered, and renders our love for God dependent on the beatitude we seek in this love. Moreover it is not any natural inclination, necessary and instinctive, that we are concerned with here. Is it to be feared that men fall into illusion by evading what is necessary and instinctive? These instinctive desires, which are less desires than [658] necessary inclinations, can no more be lacking in men than gravity can be lacking in rocks. What are in question here are only our voluntary and deliberate actions, what we can do or not do. With regard to these free actions, the motive of our own beatitude is not forbidden. God wants us to find our own interest in our union with Him; but it is necessary that this motive be secondary, and the least of the created being's concerns. It is necessary to desire God's glory more than our beatitude: it is necessary to desire this beatitude only insofar as it concerns His glory, as the thing that one wants less, as compared to the thing that one wants more. It is necessary that our interest touches us incomparably less than His glory. This is what the created being, attached to himself as a result of sin, has so much trouble understanding. This is a truth that is the very essence of the created being, which must tame all hearts, and which nevertheless shocks them when they examine it more deeply. But we must do justice to ourselves and to God. Did we make ourselves? Are we made for God or for ourselves? What are we made to become? Is it for our own beatitude or for His glory that God has created us? If it is for His glory, it is then necessary for us to conform to the essential order of our creation; it is necessary to desire His glory more than our beatitude, such that we relate our beatitude to His own glory.

It is thus not a question of a natural and instinctive inclination of man for beatitude. How many natural tendencies or inclinations are there in men that they can never either destroy or diminish, and which even so they do not always follow! For example, the inclination toward self-preservation is one of the strongest and most natural of our inclinations; the desire we have for happiness cannot be more ineradicable than that which we have for existence. Beatitude is only *greater being*, as St. Augustine says.[4] The inclination toward happiness is then only an extension of the desire for self-preservation. However, one can choose not to follow this inclination in intentional acts. How many Greeks and Romans freely condemned themselves to certain death? [659] How many of them have we seen who committed suicide, in spite of this raging inclination at the depth of our natures?

Again, we are only concerned with our free acts of love for God, and of the motives for beatitude that can enter into these. We come to see that the motive of our self-interest for beatitude is permitted only insofar as it is the least desired by us, and it is desired only in relation to the primary motive, which it is necessary to desire from a superior will, namely the glory of God. It is thus only a question of comparing two different ways of preferring God to ourselves. The first is of loving Him wholeheartedly and as perfect in Himself and as necessary for our beatitude; such that the motive of our beatitude, although less strong, nevertheless supports the love we have for divine perfection, and we would love God a little less if He were not beatifying for us. The second way is to love God knowing that He is beatifying for us and from whom one can receive beatitude because He has promised it—not loving Him solely out of self-interest for the beatitude that follows from it, but loving Him above all for Himself because of His perfection, such that we would love Him even if (speaking wholly hypothetically) He never wanted to be beatifying for us. It is clear that the last of these two loves, which is the disinterested one, more perfectly promotes the total and singular attachment of the created being to His end—leaving nothing to the created being and giving everything to God alone—and as a result is more perfect than that other love of God in which our interest is mixed.

It is not that the man whose love is free of self-interest does not love reward; he loves it insofar as the reward is God Himself, and not his own interest. He desires it because God desires that it should be so; it is the order and not his interest that he seeks. He loves himself, but he loves himself only from love of God, as he would love a stranger, and in order to love that which God has made.

What is clear is that while God is infinitely perfect in Himself, He alone cannot prop up the love of one who needs to be animated by the motive of his [660] own beatitude, which he finds in God. The other has no need of this motive; it is not necessary for him in order to love what is perfect in itself and to know its perfection. The one who has need of his own beatitude as a motive is only attached to this motive because he feels his love would be less strong if one stripped him of this support. The lame man who cannot walk without a crutch cannot consent to it being taken away from him; he feels his weakness and he rightly fears to fall, but he must not be shocked at the sight of a healthy and vigorous man who has no need for such support. The healthy man walks more freely without crutches; but he must never despise those who cannot get by without them. Even the man who still needs to add the motive of his beatitude to that of the supreme perfection of God in order to love Him, recognizes humbly that there is in the treasures of the grace of God a perfection higher than his own, and renders glory to God for the gifts which are in others without being jealous of them. So too even the one who is brought to love without interest follows this attraction, but he judges neither him nor others; he claims nothing for himself, he would be ready to believe that he is not in the state which he seems to be, he would be docile, submissive, mistrustful of himself, and appreciative of all virtue he could see in his neighbors who still have need of a love mixed with self-interest. But in the end, love without any motive of self-interest for beatitude is manifestly more perfect than that in which self-interest is mixed.

If someone imagined that this perfect love is impossible and chimerical, and that it is an empty refinement that can become the source of illusion, I have only these words to say to him: Nothing is impossible with God. He calls himself the jealous God; He subjects us to the wayfaring of this life in order that we might be led to perfection. To regard this love as one of chimerical and dangerous refinement is foolishly to condemn as illusory the greatest saints of all the ages who have testified to this love, and who have regarded it as the pinnacle of spiritual life.

But if my reader still refuses to recognize the perfection of this love, I ask him to respond precisely and directly to the following questions that I want to put to him. [661] Is not eternal life a pure grace and indeed the pinnacle of all the graces? Is it not a matter of faith that the kingdom of Heaven is owed to us only as a result of the purely free promise and on the equally free application of the merits of Jesus Christ? The benefit would not be less free than the promise on which it is founded: this is what we never cease to say to our errant brethren; we justify ourselves to them on the notion of *merit*, of which the Church makes use in protesting that all our merits are not founded on strict right, but only on a promise made out of pure pity. Thus eternal life, which is the end of all that God has decreed, is of all ends the most free; all the other graces are given in relation to this one. This grace, which itself contains all others, is founded on no other title than on the purely free promise and following the application similarly free of the merits of Jesus Christ. The promise itself, which is the foundation of everything, is only applied based on God's pure pity, on the good pleasure and good intention of His will. In this order of the graces everything reduces itself evidently to an absolutely free and freely given will.

With these indubitable principles in place, I propose to venture a conjecture. Say that God wanted to destroy my soul at the moment at which it detached itself from my body. This conjecture is only impossible because of the promise freely given. God would have then been able to exempt my individual soul from His general promise toward others. Who will dare deny that God could not destroy my soul in accord with my conjecture? The created being, which is not created by itself, exists only as far as the unrestricted will of the Creator makes it exist. In order for it not to fall into nothingness, it is necessary that the Creator constantly renew the benefit of His creation, conserving it by the same power by which He created it. I suppose then a thing quite possible since I suppose only a simple exception to a purely free and unrestricted rule. I suppose that God, who renders all other souls immortal, will bring mine to an end at the moment of my death, and I suppose also that God revealed His project to me. Nobody would dare say that God could not do it. [662]

These quite plausible conjectures having been granted, there is no longer any promise or reward or beatitude or hope of a future life for me. I can no longer hope to possess God, or to see His face, or to love Him eternally, or to be loved by Him in the life beyond. I suppose that I am to die, and only a single moment of life still remains for me, which must be followed by eternal and entire extinction. I imagine my reader asking me to respond with exact precision to the question of how I would spend this moment? In this final instant, would I excuse myself from loving God, as a consequence of regarding Him as a reward? Would I renounce Him for what will produce more happiness for me? Would I abandon the final end of my creation? God, in excluding me from blessed eternity, which He doesn't owe me, has He cast off what He essentially is? Did He cease to do His work for the sake of His pure glory alone? Has He lost the right of the creator in creating me? Has He dispensed of the duties of the created being, who must essentially owe all that he is to the one by whom he is? Is it not evident that in this quite plausible conjecture I must love God solely for Himself, without hoping for any further reward from my love, and with certain exclusion of all beatitude, such that this last moment of my life, which will be followed by an eternal destruction, must necessarily be filled by an act of pure and wholly disinterested love?

But if the one to whom God grants no eternity yet owes everything to God, what does the one to whom He gives Himself entirely owe? I will be destroyed in a little while, I will never see God, He refuses me His kingdom that He gives to others, He wants neither to love me nor to be loved by me eternally. I am obliged nevertheless even in dying to love Him with all my heart and all my strength; if I fall short there, I am a monster and a denatured creature. And you, my reader, for whom God makes ready, without owing it to you, the eternal possession of Himself, would you fear as a chimerical refinement this love of which I am obliged to give you an example? Will you love God less than me, because He loves you more? Would not the reward render [663] your love self-interested? Even if God were to love you less than He does, it would be necessary for you to love Him without any motive of interest. Is this then the fruit of the promises and the blood of Jesus Christ, to keep men from a generous and disinterested love of God? To the degree that He offers you full beatitude in itself, will you only love Him insofar as you are supported by this infinite interest? The kingdom of Heaven, offered to you while I am excluded from it—is it desirable to you and do you want to love God only in order to seek there your own glory and your own felicity?

Do not say that this felicity is God Himself. God could, if He so desired, be no more beatifying for you than for me. It is necessary that I love Him although He would not be so for me; why is it impossible for you to resolve yourself to love Him without being sustained by this motive that He is beatifying for you? Why do you tremble at the mere mention of a love that is wholly independent of this support of self-interest?

If we were entitled to eternal beatitude, and if God, in creating men, was required to provide for their eternal life, one could deny my conjecture. But one could not deny it without a manifest impiety. Eternal life, the greatest of gifts, would no longer be a gift; the reward would be owed to us independently of the promise. God would owe to his creature eternal existence and felicity. He could not remove Himself from it; it would become a necessary being. This doctrine is monstrous. On the other hand, my conjecture clearly testifies to God's rights, and offers examples of possible cases where love without interest would be necessary. If it is not so in this case from the order established by the free promise, this is only because God does not judge us worthy of these great proofs. He is content with an implicit preference of Him and His glory to us and to our beatitude, which is like the germ of pure love in the hearts of all just souls. But in the end my supposition, in comparing the man ready to be destroyed with the one who has received the promise of eternal life, reveals the degree to which love mixed with interest is inferior to disinterested love. [664]

Testimonies of the Ancients

Even as I expect that Christians would be capable of understanding God's infinite rights over His creature, I want to try at least to make them return into their own heart in order to reexamine their idea of what they call friendship. Each wants, in the company of his friends, to be loved solely for himself and not out of interest. Alas! If the man unworthy of all love cannot suffer to be loved by interest, how do we dare to believe that God would not have the same sensibility? We go to the farthest degree to disentangle the subtle motives of interest, of propriety, of pleasure, or of honor that attach our friends to us; we despair being loved by them out of indebtedness, and even more so out of other more shocking motives. We want to be loved out of pure inclination, out of esteem, out of admiration. Friendship is so jealous and so delicate that one atom that mixes with it injures it; it can suffer in the friend only simple gifts given without reserve from the depths of his love. The one who loves, in the transport of his passion, wants only to be loved for himself alone, to be uniquely valued above everything, to be such that the entire world would be sacrificed for him, to be of the sort that one forgets oneself and counts oneself for nothing in order to be everything for him: such is the frenzied jealousy and the extravagant injustice of passionate loves; this jealousy is only a tyranny of self-love.

One need only sound oneself to find these depths of idolatry; and whoever does not disentangle these mixed motives will never wholly know themselves. The most ridiculous and odious injustice in us is supreme justice in God. Nothing is so common and so shameful in men than to be jealous; but God, who cannot cede His glory to another, calls Himself *the jealous God*, and His jealousy is essential to His perfection.[5] Examine then, you who read this, the corruption of your heart, and see that the jealousy of your friendship serves to make you understand the infinite subtleties of divine love. When you find these subtleties in your heart for the kindness that you feel for your friend, you never regard them [665] as chimerical refinements; on the contrary, you would be shocked by the coarseness of friends whose friendship had none of these delicacies. It is only with regard to God that you want to defend them; you do not wish that He seeks to be loved as you pretend that your friends love you; you cannot believe that His grace could form adorers who love Him as you wish to be loved; judge yourself, and render glory to God in the end.

I admit that irreligious men, who have this idea of pure friendship, do not follow it, and that all their graceless friendships are only a subtly disguised self-love, but they still have an idea of pure friendship. Would they need to have it if it were only about loving the vile and corrupted created being, and if we were the only ones to fail to recognize it as soon as it concerns loving God?

The ancients themselves had this pure idea of friendship; and we have only to read them in order to be astonished that Christians would not desire that one could love God by His grace, as the ancients believed that it would be necessary to love each other in order to merit the names of friends.

Thus Cicero: "To be impatient of the things that one suffers in friendship is to love one's self and not one's friend." He adds in what follows that "friendship can be only between the good," that is, between those who, following its principles, always prefer the decent to that which the vulgar call useful. "Otherwise," he says, "interest being the rule and the motive for friendship, the least virtuous, who have more needs and desires than others, would be the most suitable to become friends with others, though they are the most avid to love what is useful to them."

"We thus think" (this is again Cicero speaking) "that it is necessary to seek friendship, not by the hope of advantages that one draws from it, but because all the gifts of friendship are in friendship itself. . . . The self-interested are excluded from this excellent and very natural friendship that must be sought by itself and for itself; they cannot profit from their own examples in order to learn where the power of friendship comes from; because each loves himself, not in order to draw [666] from himself some reward for his love, but because each is dear to himself. . . . If one does not apply this same rule to friendship, one will never find a true friend; the true friend is like another self. . . . But the majority of men desire unjustly, and almost with impudence, the sort of friend that they would not wish to be themselves, and demand of them what they would not themselves be willing to give to them."[6]

Cicero cannot more clearly express the disinterestedness of friendship, which desires that our friend be valued for himself alone, without any other motive, in the same way that we ourselves are valuable to ourselves without any hope that excites this love in us. Self-love is without doubt in this sense the perfect model of disinterested friendship.

Horace, although an Epicurean, did not fail to examine this principle of the union of friends when, speaking of the philosophical conversation that occupied him in the countryside, he says that one should ask if men are happy by wealth or by virtue; if it is our own utility or perfection in itself that is the motive of friendship:

> Utrumne divitiis homines, an sint virtute beati?
> Quidve ad amicitias, usus rectumne, trahat nos?[7]

Thus what the ancients, and the ancient Epicureans, thought with regard to friendship for beings unworthy of being loved. It is with regard to this notion of pure friendship that the theologians distinguish, with regard to God, the love that they label friendship from other loves, and the friends of God from His servants.

This pure idea of friendship is not only (as we have seen) in Cicero; it could have also been drawn from the doctrines of Socrates, as presented in Plato's works. These two great philosophers, the latter of whom reports the discourse of the former in his *Dialogues*, want us to attach ourselves to what they call *to kalon*—that is, "the good and the beautiful" or "the perfect"— solely by the love of the beautiful, the good, the true, and the perfect in itself. This is why they often say that it is necessary to despise "*becoming*," [667] *to ginomenon*—that is to say, "*ephemeral being*"—in order to unite oneself to "*that which is*"—that is to say, "*perfect and eternal being*"—which they call *to on*, that is to say, "*that which is*."[8] On such grounds Cicero, who merely repeats their maxims, says, "if we could see with our own eyes the beauty of virtue, we would be overwhelmed by love of its excellence."[9]

Plato has Socrates say in his *Symposium* that "there is something more divine in that which loves than that which is loved."[10] Here we have all the delicacy of the purest love. The one who is loved and who wants to be loved, is occupied with himself; the one who loves without any thought of being loved, expresses the most divine side of love: transcendence, forgetting of the self, disinterestedness. "The beautiful," this philosopher says, "consists not in any individual things, such as the animals, the earth or the heavens . . . rather the beautiful is itself by itself, being always uniform with itself. All other beautiful things participate in this beauty such that if they are born or die, they neither diminish nor add anything to this beauty, and it suffers no loss. If then someone ascends to the level of true friendship, he begins to see the beautiful, he almost touches the final end."[11]

It is easy to see that Plato speaks of a love of the beautiful in itself, independent of all interest. It is the universal beauty that elevates the heart and that makes it forget all particular beauty. This philosopher insists in the same dialogue that love renders man divine, that it inspires him, that it transports him. "There is no one so base," he says, "that love could not make him a god, such that he would become similar to the beautiful by nature; and as Homer says that a god inspired some heroes, this is what love gives to the lovers he forms; those who love want only to die for each other."[12] Plato goes on to cite the example of Alcestis, dying so that her husband might live. Thus, following Plato, what makes man divine is to prefer by love the other to one's self, such that one forgets oneself, sacrifices oneself, counts oneself for nothing. This love is, according to him, a divine inspiration; it is the eternal beauty that renders man astonishing to himself and that raises man by virtue to a level similar to it. [668]

Such was the idea of friendship among the ancients. Pythias and Damon, taken by Dionysius, wished to die for each other, and the astonished tyrant could only sigh when he saw two such disinterested friends. This idea of perfect disinterestedness reigned in the politics of all the ancient legislators; they necessarily preferred the law and the fatherland to themselves, because justice demanded it, and because one must prefer to one's self the beautiful, the good, the just, the perfect. It is to this order that they believe everything must be referred, and which itself orders all the rest. It is not about rendering oneself happy in conforming one's self to this order. It is necessary on the contrary to sacrifice oneself, to die, and to abandon one's self for the love of this order. Thus Socrates, in Plato's *Crito*, prefers to die rather than to flee, from fear of disobedience to the laws that held him in prison; so too this same Socrates, in the *Gorgias*, depicts a man who accuses himself, and who condemns himself to death rather than elude by his silence the rigorous laws and the authority of the magistrates.[13] All the legislators and all the philosophers who have examined the laws have supposed as a fundamental principle of society that it is necessary to prefer the public to the self, not by the hope of some interest, but solely by the disinterested love of order that is beauty, justice, and virtue itself. It is for this idea of order and of justice that it would be necessary to die, that is to say, following the ancients, to sacrifice everything, to be reduced to a vain shadow, not knowing even if this shadow was only a ridiculous fable of the poets. Will Christians refuse to grant as much to the infinitely perfect God who they know as these ancient pagans believed it was necessary to give to an abstract and obscure idea of order and justice and virtue?

Plato often says that the love of the beautiful is the whole good of man—that man cannot be happy in himself, that the more divine end for him is to leave himself through love, and that the pleasure that one experiences in the transport of the passions is essentially only an effect of the inclination of the soul to leave its narrow limits, and to love the infinite beautiful that lies beyond.[14] When this journey ends at the deceitful and ephemeral beauty [669] that glitters in created beings, it is divine love that is displaced and lost. It is a divine trait unto itself, but it can lead to errors; that which is divine in him becomes illusion and folly when it falls on a vain image of the perfect good, such as the created being, which is itself only the mere shadow of the supreme Being. But finally this love that prefers the absolutely perfect to itself is a divine and inspired movement, as Plato says. This impression is given to man by nature. His perfection consists in leaving the self by love, such that he never stops trying to persuade both others and himself that he loves without self-interest the friends to whom he attaches himself. This idea is so strong, self-love notwithstanding, that one would be ashamed to admit that one only loves others in ways that allow for some degree of self-interest. One cannot so subtly disguise all the motives of self-love in friendships as to save the shame of appearing to seek out one's self in the others. Nothing is so odious as this idea of a heart always occupied with itself; nothing flatters us so much as certain generous actions that persuade the world and ourselves that we do good from the love of good in itself without seeking to advance ourselves by so doing. Even self-love renders homage to disinterested virtue by the subtleties with which it wants to take on its appearance: so much that it is true that man, who is not his own creator, is not made to find himself, but to exist solely for the sake of the one who made him! His glory and his perfection consist in leaving himself, forgetting himself, losing himself, and passing into the simple love of infinite beauty.

This thought frightens the self-lover accustomed to regard himself as the center of everything. This thought alone suffices to make self-love tremble, and shocks a secret and inner pride, which always imperceptibly returns the self to the end to which we ought to bind ourselves. But this idea that astonishes us is the foundation of all friendship and all justice. We can neither reconcile self-love with this idea, nor abandon it; it is what is *most divine* in us. This thought cannot be said to be merely imaginary. When men invent chimeras, they invent them to please and flatter themselves. Nothing is less natural to [670] the unjust man, vain and drunk on pride, than to think in ways counter to his self-love. Not only is the exercise of such thought an exceptional act of virtue beyond man, but this very thought is itself a marvel that we must be astonished to find within us. Only a principle infinitely superior to us could teach us to raise ourselves so wholly above ourselves. Who could have given to the human being, suffering from an excess of self-love and self-idolatry, this elevated idea of counting himself for nothing, of becoming a stranger to himself, of loving himself only by charity, like his neighbor? Who could have taught him to be jealous of himself against himself for the sake of an invisible object that must forever obliterate the *self*, and leave no trace of it? This idea alone renders *man divine, it inspires him, it instills the infinite within him.*

I admit that the ancients, who all praised disinterested virtue, practiced it poorly. Nobody believes more than I that all love without grace and separate from God can never be anything but a disguised self-love. Only an infinitely perfect Being could, as a consequence of his infinite perfection and his infinite strength, raise us above ourselves, and make us prefer what is not us to our own being. I accept that among the ancients self-love vainly gloried in the appearance of a pure love, but in the end it gloried in it; even those who most mastered their pride were charmed by this beautiful image of virtue and friendship free of self-interest. They carried it within them, and they could neither ignore it nor destroy it, they could neither follow it nor resist it. And the Christians, do they resist it? Do they not content themselves, like the ancients, to admire it without faithfully following it? The very vanity of the ancients with regard to this virtue testifies to how excellent it is. For example, the praise that all Antiquity gave to Alcestis would have been both mistaken and ridiculous had it not been truly beautiful and virtuous for her to die for her husband; without this fundamental principle, her act would have been a furious extravagance, an act of horrible despair.[15] [671] All of pagan antiquity however reaches an opposite conclusion, saying with Plato that *what is most divine in us is to forget ourselves for what we love.*[16]

Alcestis earned the admiration of men for having wanted to die and to be reduced to a mere shadow so as to preserve the life of the one she loved. This forgetting of the self, this total sacrifice of her being, this total loss of herself forever, is in the eyes of the ancients what is most divine in the human being. It is what renders us godlike; it is what makes us come close to realizing our purpose.

Thus the idea of virtue and pure friendship, imprinted on the heart of men who never knew the truth of creation, who were blinded by self-love, and who were alienated from the life of God.

Notes

Introduction

Author's note: This introduction is an adaptation of material to be found in the opening chapter of my monograph *The Political Philosophy of Fénelon*, also published by Oxford University Press and intended as a companion to the present volume.

1. This claim has become a staple of English-language scholarship; see, e.g., Patrick Riley, "Rousseau, Fénelon, and the Quarrel between the Ancients and the Moderns," in *The Cambridge Companion to Rousseau*, ed. Riley (Cambridge, 2001), 81; and Istvan Hont, "The Early Enlightenment Debate on Commerce and Luxury," in *The Cambridge History of Eighteenth-Century Political Thought*, ed. Mark Goldie and Robert Wokler (Cambridge, 2006), 383. The commonly credited source for the claim is Albert Chérel, *Fénelon au XVIIIe siècle en France (1715–1820): Son prestige—son influence* (Hachette, 1917).

2. Peter Gorday's *François Fénelon: A Biography—The Apostle of Pure Love* (Paraclete, 2012) is by far the best source on Fénelon's life currently available in English; most of the details of the brief biographical sketch that follows are drawn from his account, supplemented by reference to the helpful chronology included in Le Brun's Pléiade edition (Pl. 1:xxix–xxxix) and the outstanding chronologies that conclude each commentary volume in CF. Shorter but also valuable to English readers will be the brief sketches of Fénelon's life to be found in James Herbert Davis, *Fénelon* (Twayne, 1979), 15–34; as well as the introduction to Riley's edition of *Telemachus* (Cambridge, 1994), xiii–xvii); and H. C. Barnard's introduction to the education writings [*Fénelon on Education* (Princeton, 1966), vii–xxx].

3. Thus Gorday's observation that this task, which so often "lent itself to mean-spirited intimidation and bullying," was generally regarded to have been conducted by Fénelon in a "sensible, reasonable, even compassionate" manner (*François Fénelon: A Biography*, 24–28, quote at 27).

4. See respectively CF 8:101; CF 8:188. See also CF 8:128; CF 8:179; CF 8:197.

5. Details on the texts and their publication history are principally drawn from the excellent editorial notes in Le Brun's Pléiade edition.

6. Fragments of this memoir were published in OF 7:661–666.

7. As reproduced in OF 7:665.

8. For a helpful guide to the context that emphasizes the impact of the climatological events of the 1690s, see Pierre-Eugene Leroy's preface to his edition of the *Lettre à Louis XIV et autres écrits politiques* (Bartillat, 2011), esp. 24–25.

9. See, e.g., Leroy, in *Lettre à Louis XIV et autres écrits politiques*, 39.

Chapter 1

1. Iris: mythological goddess of the rainbow.
2. Tethys: mythological daughter of Earth and Heaven and wife and sister of Ocean.
3. Alexandretta (modern Iskenderun) is a coastal city in south-central Turkey; Aleppo is roughly one hundred kilometers to the southeast, in modern Syria.
4. Pasha: title given to high-ranking political or military officials in the Ottoman Empire whose honorary status was conferred by the sultan.
5. Great Lord: sultan of Constantinople, head of the Ottoman Empire, which had been in a state of more or less constant war with the Persian Empire since the early sixteenth century.
6. Aristonoüs and Sophronime: essentially fictional characters of Fénelon's invention.
7. Clazomenae: ancient Greek city on a peninsula of the western coast of Asia Minor, near modern Izmir (referenced later as "Smyrna") in Turkey. Teos and Erythrae (mentioned later) lie further west on the same peninsula, close to the island of Chios.
8. Patara: an important commercial center within Lycia located on the southwestern coast of Asia Minor.
9. Early published versions of the text include at this point a different story, drawn from Herodotus, in which Alcine sends Aristonoüs to Polycrates, tyrant of Samos; see Pl. 1:1325–1327.
10. Lycaonia: inland region in modern central Turkey.
11. Karpathos: southern Aegean island lying roughly midway between Patara on the coast and Crete.
12. Delos: Greek island in the central Aegean.
13. For his killing of the Cyclops, Apollo was banished to a year of serfdom in Admetus's kingdom in Thessaly.
14. Hebe and Ganymedes: cupbearers to the gods; the former was daughter of Hera and Zeus, the latter a Trojan prince kidnapped by Zeus and brought to Olympus.
15. Caria: inland region of western Asia Minor; Meander and Cayster and Pactolus: rivers in southwest Asia Minor; Pamphylia: coastal region of Asia Minor east of Lydia. Ceres, Pomona, and Flora: respectively the Roman goddesses of growth, of fruit, and of flowering plants.

Chapter 2

1. French interest in and knowledge of China began to blossom in the second half of the seventeenth century in the wake of the Jesuit missions and the delegation of Jesuit scholars sent by Louis XIV to Beijing in 1685.
2. "Chroniclers" translates *relateurs*; the French missions to China resulted in numerous texts, sometimes titled *Relations* (e.g., Jean-François Gerbillon, *Relations de huit voyages . . .* (1698).
3. Fernão Mendes Pinto (1509–1583), Portuguese explorer whose travel memoirs were first published in 1614; despite their exaggerations, they served as a source of

European knowledge about China before being supplanted by the accounts of later Jesuit missionaries.

4. King Yao: legendary Chinese emperor and model philosopher-king for Confucius.

5. Legendary ancient Greek figures. Cecrops: oldest of the Athenian kings; Inachus: ancestor of the Argive kings; Pelops: ancient hero who gave his name to the Peloponnesians.

6. Justinian (AD 482–565), Roman emperor from 527, was renowned for his Codex (534), an authoritative compilation of extant Roman law.

7. "Legal experts" here translates *jurisconsultes*.

8. Tribonianus (AD 500–547), Roman jurist, contributed to preparation of the Codex and appointed by Justinian to supervise preparation of the Digest.

9. Procopius (AD 6th c.), Roman historian; his *Secret History* (c. 550) "unmasked" Justinian by detailing scandals not mentioned in the official histories.

10. Lysander (d. 395 BC), Spartan military commander; his blockade of Athens in 404 compelled its surrender.

11. Aristophanes (c. 450–386 BC), Athenian playwright; satirized Socrates in his *Clouds*.

12. Herms: stone formations revered as representations of the god Hermes; Alcibiades was accused of mutilating them and of committing other sacrileges, prompting his exile from Athens in 415 BC.

13. The Athenians laid siege to the Corinthian colony of Potidaea in 430 BC and conquered it the following year.

14. See, e.g., Plutarch, *Life of Alcibiades*, sec. 8.

15. Helots: Greek slaves whose treatment at the hands of the Spartans was renowned as especially harsh.

16. Proteus: sea-god renowned for his shape-changing capacities.

17. See Aristotle, *Nicomachean Ethics*, 4.3.

18. Gnaeus Marcius Coriolanus (5th c. BC), Roman statesman who defected to lead the Volsci after being accused of tyranny. Marcus Furius Camillus (c. 445–365 BC), Roman tribune and dictator who fled Rome in voluntary exile after having been unjustly accused of embezzlement.

19. "Regulation" here translates *police*.

20. Publius Cornelius Scipio Africanus (236–183 BC), Roman military commander who left Rome for voluntary exile in Liternum in 184, escaping his and his brother's trials for bribery and embezzlement.

21. The Battle of the Allia River in 390 BC resulted in the defeat of the Romans by the Gauls.

22. Livy, *History of Rome*, 5.49; Plutarch, *Life of Camillus*, 29.

23. The Battle of Thapsus of 46 BC marked the defeat of the Optimate resistance to Caesar.

24. Timoleon (c. 411–337 BC), Greek military commander who allowed the assassination of his brother Timophanes after the latter's tyrannical seizure of the acropolis of Corinth. Lucius Junius Brutus (6th c. BC), founder of the Roman Republic; as consul in 509 BC he sentenced two of his sons to death for their participation in the Tarquinian conspiracy.

25. Marcus Junius Brutus (85–42 BC), Roman statesman and descendent of Lucius Junius Brutus ("Junius"); a leader of the assassination of Caesar in 44 BC.

26. The conspiracy of Catiline of 63 BC sought to overthrow the Roman Republic, but was exposed by Cicero.

27. As Le Brun explains (Pl. 1:1375n), in *De officiis*—a text to which this particular dialogue is much indebted—Cicero reports that Caesar was fond of quoting a line of Euripides (*Phoenicians*, ll. 524–525; see *De officiis* 3.82).

28. Lucius Cornelius Sulla (138–78 BC), Roman military commander who marched on Rome and claimed the dictatorship but ultimately relinquished his office voluntarily.

29. Louis XI (1423–1483), King of France, 1461–1483. Jean Balue (1421–1491), church official and minister of Louis XI.

30. All influential figures surrounding Louis XI. Louis Tristan l'Hermite, or *prévôt Tristan* (d. 1478), soldier and military official; Jacques Coitier or Coctier (c. 1430–1506), chief court physician; Olivier le Daim, or Olivier le Diable (c. 1428–1484), courtier and barber to the King. The reference to "Janfredy" is untraced.

31. The Pragmatic Sanction of Bourges (*La pragmatique*) was issued by Charles VII in 1438 and laid the foundation for the increasing independence of the Gallican Church from the Pope. Louis XI revoked it in 1461, and Balue was made a cardinal by Pope Paul II in 1467 for his role in negotiating the revocation.

32. "Miserable document" translates *pancarte crasseuse*, presumably referring to *La pragmatique*.

33. Plessis-lez-Tours: Loire Valley château and preferred residence of Louis XI.

34. Charles de Valois, Duke of Berry and Guyenne (1446–1472), brother of Louis XI, who joined forces with Charles the Bold, Duke of Burgundy (1433–1477) to oppose Louis XI.

35. Balue's rapid political rise ended with his arrest for treason and an eleven-year imprisonment (1469–1480) after the interception of his correspondence with Charles the Bold.

36. Louis XII (1462–1515), King of France, 1498–1515.

37. The Duke of Burgundy lured Louis XI to Péronne in 1468 and had him briefly imprisoned there.

38. Episodes in the reign of Louis XI. "Ridding yourself of a brother": reference to his outmaneuvering of Charles de Valois. "Misfortunes of the Duke of Burgundy": reference to the outmaneuvering of Charles the Bold by Louis XI in signing the Treaty of Picquigny (1475). "Won the counselor": Louis XI arranged matters so that his cousin Charles, Duke of Anjou, willed him Provence on his death in 1481.

39. Episodes in the reign of Louis XII. "Legitimate alliance": Louis XII came into possession of Brittany upon his marriage to Anne, Duchess of Brittany, in 1498–1499. "Wars of Naples and Milan": Louis XII captured both territories in the Second Italian War (1499–1503), but ceded them to the Spanish after being compelled to withdraw in 1504.

40. In August 1475 Louis XI and Edward IV met to negotiate the terms of the Treaty of Picquigny. As Le Brun notes (Pl. 1:1389n), an account of their meeting, as well as an account of Louis XI's interview with the Bordeaux merchant, is given in Philippe de Commines, *Memoirs* 4.10.

41. Henry VII (1457–1509), King of England 1485–1509, and father of Henry VIII (1491–1547), King of England 1509–1547.

42. Francis I (1494–1547), King of France; and Charles V (1500–1558), Holy Roman Emperor and King of Spain, Germany and Italy.

43. The efforts of Henry VIII to secure an annulment of his marriage to Catherine of Aragon led to the establishment of the Anglican Church in 1534.

44. *Assertio Septem Sacramentorum* (1521).

45. Pope Clement VII (1478–1534) appointed Lorenzo Campeggio (1474–1539) papal legate to England and examiner of Henry VIII's suit of divorce from his first wife, Catherine of Aragon (1485–1536), aunt of Charles V.

46. Catherine of Aragon married Henry in 1509; they divorced in 1531. Anne Boleyn (1507–1536) he married in 1533, and executed three years later. Jane Seymour (1509–1537) he married in 1536; they stayed married until her death following birth of her son Edward VI. Anne of Cleves (1515–1557) he married in early 1540; their marriage was annulled months later. Catherine Howard (c. 1524–1542) he married in July 1540, and had executed in 1542. Catherine Parr (1512–1548) he married in 1543; they remained married until his death in January 1547, after which she married Sir Thomas Seymour.

47. Thomas Wolsey (c. 1475–1530), cardinal and influential diplomat; Thomas Cranmer (1489–1556), Archbishop of Canterbury, presided over divorces from both Catherine and Anne Boleyn.

48. Reginald Pole (here *Renauld de La Poule*, 1500–1558), cardinal from 1538 and final Catholic Archbishop of Canterbury.

49. Henry III (1551–1589), King of France, 1574–1589; Henry IV (1553–1610), King of France, 1589–1610.

50. "Minions" here translates *mignons*; "*les mignons*" were young male court favorites of Henry III who were subjects of considerable rumor.

51. The two brothers Louis, Cardinal of Guise (1555–1588) and Henri de Lorraine, Duke of Guise (1550–1588) were assassinated at the order of Henry III at a meeting of the Estates-General at Blois.

52. The Marquis du Guast was a favorite of Henry III; the Elbènes were a Florentinian family influential in France, and included Alexandre d'Elbène (1554–1610), who served Henry III as *Gentilhomme ordinaire*.

53. Key counselors to Henry IV: Maximilien de Béthune, Duke de Sully (1560–1641), nobleman and memoirist; Pierre Jeannin (1540–1622), statesman and diplomat; Arnaud d'Ossat (1537–1604), diplomat and cardinal.

54. Diane d'Andouins, Countess of Guiche (1554–1621), mistress of Henry IV from 1582–1591.

55. Coutras, Ivry, Arques, Fontaine-Française: military victories won by Henry IV and his Protestant forces between 1587 and 1595 in the later stages of the Wars of Religion.

56. Jarnac and Moncontour: military victories won by Henry III and his Catholic forces in 1568–1569 in the early stages of the Wars of Religion.

57. The future King Henry III was the Duke of Anjou until 1574; the future King Henry IV was the King of Navarre from 1572.

58. Gabrielle d'Estrées, Duchess of Beaufort (1573–1599), mistress to Henry IV; Catherine Henriette de Balzac d'Entragues, Marquise de Verneuil (1579–1633), succeeded the Duchess of Beaufort as Henry's mistress.

59. Armand Jean du Plessis, Cardinal Richelieu (1585–1642), Church official and statesman and de facto prime minister; Jules Raymond, Cardinal Mazarin (1602–1661), Church official and statesman who succeeded Richelieu as de facto prime minister.

60. Richelieu was prime minister under Louis XIII (1601–1643), son of Henry IV and King of France from 1610. The Battle of La Rochelle (1628) marked a decisive victory for the royal Catholic forces over the Huguenots.

61. Allusions to several French alliances established by Richelieu. "Revolt of Catalonia": Under Richelieu, France launched the Franco-Spanish War (1635–1659); Catalan declared itself an independent republic in 1641, and sided with France. "Portugal": Portugal likewise rebelled against Spain in 1640 and allied with France. "Dutch": France's intervention on behalf of the Dutch against the Spanish helped bring to a close the Dutch Revolt (1568–1648). "Allies of the North": in 1631 France allied with Sweden under King Gustavus Adolphus, pledging to support the Swedish efforts against the Holy Roman Emperor in the Thirty Years' War.

62. Key episodes and figures in France during the ministry of the Italian-born Mazarin. "The queen's mind": Anne of Austria (1601–1666), served from 1643 to 1651 as regent during the minority of her son Louis XIV, with Mazarin as her chief minister. Parlement and the Fronde: from 1648 Mazarin stood in tension with both the populace and the Parlement owing to his war expenses and tax schemes; these tensions culminated in the Fronde, an open rebellion led by the nobility that lasted until 1653. "Audacious cardinal": Jean-François-Paul de Condi, Cardinal de Retz (1613–1679), French priest and a leader of the Fronde. "Prince": Louis de Bourbon, Prince de Condé (the Great Condé) (1621–1686), military commander and leader of the Fronde.

63. "A glorious peace": The Peace of Westphalia (1648), which concluded both the Thirty Years' War and the Dutch Revolt. "Young king": Louis XIV.

64. In January 1650 Mazarin arrested and had imprisoned at Vincennes the Prince de Condé, along with Armand de Bourbon, Prince de Conti (1629–1666) and Henri II de Orleans, Duke of Longueville (1595–1663); all three were prominent in the Fronde.

65. See Machiavelli, *Prince*, ch. 18.

66. Pierre Corneille (1606–1684), French poet and dramatist; originally supported by Richelieu, their rupture came to a head in the public quarrel over Corneille's play *The Cid* (1637).

Chapter 3

1. "Administration" here translates *police*.

2. Sesostris: legendary king of ancient Egypt described by Herodotus.

3. Tyre, meaning "rock," takes its name from the sharp promontory jutting out into the Mediterranean on which it sits.

4. Strait of Gades: passage between the Pillars of Hercules.

5. Minos: legendary first king of Crete, said to be a son of Zeus.

6. "Civilization" here translates *police*.

7. Tartessus: harbor city on the Iberian peninsula with which the historical Phoenicians had extensive contact; also associated with the traditions of Atlantis and the biblical Tarshish.

8. Astraea: Greek goddess of purity often connected to the goddess of justice (Diké); she was said to have fled the world of men at the dawn of the Iron Age, but her expected return to earth will herald the beginning of a new Golden Age.

9. Modern-day Cadiz.

Chapter 4

1. Fénelon's letter begins with the feminine noun *personne*, which requires use of the first-person singular feminine pronoun *elle* as the subject of the sentences that follow. I have preserved the feminine constructions here (and in the concluding sentences of the letter), partly to preserve literal consistency, and partly with reference to the possibility that Fénelon intended the letter for Mme de Maintenon.

2. Ministers Fénelon likely has in mind include at least Jean-Baptiste Colbert (1619–1683), minister of finance from 1661; and François Michel le Tellier, Marquis de Louvois (1641–1691), secretary of state for war from 1666.

3. Louis XIV launched the Franco-Dutch War in 1672; this was in part resulting from tensions between the two countries over escalating import taxes.

4. The Treaty of Nijmegen (1678) that ended the Franco-Dutch War awarded France the Franche-Comté and several other areas along its modern northern border, including Cambrai.

5. In commemoration of the Peace of Aachen (1668), the Dutch arranged for a medallion to be struck celebrating their republican virtues, to which Louis XIV took offense. Voltaire gives its inscription as: *Assertis legibus, emendaits sacris, adjutis, defensis, conciliatis regibus, vindicata marium libertate, stabilita orbis Europae quiete* ("The laws asserted, religion amended, princes succored, defended, and reconciled, the freedom of the ocean vindicated, and peace restored to Europe"); see Voltaire, *Age of Louis XIV*, in *The Works of Voltaire*, trans. William R. Fleming (E.R. DuMont, 1901, vol. 12, p. 145 (Fleming's translation).

6. *Chambres des réunions*: system of courts established by Louis XIV to examine peace treaties and exploit loopholes going back to feudal law, thereby enabling France to annex additional lands and further solidify its northern border.

7. Louis XIV seized independent Strasbourg in 1681.

8. *La grande famine* of 1693–1694 claimed the lives of over one million French subjects (perhaps as much as 10 percent of the nation's population).

9. Isaiah 29:13.

10. François de Harlay de Champvallon (1625–1695), Archbishop of Paris, 1671–1695.

11. François de la Chaise (1624–1709), Jesuit priest and confessor of Louis XIV.

12. Luke 6:39.

13. François-Michel le Tellier, Marquis de Louvois (see n2, earlier). The Order of St. Lazarus was a French Catholic military order; Louvois managed the united orders of St. Lazarus and Mount Carmel after 1673.

14. Françoise d'Aubigné, Marquise de Maintenon (1635–1719), morganatic second wife of Louis XIV from c. 1683; Paul de Beauvillier, Duke de Saint-Aignan (1648–1714), political official, governor of the Duke of Burgundy, and member of Fénelon's reformist circle.

15. Charles Auguste d'Allonville, Marquis de Louville (1664–1731) was Gentleman of the Chamber and chief advisor to another of Fénelon's former pupils, the Duke of Anjou. The Duke of Anjou was younger brother to the Duke of Burgundy and in 1700 himself succeeded to the throne of Spain as King Philip V.

16. A reference to Molière's *Le bourgeois gentilhomme* (1670).

17. Sixtus V (1520–1590) was elected Pope in 1585, and was renowned for his stringency.

18. 1 Kings 3:28.

19. In 1515, King Francis I (1494–1547) led French troops to victory over the Swiss confederacy at the battle of Marignan; he later earned a reputation for his mistresses.

20. Charles V (1338–1380), King of France from 1364.

21. French forces overseen by Louis XIV engaged in an extended siege of the citadel of Namur in 1692; the siege lasted over a month before Namur capitulated.

22. Fénelon here refers to James Francis Edward Stuart (1688–1766), son of James II and VII, who claimed the crown of England (and Scotland and Ireland) on the death of his father in 1701. The Stuarts were allied to Louis XIV, and James served in the French armies active in Flanders between 1708 and 1710.

Chapter 5

1. I Corinthians 9:19. English translations of Fénelon's biblical citations are drawn from the Douay-Rheims edition; Fénelon here also gives the Latin of the Vulgate.

2. Joseph-Clément was a member of the House of Wittelsbach, which comprised a Bavarian branch and a Palatinate branch. Louis IV (1282–1347), Holy Roman Emperor from 1328, was of the Bavarian branch; Charles XII of Sweden (1682–1718), King of Sweden from 1697, was of its Palatinate branch.

3. *Henri le Grand* (Henry IV; see ch. 2, n49) was great-grandfather of Joseph-Clément on his mother's side.

4. Marie-Anna Victoria of Bavaria (1660–1690), Dauphine of France, was sister of Joseph-Clément, wife of Louis of France (the Grand Dauphin), and mother of the Duke of Anjou, the Duke of Berry, and the Duke of Burgundy.

5. Maximilian II Emanuel, Elector of Bavaria (1662–1726), won multiple military victories for Austria against the Turks in the 1680s, and fought with the French in the War of Spanish Succession.

6. Bernard of Clairvaux, *On Consideration*, Prologue.

7. Here and throughout the remainder of the *Discourse*, "bridegroom" translates *époux* and "bride" translates *épouse* in accord with the traditional Gospel imagery of the relationship of Jesus to the Church (and in accord with the terminology used in the Douay-Rheims translation; see, e.g., John 3:29).

8. Jeremiah 17:5.

9. I Corinthians 1:17.

10. Luke 21:33.

11. Revelations 1:5; I Timothy 1:17.

12. All quoted passages in this paragraph are from Isaiah; see respectively 60:16; 49:23; 60:3; 60:11; 49:23; 52:15; 60:12.

13. Psalms 2:10–12.

14. Ben Sira 10:17.

15. Ben Sira 10:18.

16. Ben Sira 10:21.

17. Isaiah 40:6–8.

18. Isaiah 60:12.

19. Luke 1:33; cf. Isaiah 9:7.

20. I Maccabees 12:9.

21. I Corinthians 1:25–29.

22. Tertullian, *Apology*, sec. 21.

23. Ambrose, *Letter 18 to Valentinian*, sec. 17.

24. Isaiah 49:23.

25. Ambrose, *Sermon against Auxentius on the Giving up of the Basilicas*, sec. 36.

26. See n24 above.

27. Ambrose, *Sermon against Auxentius*, sec. 36.

28. Tertullian, *To Scapula*, ch. 4. Fénelon himself provides a translation of the Latin in the sentence that follows his quotation of it.

29. Matthew 21:44.

30. Isaiah 53:3, 53:10; Lamentations 3:30.

31. Ambrose, *Sermon against Auxentius*, sec. 33.

32. Matthew 28:18–19.

33. Daniel 7:22.

34. Daniel 7:25–27.

35. Ibid.

36. Psalms 2:2.

37. Psalms 2:3–4.

38. Psalms 2:8.

39. Psalms 2:9.

40. Acts 4:19.

41. The term "bishop of the external" (*évêque du dehors*) is traditionally attributed to Eusebius, *Life of Constantine*, 4.24; in the seventeenth century it had come to denote the superiority of the crown in secular matters.

42. A reference to Henry VIII (see chapter two, note 41).

43. II Timothy 2:9.
44. Augustine, *Letter 100 to Donatus*, sec. 1.
45. Cyprian, *Letter 54 to Cornelius*, sec. 17.
46. Maximilian I (1573–1651), Elector of Bavaria and grandfather of Joseph-Clément, was a key figure in the Thirty Years' War and played an important role in helping to consolidate the Catholic League in Germany.
47. Matthew 20:28.
48. Hebrews 1:3.
49. II Corinthians 4:5 ("ourselves your servants through Jesus").
50. Esther 14:16.
51. The Golden Bull of 1356 granted electoral authority to the Archbishop of Cologne.
52. Matthew 11:28–29.
53. Bernard of Clairvaux, *On Consideration*, Prologue.
54. Bernard of Clairvaux, *On Consideration*, 2.6.
55. See notes 24 and 26.
56. Fénelon's editors traditionally attribute this to Cyprian, *On the Unity of the Church* (e.g., sec. 5). Yet it may be that he has a biblical passage in mind here, e.g., 1 Corinthians 1:10–12.
57. Psalms 45:10; see also Luke 13:27; Matthew 25:12.
58. II Samuel 6:22.
59. I Peter 5:4.
60. Philippians 2:6–7.
61. Romans 1:14.
62. I Kings 3:8–9.
63. Psalms 85:8.
64. Cyprian, *Letter 73 to Pompey*, sec. 10.
65. Fénelon here uses the word *COMPRÊTRES* (in all caps) to stand in for the names of Donatus, Fortunatus, Novatus, and Gordius mentioned in Cyprian's letter.
66. Cyprian, *Letter 5*, sec. 4.
67. Augustine, *Confessions*, 6.3.3. The Loeb translation renders this "tending to their frailties."
68. I Peter 4:10.
69. I Corinthians 9:20–22.
70. II Corinthians 11:29.
71. I Thessalonians 2:7.
72. II Timothy 4:2.
73. Augustine, *Confessions*, 6.5.7. Fénelon's preceding sentence is a translation of the Latin.
74. "Administration" here translates *police*.
75. Augustine, *Letter 140 to Honoratus*, sec. 18. In the English translation of Wilfrid Parsons: "He is not worshiped but by love" (*Saint Augustine: Letters, vol. 3 (131–164)* [Catholic University Press, 1953], p. 95).
76. Augustine, *Of True Religion*, 16.31. Fénelon's preceding sentence is a translation of the Latin.
77. Luke 9:54.

78. Luke 9:55.
79. II Corinthians 10:1.
80. John 16:12.
81. Augustine, *On the Morals of the Catholic Church*, 32.69.
82. Matthew 13:30.
83. Matthew 9:12–13.
84. James 2:13.
85. Cyprian, *Letter 54 to Cornelius*, sec. 16.
86. Cyprian, *Letter 1 to Donatus*, sec. 10.
87. Fénelon's French editors customarily attribute this reference to Augustine, *Letter 54 to Januarius*, 5.6. Yet here again Fénelon may have a Bible verse in mind.
88. Acts 9:16.
89. Luke 17:10.
90. Augustine, *Rule* (*Regula ad servos Dei*), 7.3. For the complex history of this text as well as an authoritative translation of this passage, see George Lawless, *Augustine of Hippo and His Monastic Rule* (Oxford, 1987), esp. p. 101.
91. Romans 10:12.
92. John 21:15–17.
93. Isaiah 55:1.
94. I Thessalonians 5:17.
95. I Corinthians 2:6.
96. Psalms 34:8.
97. Otto I (912–973), Holy Roman Emperor from 962; his brother, Bruno the Great (925–965), was Archbishop of Cologne from 953.
98. Isaiah 40:1; 40:4; 40:9.
99. Isaiah 49:12; 49:18; 49:20–21.
100. Wisdom 4:12.

Chapter 6

1. The manuscript (BnF Fr. 14944) carries includes topical headings for some but not all of the numbered sections of the *Examination*. These are in Fénelon's hand and appear in the margin of the manuscript directly across from the section number; in this version they are given in brackets.
2. The laws of nations or peoples (*le droit des gens*) refers to the body of early modern natural law that in developing the Roman concept of *jus gentium* sought to establish laws universally applicable to all peoples and that formed the foundation of modern conceptions of international law and human rights.
3. In the ms (BnF Fr. 14944), another hand has changed this to read "ancient parlements of the nation."
4. Luke 17:2.
5. Francis I (1494–1547), King of France from 1515, was known for welcoming women to his court.

6. Charles VIII (1470–1498), King of France from 1483, invaded Italy in 1494 and was crowned King of Naples a year later.

7. In conceiving of *"le Parlement"* as a representative body responsible for fiscal appropriations, Fénelon suggests a broader conception of its authority than most would have recognized at a time when the responsibilities of the *parlements* were chiefly dedicated to serving as courts of appeal and registrants of royal law.

8. *Edits bursaux* raised revenue for the sovereign by making it possible to sell offices and create other revenue-generating institutions in times of public necessity.

9. Psalms 49:21 ("Thou thoughtest unjustly that I should be like to thee").

10. "Law of peoples" here translates *droit des gens*; see earlier note for its relationship to the concept of international law. "Law of nations" two sentences later translates *droit des nations*.

11. Proverbs 31:10 ("far, and from the uttermost coasts is the price of her").

12. Fénelon here refers to officials dedicated to the king's personal service; within the royal household, or *Maison du Roi*, numerous inferior *valets de chambre* and *valets de garde-robe* attended to the king's domestic needs.

13. "Reporters" translates *rapporteurs*; the 1694 *Dictionnaire* emphasizes its use with regard to those who report "maliciously."

14. Augustine, *Letter 220 to Boniface*, sec. 5. The Loeb translation renders this "few, indeed, by you, but many because of you."

15. Charles V (1500–1558), Holy Roman Emperor from 1519; through inheritance he came into possession of Spain and the Netherlands, leaving him effectively the ruler of nearly all of Europe except France. Francis I was taken prisoner by Charles V at the Battle of Pavia (1525).

16. Philip II (1527–1598), King of Spain from 1556, conquered Portugal in 1581 and married Mary Tudor (1516–1558), Queen Mary I of England from 1553. Parliament bestowed on Philip the title of King of England until Mary's death. Elizabeth I (1533–1603) succeeded her Catholic half-sister Mary as the first Protestant Queen of England, reigning from 1558 until her death, and in spite of the claims made on behalf of the Catholic Mary Stuart or Mary, Queen of Scots (1542–1587).

17. "Extreme justice is extreme injustice."

18. The Carolingian Empire established by Charlemagne covered most of western Europe at the time of his death in 814; it was partitioned into France and Germany in 843 and divided to the point of dissolution in 887. Alexander's generals partitioned his eastern empire after his death in 323 BC, but soon fell to infighting.

Chapter 7

1. In the previous year Daniel Voysin de la Noiraye (1655–1717) had succeeded Michel Chamillart (1652–1721) as secretary of state for war.

2. The French credit crisis of 1709, partly the result of excessive military expenditure on the part of Louis XIV, had led to a significant depreciation in value of existing bank notes.

3. Hainaut: borderland that is today part of Belgium.

4. Menen and Tournai: heavily fortified French border towns that fell to the allies led by Marlborough in 1706 and 1709 respectively.

5. Valenciennes, Bouchain, Douai, Cambrai: northern French towns of the modern Hauts-de-France region.

6. Tournai: Like several of the aforementioned towns, on the river Scheldt but today part of modern Belgium.

7. Somme: river running east–west across northern France, parallel to and located roughly halfway between the modern Belgian border to the north and the Seine to the south.

8. Jean-Baptiste Colbert, Marquis of Torcy (1665–1746) and Pierre Rouillé de Marbeuf (1657–1712) were French diplomats who each played prominent roles in negotiating various settlements during the War of Spanish Succession (1701–1714). Fénelon here refers to their diplomatic mission to The Hague in 1709.

9. A reference to the most controversial article of the Barrier Treaty of 1709.

10. On Castille, see CF 15:375n19, as per Le Brun in Pl. 2:1709n.

11. The Duke of Burgundy had become Dauphin on the death of his father in April 1711.

12. All prominent military officers in the service of Louis XIV: François de Neufville, duc de Villeroy (1644–1730); Claude-Louis-Hector, duc de Villars (1653–1734); Henri, duc d'Harcourt (1654–1718); James Fitzjames, 1st Duke of Berwick (1670–1734); Jacques Bazin, Marquis de Bezons (1646–1733); and Pierre de Montesquiou, Comte d'Artagnan (1640–1725).

13. *Hôtel des Invalides*: built under Louis XIV in Paris between 1670 and 1676 to provide refuge and assistance for retired and injured soldiers. A military pension system akin to that envisioned by Fénelon did not emerge until the 1760s.

14. All noblemen and military leaders: on Harcourt, see n12 earlier; Camille d'Hostun de la Baume, duc de Tallard (1652–1728); Jacques François de Chastenet, Marquis de Puységur (1656–1743).

15. Across from these lines, in another hand: "Militias throughout the realm, etc."

16. *Rentiers*: members of the propertied nobility and bourgeoisie who received regular payments on government-backed annuities in their possession.

17. *Assiette*: a type of representative committee in Languedoc responsible for distributing the tax burden across communities according to a predetermined rate.

18. *Etats de la province* (or *Etats provinciaux*): local representative assemblies that held principal administrative authority throughout much of France prior to the shift towards administrative centralization in the seventeenth century.

19. *Gabelle*: a specific salt tax, the rate of which differed across the six regions into which France had been divided for the purpose of salt taxation. The inequities of its application were a source of considerable resentment.

20. *Grosses fermes*: the five regional tax farms that had been consolidated in the early seventeenth century into a single administrative district subject to a complex and inefficient system of tariffs and tax farming procedures.

21. *Capitation*: a direct tax on individuals, established in 1695 to help finance the foreign wars of Louis XIV. Fénelon had extensive personal experience with the collection of

capitation, as has been noted (CF 11:17n3); see, e.g., CF 10:261 and also CF 10:15, 157, 167, 172, 182, 203; CF 12:160; CF 18:42.

22. *Dîme royale*: a universal flat tax of 10 percent on all incomes imposed in October 1710 as a wartime measure. It was inspired by the famous proposal of Vauban in a manuscript of the 1690s (published 1707). But where Vauban's *dîme royale* was proposed as a substitute for the complex and much-abused tax system then in place, the *dîme royale* that was enacted in 1710 was merely added on top of existing taxes; cf. CF 14:286.

23. *Fermiers*: "tax farmers" who purchased from the king the authority to collect various taxes, including, among others, the *gabelles* and the *aides*.

24. *Traitants*: financial speculators who contracted with the king for rights related to lending money. Like the *fermiers*, the *traitants* were at once an important source of revenue for the king and widely unpopular.

25. *Etats généraux*: national representative body including delegates from each of the three estates in French society charged with advising the crown. It had last been assembled in 1614.

26. Across from this line, in another hand: "By means of representation."

27. At the end of this line, in another hand: "new, fix number of plots, if there is not labor."

28. At the end of this line, in another hand: "because of too many deer, rabbits, etc. which spoils the grains, vines, meadows, etc."

29. *Capitaineries*: land areas governed by specific hunting regulations. In those claimed by the crown, the feudal lords who would ordinarily be considered owners of the land were forbidden to hunt there except by permission of the administrating *capitaine*.

30. At the end of this line, in another hand: "—abusive."

31. The four lines that follow are bracketed next to this line, but seem to gloss the previous line's reference to the ancient Church. See also in this context Fénelon's comments at CF 12:181.

32. At the end of the line the two words "in secret" have been struck.

33. *Evêque du dehors*: see n41 to the *Discourse*.

34. Next to these lines, in another hand: "Note, this is only since Francis I."

35. *Capitulaires*: collections of laws and administrative edicts divided into chapters and promulgated by royal courts from the time of Charlemagne.

36. Amphictyons: in ancient Greece, delegates to a confederation of towns and states bound together by political and religious ties.

37. Pepin the Short (714–768) came to be King of the Franks after having arranged for the deposition of the previous king, Childeric III, by Pope Zachary (679–752) in 751.

38. Louis the Pious, or *Louis le Débonnaire* (778–840), King of the Franks and successor to his father Charlemagne as Holy Roman Emperor from 814, was briefly deposed in 833–834.

39. Charlemagne (c. 747–814), King of the Franks from 768 and Holy Roman Emperor from 800, was the eldest son of Pepin; Carloman I (751–771), his younger brother, · shared in tension with him the crown of King of the Franks.

40. Hugh Capet (938–996), King of the Franks from 987.

41. Respectively: Peter the Cruel (1334–1369), King of Castile; John (1166–1216), King of England; Henry IV (1050–1106), Holy Roman Emperor; Frederick II (1194–1250), Holy Roman Emperor; Raymond VI (1156–1222), Count of Toulouse; Henry IV (1553–1610), King of France (see also note 49 in *Dialogues* earlier); Gregory II (669–731), Pope from 715.

42. Ultramontanes: Catholics who regarded the Pope's authority as superior to the crown's; generally regarded as supporters rather than critics of papal infallibility.

43. Ossius of Cordova (c. 256–358), presided over the Council of Nicaea in 325, convened to resolve a number of emerging points of dispute and bring unity to the early Church.

44. Added in another hand: "though fallible."

45. Added below this line, in another hand: "by consultation, but deposition brings nothing of it."

46. The remainder of this line and the three lines that follow have been struck in the manuscript. They are provided however by another hand in a page that has been interleaved with the manuscript (A.S.-S. 2027, f106r).

47. Across from this line, in another hand: "Note: To collect that which is consecrated to God, is this not a kind of sacrilege."

48. Added below this line, in another hand: "Would they not need to contribute to the charges of the state? Yes by the revenues."

49. *Libertés gallicans*: The "Liberties of the Gallicans" were a series of freedoms codified in 1682 that asserted the general independence of the French church (in local ecclesiastical matters) and the French monarchy (in temporal matters) from papal authority, in opposition to the deference supported by the ultramontagnes.

50. *Arrêt d'Agen*: decree issued by a royal council in 1669 order to support the efforts of Claude Joly, Bishop of Agen, to establish his authority over his priest; see Bergin, *Politics of Religion*, 427.

51. A royal council of 1702 judged in favor of the Archbishop of Rouen's suit that sought to limit the authority of the Archbishop of Lyon (the "Primate of the Gauls").

52. *Appel comme d'abus*: a formal appeal to parlement to review ecclesiastical judgments in instances where such judges are believed to have exceeded their authority. For Fénelon's experiences with the *appel*, see, e.g., CF 10:77; cf. CF 12:39–40; CF 16:223.

53. *Possessoire* refers to actions intended to protect or recover possession; *pétitoire* refers to actions intended to establish one's right to ownership.

54. Added in the margin, in another hand: "which might be useful if the clergy were not required to contribute to the state. They are new."

55. Added at the end of this line, in another hand: "which will constitute their functions in this regard." Below this line, at the base of the page, the same hand adds: "To know if the property of the bishops and abbeys, ancient fiefs given to the Church on condition of furnishing troops have since been exempt from them, and if these troops were only in times of war. In order to judge if the clergy must contribute to the charges of the state."

56. Charles-Bénigne Hervé (1652–1722), Bishop of Gap until stripped of his position in 1705. This example may be in another's hand.

57. Cluny Abbey was the principal monastery of the Benedictines; *cordeliers* are Franciscans.

58. *Appel simple*: like the *appel comme d'abus*, an appeals request for review of ecclesiastical judgments, but in this case an appeal to a higher ecclesiastical court rather than to a secular court.

59. Fénelon was a prominent voice in the opposition to Jansenism, a Catholic theological movement inspired by the works of Cornelius Jansen (1585–1638), and which emphasized the fallenness of humanity, predestination, and an austere form of moral asceticism.

60. Not the much-better known bull *Unigenitus*, which would not be issued by Pope Clement XI until 1713, but the anti-Jansenist bull *Vineam Domini Sabaoth* (1705).

61. *Chambre des Comptes*: the system of royal courts responsible for matters of financial and legal administration pertaining to the crown's accounts and domains, chief of which was the Paris branch.

62. *Trésor des Chartes*: the official archive of state papers.

63. The military branch of the royal household was composed of several classes of soldiers and officers, including the guards (*gardes du corps*), the heavy cavalry (*gendarmes de la garde*), and the light cavalry (*chevau-légers*).

64. Added at end of line, in another hand: "Chamberlains or gentlemen of the chamber rather than valets of the chamber, ushers, and only valets or chamber boys for meaner services. All other more significant duties to the verified nobles."

65. *Majorasgo* (or *mayorazgo*): right established by Spanish law providing for bequest of property to an eldest son. Added after this line, in another hand: "for the Houses of the high nobility, not lesser. In [illeg.] for mediocre."

66. Added between phrases, in another hand: "of the name of surviving noble families."

67. Added below, in another hand: "no Duke not peer."

68. Added in other hand: "viscounts."

69. *Honneurs*: Privileges awarded on basis of nobility regarding matters of court etiquette (e.g., the right to enter the royal residence by carriage, the right of women to sit on a stool in the presence of the queen or on a cushion at masses attended by the king, etc.), which served as marks of distinction.

70. The complexities of and relationships between the Bouillon and Rohan families are chronicled in other seventeenth-century French sources, esp. the *Mémoires* of Saint-Simon.

71. *Maîtres des requêtes*: administrative officials chiefly responsible for transmitting requests sent to the king; under Louis XIV their duties evolved and expanded to include a wide variety of legal and administrative and fiscal responsibilities.

72. *Paulette*: tax on political and administrative offices in the amount of one sixtieth the value of the office, which officeholders paid annually to the crown in order to secure the right of transferring their offices to their chosen designees. It was established in 1604 and not abolished until the French Revolution.

73. Added on facing manuscript page across from this line, in another hand: "Council of State where the king is always present. Other six councils for all the affairs of the realm." Added beside this, in yet a different hand (perhaps Fénelon's): "as it is recorded in the particular memorandum, etc."

74. Added on facing manuscript page across from this line, in another hand: "No remnants of charges, governments, etc."

75. *Premiers présidents*: heads of sovereign courts and parlements, whose authority was granted by the king and could not be sold or transferred.

76. *Procureurs généraux*: chief representative of the king's interests in certain courts of appeal and financial courts.

77. Added below, in another hand: "Magistrates of the sword and with the sword in place of Robe when possible."

78. *Bailliages*: tribunal system responsible for administrating justice in ordinary matters; presided over by a *bailli* who held the rank of nobility and pronounced justice in the king's name.

79. *Presidiaux*: system of intermediary tribunals superior to the *bailliages* but inferior to the *parlements*.

80. Added at the end of this line, in another hand: "Same as above. Nobility 40 years and beyond."

81. Two high posts in the central civil administration: the *lieutenant général de police* was responsible for oversight over all matters of public order and safety; the *lieutenant criminel* was responsible for preventing and prosecuting criminality.

82. Added below this line, in another hand: "Reserve to them jurisdiction over land revenue, honors of the parish, rights of the hunt, etc."

83. Added below this line, in another hand: "Regulate hunting rights between the lords and vassals."

84. In the margin, heading of "Office of commerce" struck.

85. *Grand Conseil*: superior tribunal, convened directly by the king, that ruled in especially contentious matters in which *Parlement* was not thought sufficiently independent.

86. *Cour des Aides:* system of tribunals responsible for judging matters of trade and taxation. The *élections* similarly attended to legal matters concerning trade, and were presided over by the "elected" (*élus*).

87. "Commerce" here translates *mercature*, a word uncommon in seventeenth-century French.

88. *Mont-de-piété*: charitable lending institution sponsored by the Catholic Church; designed to provide low-interest loans on terms advantageous to borrowers.

89. Added below, in another hand: "and for each station."

90. This is the final line of the manuscript in Fénelon's hand. The remaining four entries are in another hand.

91. *Missi dominici* ("envoys of the lord") were sent into the provinces to administer justice in the king's name.

92. Added in another hand: "15 March 1712."

93. Fénelon refers here to Philippe II, duc d'Orléans (1674–1723), nephew of Louis XIV and Regent of France during the minority of Louis XIV from 1715. The Duke of Burgundy earlier in the year had died of measles caught while attending to his wife on her deathbed; rumors circulated widely about the possibility of poisoning.

94. Added at end of line: "without a solid foundation."

95. Fénelon originally wrote "the young princes" in the plural, which he here and elsewhere throughout the memorandum corrected to the singular. As Le Brun notes (Pl. 2:1716n), these corrections were made after Fénelon came to know of the death of the Duke of Brittany, the oldest son of the Duke of Burgundy, who died on March 8, which left the Duke of Anjou, younger son of the Duke of Burgundy and the future Louis XV, the only remaining prince.

96. Marie-Louise-Elisabeth d'Orléans, Duchess of Berry (1695–1719), daughter of the Duke of Orléans. Her tumultuous personal life and several pregnancies were the subject of considerable gossip.

97. Added at end of line: "He is ambitious, and focused on the future."

98. *Petits-fils de France*: sons of the Dauphin.

99. Added here: "the father who would have been."

100. Added here: "damning and."

101. Charles, Duke of Berry (1686–1714), son of *le Grand Dauphin* and husband of Marie-Louise-Elisabeth d'Orléans.

102. Struck in the manuscript is an opening line: "If one were to take the path of detaining his daughter for her whole life."

103. Maria Theresa of Spain (1638–1683), wife of Louis XIV and Queen of France from 1659; Fénelon examines her claims to the throne and their effect on future claims to succession in Spain in a separate memoir (*Examen des droits de Phillippe V à la couronne d'Espagne*).

104. This and the following entry seem to have been added at a different time, and may be in a different hand.

105. Added in another hand: "15 March 1712."

106. Added above: "Otherwise they will cross you—a very easy thing to do."

107. This final line seems to be a later addition.

108. Hercule Mériadec, Duke of Rohan-Rohan (1669–1749). Added at the end of this line: "One can very well do without this."

109. Respectively: Charles-Honoré d'Albert, duc de Chevreuse (1646–1712); François de Neufville, duc de Villeroy (see note earlier); Paul de Beauvillier (see note earlier); Louis de Rouvroy, duc de Saint-Simon (1675–1755); Armand de Béthune, duc de Chârost (1662–1747); Henri duc d'Harcourt (see notes earlier); Louis Auguste d'Albert, duc de Chaulnes (1676–1744).

110. Respectively: Nicholas Chalon du Blé, Marquis d'Uxelles (1652–1730); Camille d'Hostun de la Baume, duc de Tallard (see note earlier).

111. Respectively: Antoine V de Gramont, duc de Guiche (1671–1725); Adrien-Maurice, duc de Noailles (1678–1766); Louis Antoine de Pardaillan de Gondrin, duc d'Antin (1664–1736); Victor-Marie, maréchal d'Estrées (1660–1737).

112. *Lit de justice*: formal meeting of the *Parlement* of Paris over which the king would preside in order to compel registration of royal edicts that the *Parlement* had

resisted; its name derives from the reclining throne or "bed" on which the king would sit while in session.

113. Added above: "in the last resort"

114. See n109.

115. Respectively: Henri-Pons de Thiard de Bissy (1657–1737), Bishop of Meaux from 1704; Fabio Brulart de Sillery (1655–1714), Bishop of Soissons from 1692; Jules-César Rousseau de la Parisière (1667–1736), Bishop of Nîmes from 1710; Charles-François d'Hallencourt de Drosmesnil (1674–1754), Bishop of Autun from 1710; François de Blouet de Camilly (1664–1723), Bishop of Toul from 1704.

116. Melchior de Polignac (1661–1742), prominent church official and literary figure.

117. *Gentilshommes de la manche*: nobles charged specifically with overseeing the welfare of the Dauphin. On the *valet de chambre*, see note earlier.

118. "Unfit for good company" translates "*de contrebande*"; see DAF.

119. Michel Colin, Lord du Chesne, *valet du chambre* to the Duke of Berry; and possibly, as LeBrun suggests (Pl. 2:1720n), Hennequin de Charmont, secretary to Louis XIV.

120. "Bourdon" was the name that Fénelon used in his correspondence to refer to Michel le Tellier (1643–1719), priest and influential anti-Jansenist polemicist, as LeBrun notes (Pl. 2:1720n).

121. Added in another hand: "15 March 1712."

122. On the *rentiers*, see note earlier.

123. Added here: "in order to bring her closer to him."

Chapter 8

1. Proverbs 16:4.

2. *City of God* 14.3.

3. LeBrun suggests that Fénelon's reference here is "*sans doute*" to Louis-Antoine de Noailles and his *Instruction pastorale* of October 27, 1697; see Pl. 1:1445n.

4. Reference untraced.

5. Exodus 20:5.

6. Cicero, *De amicitia* 3.10, 5.18, 9.29–31, 21.80, 22.82.

7. Horace, *Satires* 2.6.73–75 (Fénelon's preceding sentence is essentially a direct translation of the Latin).

8. Plato, *Republic* 7, 518c and 521d.

9. Cicero, *De officiis*, 1.5.15; cf. Plato, *Phaedrus*, 250d.

10. Plato, *Symposium*, 180b.

11. Plato, *Symposium*, 211a–b.

12. Plato, *Symposium*, 179a–b.

13. Plato, *Crito*, 52e–54c; *Gorgias*, 521d–522e.

14. Plato, *Symposium*, 206a–b, 210e–211c.

15. Alcestis: wife of Admetus, king of Thessaly; her self-sacrifice is memorialized in Euripides's *Alcestis*.

16. Plato, *Symposium*, 211d–e.

Index